Analysing Real Texts
Research Studies in Modern English Language

HILARY HILLIER

First published 2004 by
PALGRAVE MACMILLAN
Houndmills, Basingstoke, Hampshire RG21 6XS and
175 Fifth Avenue, New York, N.Y. 10010
Companies and representatives throughout the world

PALGRAVE MACMILLAN is the global academic imprint of the Palgrave
Macmillan division of St. Martin's Press, LLC and of Palgrave Macmillan Ltd.
Macmillan® is a registered trademark in the United States, United Kingdom
and other countries. Palgrave is a registered trademark in the European
Union and other countries.

ISBN 0–333–58470–8 hardback
ISBN 0–333–58471–6 paperback

This book is printed on paper suitable for recycling and made from fully
managed and sustained forest sources.

A catalogue record for this book is available from the British Library.

Library of Congress Cataloging-in-Publication Data
Hillier, Hilary.
    Analysing real texts : research studies in modern English language / Hilary Hillier.
        p. cm.
    Includes bibliographical references and index.
    ISBN 0–333–58470–8 — ISBN 0–333–58471–6 (pbk.)
        1. English language—Discourse analysis. 2. English language—Written English.
    3. English language—Variation. I. Title.

PE1422.H55 2004
420.1'41—dc21   2003055268

10   9   8   7   6   5   4   3   2   1
13 12 11 10 09 08 07 06 05 04

Printed and bound in Great Britain by
Creative Print & Design (Wales), Ebbw Vale

For MWD – who began to bring things together

Contents

List of Figures

List of Texts

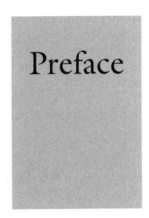

Preface

Overall aims of the book

This book arises from my experience of teaching (and supervising the projects of) a wide range of students of the English language. These have included undergraduates and postgraduates in the School of English Studies, University of Nottingham, and – latterly – undergraduates in the Faculty of Education and Language Studies, The Open University, East Midlands Region.

The book addresses all those who wish to carry out close and detailed study of the way the English language is used in a range of 'real' texts, produced in clearly identified situations. It attempts to synthesise two broad approaches to the study of Modern English Language: the work on style/register by, for example, Crystal and Davy (1969), Ghadessy (1988), Carter and Nash (1990), Freeborn et al. (1993), Carter et al. (2001), and the practical guides to project methodology by, for example, Berry (1987), Sebba (1993), Wray et al. (1998). It may to some extent be regarded as complementing Delin (2000) – partly through the kinds of text examined. The aim of the current book, however, has been to use the chosen range of texts to carry out a series of principled and fully explicated research studies. These studies are intended:

- to provide students (and their tutors/supervisors) with detailed demonstrations of the kinds of things that can be done in the analysis of 'real' Modern English Language texts, written and spoken;

- to spark ideas for comparable, analogical, studies according to students' own interests, background and experience;

- to suggest how they themselves might set about doing such studies.

My own experience – first as a mature student and then as a tutor/supervisor – has convinced me that the 'learning by doing' which the project approach requires is the most significant, long-lasting, and potentially fulfilling way to engage with English language in use. The book's overriding aim, therefore, is to show the way, and in two senses: to point out intriguing paths which enquiring and adventurous students will, I hope, want to explore, and to demonstrate some of the ways in which their explorations might be carried out.

Scope of the book

There are, of course, many kinds of text that might have been examined, and it has been necessary to be selective. This book takes as its main focus a group of texts which I have worked on and used successfully with students – sometimes over a number of years. Some of the chapters feature texts which have been used many times with students (for example Chapters 3, 5 and 6); some feature texts which were specially collected for this book but draw on insights and experience gained from earlier, comparable, texts (for example Chapters 7 and 8); some involve a mixture of both (Chapters 2 and 4). The range is wide and varied and the texts themselves have many interesting and often thought-provoking things to say about some specific uses of English in Britain today. The fact that the texts are firmly rooted in a particular UK-based cultural environment should <u>not</u> be regarded as limiting the scope of the book. Experience with students (including international students) suggests that a specifically anchored instance, far from hindering the imaginative leap required in the sparking of ideas, can in fact actively <u>encourage</u> the analogical aspirations expressed under 'aims'. Some suggestions for further work are offered at the end of each chapter, and I hope that, given <u>both</u> the specific instance <u>and</u> these further suggestions, readers will be moved to take that imaginative leap.

The chapters are presented as 'independent' studies, but they have been placed within a coherent and mutually supportive overall framework. Each chapter is intended to reinforce and be reinforced by the others in the book, encouraging as much cross-fertilisation of ideas as possible, with application to other kinds of text being suggested at appropriate points.

As with the kinds of text chosen, the range of linguistic features which might have been investigated at the analysis stage is very wide indeed, and it was not practicable to try to cover everything. The aim has been to present analytical approaches used successfully during teaching – those which seemed most suitable to the different kinds of text involved. It is not, of course, suggested that a chosen descriptive framework is the only one which might have been applied, merely that it seemed to offer the potential for illuminating some particular aspects of that data. The application of a <u>different</u> framework might well throw valuable light on <u>other</u> aspects. Indeed, one of the purposes of this book is to show the application of a range of different frameworks in different contexts, and one particular study might well prompt ideas which could be applied to another.

Only a small number of features could be investigated in each case, given the inevitable limits of space. Each feature, however, is examined in some depth. Such an approach seemed likely to allow both a fuller <u>explication</u> of the principles involved at each stage and an explicit <u>demonstration</u> of actual procedures. The degree of detail presented in the analyses may or may not be considered appropriate to a particular student or type of study. The strategy has been to offer a highly detailed model which will at the same time allow students and tutors/supervisors ample room for discriminating selection according to need.

A Glossary is provided in Appendix 2 giving brief definitions of technical terms used, but not fully defined, in this book. Those which are explained in the text have not, in the main, been included in the Glossary. These terms can be found via the subject index, which indicates where the relevant explanations can be found.

A note on style

The 'appropriate style' for an academic text remains an area of uncertainty. Students regularly raise this issue when embarking on language assignments, especially research projects. How far should they strive for an impersonal approach, using passive constructions and tortuous third person references, such as 'the researcher'? How acceptable might be the use of the personal pronoun *I*?

My advice tends to be that judicious use of *I* is entirely appropriate, especially when describing how particular research methods were planned and implemented and relevant decisions arrived at. A more obviously impersonal approach (for example by the use of passive forms) is likely to be appropriate at the analysis and discussion-of-results stages.

I have tried to follow my own advice in this book. I have aimed to recognise distinctions between my role as researcher + collector of data (use of *I*) and my role as researcher + analyst + assessor of findings (use of 'impersonal' style), and my further, additional, role as participant (for example in Chapters 4 and 5) where reference is made to *H*. These distinctions are not always easy to draw clearly, but they are nevertheless aimed at.

The principle of 'gender-free' language has been followed. No assumptions have been made about gender in the use of non-specific third person singular pronoun reference (see Section 6.6.1). Various avoidance strategies have been adopted, including the deliberate choice of plural forms, the use of singular *they*, and explicitly stated alternatives such as *s/he* and *his/her*.

Finally, some points of detail:

- Upper-case (capital) letters have been used for particular terms as specifically defined within chapters, for example, a given feature or participant role within a particular descriptive framework. An attempt has otherwise been made to restrict their use as far as possible.

- For economy of frequent use within the <u>same</u> chapter some references (particularly extensive ones) are presented in an abbreviated form, for example Bloor and Bloor 1995 (B&B), Hughes and Trudgill 1996 (H&T). Such use is made clear at each point.

- Within general discursive text emphasis is signalled via underlining; the principal use of italics is for citing illustrative extracts from texts. Other, for example analytical, uses of punctuation features are explained in individual chapters.

- The word *data* (the set of texts to be analysed) has been treated as a singular noun throughout.

Acknowledgements

I would like to express my appreciation and thanks to the following:

Nottinghamshire County Council, whose financial assistance in 1993–4 enabled me to carry out research into the dialect grammar of schoolchildren in Eastwood, Nottingham; the staff and pupils of Devonshire Drive and Greasley Beauvale Primary Schools, Eastwood; Mr Ron Coomber of Carlton Television; Donna Connelly, Clare Cully, Margaret Edbury, Ruth Henson, Daniel Hillier, Edmund Hillier, Glenda Jensen, Alan Rudd, Richard Shipman and Fred Wetherill for their willing participation (and their remarkable patience); Margaret Berry for her personal and intellectual integrity and her belief in me; Ron Carter for his constructive criticisms and many valuable comments on an earlier draft of the book; Anna Sandeman for her helpful suggestions on presentational matters; Margaret Bartley for steering the book through the early days; colleagues over the years for their support and encouragement; my students for their enthusiasm, enterprising ideas and searching questions – and their readiness to act as informants; Norman Todd for being there at some critical times; my family and friends for their loving (mainly mystified) forbearance; finally, and most of all, to Edd and Dan for their constancy – and for their unfailing good humour when rescuing me from recurrent threats of technical disaster!

The author and publisher wish to thank the following for permission to use copyright material:

Atlantic Syndication on behalf of the *Daily Mail*, for extracts from Roger Scott, 'The Miners' Day of Shame', *Daily Mail*, 23 February 1984.

Express Newspapers, for extracts from Ian Trueman, 'Miners – MacGregor knocked out in coalfield battle', *Daily Star*, 23 February 1984.

Guardian Media Group plc, for extracts from Vikram Dodd, 'Prescott Punch Up', the *Guardian*, 17 May 2001; and for material from Peter Hetherington, 'NCB Chief Fit after Incident at Pit', the *Guardian*, 23 February 1984; copyright © 2001, 1984 The Guardian.

Kellogg Company, for advertising scripts, 'Executive' (1956) and 'Early Man' (2000).

The Labour Party for the closing minutes of Tony Blair's 3 October 1995 speech to Conference.

The Rt Hon. John Major for the closing minutes of his 13 October 1995 speech to the Conservative Party Conference.

NI Syndication Ltd for frontpage headline, 'Edwina: My 3-hour Sex Romps with Major', *News of the World*, 29 September 2002; for material from 'Coal Boss is Floored by Pit Mob', *The Sun*, 23 February 1984; and 'MacGregor Knocked over at Pit Protest', *The Times*, 23 February 1984; copyright © NI Syndication Ltd, London, 1984, 2002.

Nottingham Evening Post, for extracts from Ian Drury, 'Fred's Gorra Big 'it for Issen', Nottingham *Evening Post*, 31 July 1998.

Telegraph Group Ltd, for extracts from Stanley Goldsmith, 'Surging Miners Floor the Coal Board Chief', *Daily Telegraph*, 23 February 1984; copyright © Telegraph Group Ltd 1984.

Teversal Living Memory Group, for extracts from Fred Wetherill, *Our Mam un t'Others* (1998).

Trinity Mirror Group plc, for the extracts from Oonagh Blackman and Bob Roberts, 'He's 2 Jabs', *The Mirror*, 17 May 2001; and frontpage headline, 'Sex, Strawberries, Cream . . . and Whips', *Sunday Mirror*, 29 September 2002.

J. Walter Thompson, for Persil advertising scripts of 'Woman Alone' (1959), 'Sports Kit Mother' (1998), 'Pregnant Woman' (1998) and 'Kidding Woman' (2000).

Every effort has been made to trace the copyright holders but if any have been inadvertently overlooked the publisher will be pleased to make the necessary arrangement at the first opportunity.

1

Introduction: Motivating Principles and Procedures

1.1 Theoretical and methodological principles adopted

1.1.1 Selection of texts for chapters

The studies described in this book have been placed within a framework which I have used successfully as a teaching aid over the years (see Figure 1.1). This is an adaptation of a framework produced by Gregory and Carroll (1978: 47) (G&C), who took as their starting point the basic distinction between Speaking and Writing and then identified a range of variations to be found within that simple dichotomy. (A summary of G&C's approach appears in Section 1.1.3.)

The relationship of each of the studies covered by the book to the overall framework is shown by the addition of the relevant chapter number under the appropriate node in Figure 1.1.

1.1.2 Selection of texts within chapters: the 'variables' principle

Selection of texts within chapters has been made according to the 'comparative' principle: that is, within each chapter texts have been selected which permit an investigation of the linguistic effects of 'controlled variation'. This principle requires that texts to be compared should be 'matched' in as many respects as possible (the controlled variables) in order to examine whether and how far they may differ in the chosen respect (the deliberately varying variable/s). Varying variables are to be kept to a minimum – probably a maximum of two – and in most of the chapters in this book just one variable is deliberately chosen to vary. Maximum possible control of variables is regarded as an important – indeed essential – element in the study of texts (see, for example, Berry 1987: 20–1; Wray et al. 1998: 158).

It follows that in order to make useful comparisons between specific texts both 'controlled' and 'varying' variables should be specified in as much detail as possible at the outset. The kinds of variables which may be potentially significant in any given situation are therefore identified and described in the following section.

1.1.3 Situational variables: the theoretical background

For the purposes of this book, and as shown in Figure 1.1, identification of the principal elements of a particular language situation will start by making an initial distinction between writing and speaking.

As G&C note in their chapter 'Modes of Discourse' (pp. 37–47), the medium in which 'the same language' is expressed can create variation in the kinds of patterns which occur. Such patterns will vary according to whether they are formed by visible shapes ('writing' – to be processed by the eye) or noises ('speech' – to be processed by the ear). As G&C also make clear, however, this is an over-simplification, and more delicate distinctions have to be made when particular instances of writing and speaking are considered. Writing can be specifically designed to be spoken aloud (for example as a

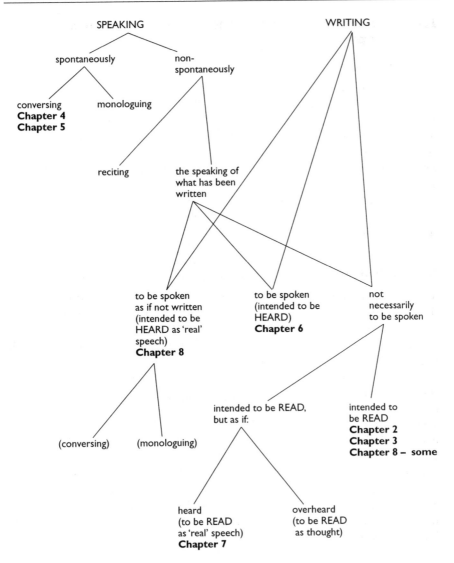

Figure 1.1 Framework for presenting the different research studies, with relevant chapters indicated under appropriate node. (Figure adapted from Gregory and Carroll's 'Suggested distinctions along the dimension of situation variation categorized as user's medium relationship' (1978: 47), itself adapted from Gregory, 1967.)

public lecture or as dialogue in a play or film) or to be read as if heard (for example as dialogue in a novel or story). Speech can be more or less spontaneous. It can, in addition, form part of a conversation, involving interchange with another speaker, or it can constitute a monologue, the latter being 'sustained, cohesive speech by one person' (p. 41). A (written) lecture can deliberately include elements which appear to be more or less informal and spontaneous, and dialogue in a play or novel can seek to create particular patterns of spontaneous speech according to the kind of 'real life' which it is intended to represent.

It will be apparent from this very brief account that there is great potential for overlap between and within the two basic concepts 'speaking' and 'writing', hence the framework shown in Figure 1.1. G&C's insights will be drawn upon throughout this book, both in providing its overall structure and in supporting some of the analytical comments made on individual texts.

It will also have become apparent that 'mode of discourse' alone will not account for variations in patterns of language in the situations exemplified. Many other factors have to be taken into account, for example the subject of, and proposed audience for, the lecture and/or play, the kinds of conversation engaged in and the relationships between the particular individuals who are conversing. Two broad theories which identify such factors are summarised in the following sections, and both will be drawn on as appropriate in this book. The theorists, in fact, have much in common, and they may be regarded as in some senses offering complementary perspectives on what each terms 'the context of situation', with Halliday representing systemic functional linguistics (within which G&C themselves are working) and Hymes representing the ethnography of communication. (The summaries given here are necessarily brief and selective, the intention being to focus on those parts most immediately relevant to the needs of this book. Readers are urged to seek out the original material for detailed explication.)

1.1.4 Halliday's features of the context of situation

Halliday's (1989a: 5–9) characterisation of 'the context of situation' acknowledges that the total environment (both linguistic and non-linguistic) plays a crucial role in creating meaning in any situation. He presents what he calls a 'simple conceptual framework' for describing the context of any situation (1989a: 12–14), which he sets out under three headings. These are 'the field, the tenor, and the mode', and they may be briefly summarised as follows:

- **Field** refers to 'the field of discourse', what kind of social action is actually happening, what the participants are engaged in;

- **Tenor** refers to 'the tenor of discourse', who the participants are, the roles they are adopting at any point, what their social relationships are to each other;

- **Mode** refers to 'the mode of discourse', the kind of role the language is playing, its function in the particular context, the channel used (spoken or written or some combination of the two) and also 'the rhetorical mode': 'what is being achieved by the text in terms of such categories as persuasive, expository, didactic and the like'.

G&C, too, characterise Field (pp. 27–36) and Tenor (pp. 48–63) as well as Mode. (There are in fact some clear correspondences between their particular account of Mode and Halliday's 'spoken or written or some combination of the two'.) There are, however, some differences of emphasis between G&C's categorisations and those of Halliday, and these are considered in Section 1.1.6 below.

1.1.5 Hymes's context of situation and the components of speech

Hymes's overall concept of the context of situation has many similarities to Halliday's, though precise categorisations and terminologies differ. Hymes (1994; an edited version of Hymes 1977) identifies what he regards as the 'fundamental notions' involved in a theory of communication. He posits a hierarchical categorisation of the elements of any instance of speech activity or communication (1994: 13–16), the term 'speech' being used by Hymes to embrace all manifestations of language, including writing. The most significant elements for current purposes are summarised as follows:

- speech event, an activity which is 'directly governed by rules or norms for the use of speech' (for example, a conversation, a lecture);
- speech act, an element having an identifiable function within a speech event (for example, a joke, a greeting, a request).

Hymes then presents (1994: 16–20) a schema consisting of a total of 16 identifiable 'components of speech acts'. The full 16, with very brief explanations, are:

1   **Message form**: precisely how something is said (or written) (see component 13);

2   **Message content**: what is being talked about, the 'topic';

3   **Setting**: the time and place of a speech act and, in general, the physical circumstances;

4   **Scene**: the culturally defined or 'psychological setting' (Hymes regards 'Setting' as the 'informal, unmarked term of the two' (1994: 18);

5–8   **Speaker, Addressor, Hearer, Addressee**: the four potential components of participant relations;

9–10   **Purposes – outcomes** and **goals**: 'conventionally recognized and expected outcomes' of a speech event from a community standpoint, and individual goals of those engaged in a speech event;

11   **Key**: 'the tone, manner, or spirit in which an act is done';

12   **Channels**: 'oral, written, telegraphic, semaphore, or other medium of transmission of speech';

13   **Forms of speech**: an organised set of linguistic resources having meaning for a particular group (for example, speakers of a particular language or dialect would have access to a stock of lexical, grammatical

and phonological resources held in common – of common provenance);

14–15 **Norms of interaction** and **interpretation**: rules of speaking, and the corresponding meanings attached, for particular groups;

16 **Genres**: categories of speech act such as poem, oration, commercial, editorial and so on (often coinciding with speech events).

Hymes acknowledges that not every single one of these 16 components may have to be specified for any particular situation. The only necessary ones, in fact, are:

> message form and some other. (It is a general principle that all rules involve message form, if not by affecting its shape, then by governing its interpretation.) (1994: 17; emphasis added)

The aim of this book is, of course, to investigate precisely this: the relationship between choice of message form and apparent meaning conveyed in the different communicative situations being examined.

Many of Hymes's most broadly defined components will be drawn on in this chapter to identify the most significant differentiating variables, for example by relating them to Halliday's as and when possible. Others of his components will also be called upon, where appropriate, in devising suitable analytical frameworks within chapters and in attempting to account for specific linguistic choices.

1.1.6 Situational variables: the approach adopted for this book

The book bases its overall approach on theories expounded by both Halliday and Hymes. These will, however, be supplemented by the insights of others, for example G&C and Hasan (1989) (also working within a systemic functional framework). Potentially significant situational variables for the purposes of this book are identified and described in the following subsections, with an attempt being made to arrive at a synthesis of the theoretical concepts outlined in the preceding sections. (Halliday himself (1978: 63 and 1989a: 8–9) in fact does this to some extent.)

The broad terminological labels used here are mainly those of Halliday – that is, Field, Tenor, Mode and so on. They should <u>not</u>, however, be interpreted too restrictively nor should a wholly systemic functional approach be inferred. The lack of a completely direct 'fit' between different theoretical approaches, and their respective terminologies, has been regarded as potentially illuminating rather than problematic. Significant differences between approaches are noted where relevant.

The particular variables have been used to identify the main characteristics of the data to be examined within each chapter and to arrive at a basis for comparisons between individual texts. Definitions of relevant terms for current purposes are presented in the following subsections.

1.1.6.1 *Field:* This term will be the predominant one used to characterise the nature of the activity being engaged in – that is, what is actually happening and the overall purpose of the speech situation. Field will tend to determine subject matter and 'topic', though some fields – for example casual conversation – can involve a wide range of topics, as can a political speech. 'Topic' has, in some circumstances, been found to have a notable influence on 'message form' (see, for example, the code-switching by bilinguals referred to by Holmes, 2001: 37–8), and it could, therefore, be investigated as a deliberately varying variable within a 'controlled' Field. (Such an approach has <u>not</u> been adopted in this book, though aspects of 'topic' are considered in relation to Tenor in Chapter 6.)

Use of the term Field will subsume Halliday's 'field' and Hymes's components 2, 9, 10 (message content and purposes), and also, perhaps, G&C's 'user's purposive role' (p. 7), although, as they acknowledge (p. 28), there is some overlap here with what they call 'functional tenor'.

1.1.6.2 *Tenor:* This term will be used to characterise the participants involved – the significant personal details of each (for example, their gender, age, regional/social origin and so on), their roles within the particular interaction and the relationships between the individual participants (for example, the degree of hierarchy and/or social distance involved). Tenor as used here will subsume both Halliday's 'tenor' and Hymes's components 5 to 8 (Speaker, Addressor, Hearer, Addressee) and also perhaps Hymes's 'provenance' mentioned under component 13.

Where appropriate and useful, reference will be made to G&C's distinction between 'personal tenor' and 'functional tenor', each being potentially independent of the other (pp. 53–4). 'Personal tenor' characterises personal factors such as those already mentioned. 'Functional tenor' characterises 'what language is being used for in the situation', for example to persuade, to exhort (p. 53). It thus overlaps in some respects with Field's 'purposive role' (pp. 8, 28) and also with Halliday's 'rhetorical <u>mode</u>' (see Section 1.1.4).

1.1.6.3 *Mode:* This term will be used for the whole range of manifestations of speaking and writing (see Figure 1.1). Mode will include Halliday's 'mode' and Hymes's 'channels' (component 12). It will also include some usefully delicate potential distinctions identified by Hasan (1989: 57–9):

- **Language role**: Is the role the language is playing in any given situation 'constitutive' (constituting the activity itself) or is it 'ancillary' (accompanying a <u>non</u>-linguistic activity)?

- **Process sharing**: Is the addressee able to <u>share</u> the process of text creation as it unfolds, or does s/he come to it as a finished product?

- **Channel**: Does the addressee come in contact with the message via sound waves (the phonic channel) or via some kind of graven image (the graphic channel)?

● **+/-Visual contact**: Is there visual contact between speaker and addressee?

Hasan stresses that each of these factors should be regarded as a continuum, as a matter of degree. Her work thus shows interesting parallels with some informal but comparable situational 'scales' posited by Brazil, for example his 'two-way . . . one-way communication' and 'shared . . . separate environment', which correspond closely with Hasan's degrees of shared process and visual contact respectively. Figure 1.2 brings together some of the ideas of Hasan and Brazil in a proposed set of situational scales.

Both Hasan and Brazil note the tendency of 'placings' on particular scales to co-occur in particular situations and for particular texts. Thus, for example, shared process and shared environment are frequently associated with phonic channel, producing the formal features characteristic of what Hasan calls the 'spoken medium'. Similarly, one-way process and separate environment are frequently associated with graphic channel and the formal features of the 'written medium'. Both writers, however, stress the theoretical independence of each scale in defining any specific situation and consequently in its capacity for influencing the form and style of language actually produced. A little reflection should confirm this: consider the positioning on the different scales of texts involving communication via, say, the telephone (see Chapter 4), answering machine/voice mail, electronic mail and so on (and see Chapter 9).

All of the different factors outlined above have been subsumed under the single umbrella term 'Mode' in arriving at a broad categorisation of the texts studied in each chapter. The more delicate distinctions have, however, been admitted where appropriate (see Section 1.1.7).

1.1.6.4 A note on Hymes's 'Setting': Hymes's components 3 and 4 – 'setting' and 'scene' – raise some questions in the context of situational variables and attempts to control and deliberately vary them for current purposes. It is unclear quite how they may be related directly to Field, Tenor and Mode. Setting (both temporal and spatial) would seem to have some links with 'Mode', since it has some correspondence with Hasan's degrees of shared

phonic channel .... graphic channel

two-way/shared process .... one-way process

shared environment (+ visual contact) .... separate environment (– visual contact)

ancillary language role .... constitutive language role

spontaneous .... prepared

informal .... formal

Figure 1.2 Situational scales: language and mode of discourse
(Drawn from Hasan, 1989: 57–9, and Brazil, 1983: 158–9; a reproduction of Brazil, 1969.)

process and visual contact between participants. (Spatial Setting has been regarded as a significant varying variable in Chapter 4.) Halliday (1978: 63), however, subsumes Hymes's 'setting' explicitly under his own field. This perhaps reflects the congruence of <u>spatial</u> setting with a particular speech situation – for example a church building and a religious service (or the conference halls and the political speeches in Chapter 6). A further, separate, dimension would seem to link a varying <u>temporal</u> setting to (personal) Tenor, especially where notably different participants are presumed to be involved, as in the advertisements and their target audiences in Chapter 8.

The following decisions were taken with regard to 'Setting':

- to define 'Setting' as the time and/or place in which the specific interaction/s being studied actually occur, or, in the case of 'one-way' written language, may be presumed to occur;

- to subsume 'Scene' under 'Setting', no attempt being made to specify in detail a separate 'psychological setting', though reference is made to 'scene' from time to time, as appropriate;

- to accord to 'Setting–temporal' and 'Setting–spatial' potentially independent theoretical values; appropriate links could thus be made to Field, Tenor or Mode as determined by the data.

1.1.7   Assignment of controlled and varying variables

Figure 1.1 shows that for this book a particular basic Mode will be one of the controlled variables within each chapter. Chapters 4, 5 and 8, however, will each introduce an element of deliberate variation <u>within</u> Mode via one of the factors identified in Section 1.1.6.3. Other significant variables will be controlled or deliberately allowed to vary as specified according to situation and type of text.

In some instances there could be factors which have effects ancillary to those of the deliberately varying variable but which are not the object of study and which are essentially unpredicted and unpredictable. An example might be varying Setting–temporal (as distinct from Setting–spatial) as in Chapter 4. Any such factors are identified at the relevant stage and their potential effects assessed as appropriate.

Table 1.1 presents a summary of the controlled and deliberately varying variables within each chapter, represented by the broad categories Field, Tenor and Mode. In some instances a particular broad category may appear under <u>both</u> headings, reflecting the specification of one of the independent factors discussed in Section 1.1.6. Such factors are shown in brackets after the relevant category. Where no separate factors are specified they are all being regarded as, at least potentially, congruent within the particular broad category.

For Chapter 7 a dual perspective has been adopted which entails a shift in the specification of variables according to the relevant perspective. This is a reflection of the dual view of Mode being taken in that chapter: the regional dialect text is <u>both</u> writing intended to be read <u>and</u> writing intended to be

Table 1.1   Summary of controlled and varying variables within each chapter

	Controlled variables	Deliberately varying variables
Chapter 2 Literary narrative	Mode Field	Tenor
Chapter 3 Newspaper reports	Mode Field	Tenor
Chapter 4 Women's talk	Mode Field Tenor	Mode (Setting–spatial)
Chapter 5 Children's talk	Mode Tenor (personal)	Mode (language role) Field Tenor (functional)
Chapter 6 Political speeches	Mode Field Tenor (functional)	Tenor (personal) (Field – topic)
Chapter 7 Dialect narrative	Mode Field Tenor (functional)	Tenor (personal)
	Field Tenor	Mode
Chapter 8 Television advertisements	Mode Field Tenor (functional)	Mode (Setting–temporal) Tenor (personal)

read <u>as if</u> heard. (Hasan cites the approximately comparable situation of writing a letter to a friend: 'I shall use the graphic channel, but I shall tend to use the spoken medium . . . I shall write <u>as if</u> I were talking to my friend' (1989: 59; original emphasis).) A full explanation is given in Chapter 7.

It will be seen that more than one deliberately varying variable is given for Chapters 5 and 8. In each case the varying variables have been regarded as being congruent in terms of the overall framework and the particular categories identified. Thus, in Chapter 5 Mode (language role) has been regarded as consistent with Field/purpose and also with Tenor (functional). In Chapter 8 Mode (Setting–temporal) is consistent with Tenor (personal). For Chapter 6 the <u>topic</u> element of Field has been regarded as a (possible) consequence of personal Tenor variation, signalled by its placing in brackets.

1.2 Practical procedures followed

An account follows of the general practical procedures adopted for each chapter, the kinds of decisions made and the factors influencing those decisions. It is intended:

- to demonstrate the overall consistency of approach adopted across all chapters;

- to provide general methodological points of reference as and when required;

- to serve as a potential model for those carrying out comparable studies.

More specific detail is given under the relevant headings within each chapter, each being structured according to the same general pattern, though with variations as appropriate.

1.2.1 Specification of the relevant variables

A full account is given of both controlled and varying variables in each chapter, including an indication of any other relevant background information.

1.2.2 Description of the data

The data is described, giving details of how and where it was obtained and the reason/s for choosing this particular data.

The collection of 'spoken' (especially spontaneous) data involved general practical considerations, as follows:

(a) The aim was to obtain as 'natural' a recording as possible, one that appeared to be representative of the speech of the participant/s and/or the overall situation. It was important, therefore, to achieve as relaxed a situation as possible, for example by ensuring subjects' familiarity with the recording process in advance of the actual taping, so that the presence of the tape recorder did not interfere or cause embarrassment – even silence!

(b) There was no recourse to covert recording. If this should be felt to be unavoidable, formal permission to use the material should always be obtained after the event. Milroy (1987: 87–91) discusses the kinds of issues involved. (See Chapter 4 for an instance of an accidental recording which was, with permission, subsequently used.)

(c) The chosen extracts had to be transcribed as accurately as possible for analytical purposes. Transcription is inevitably an interpretative process, and the possible influence of subjective and/or theoretical considerations has to be acknowledged (see, for example, Ochs, 1979; Milroy,

1987: 117; Psathas and Anderson, 1990; Hillier, 1992, 1995). The circumstances and background to any study and collection of data have therefore to be described at each stage with the intention of giving as transparent an account as possible. (Transcription conventions are set out in Section 1.2.5.)

(d)   The act of transcription itself is a laborious process, involving much rewinding and replaying of tape sections. It required intensive listening to determine what was being said and (especially in the case of the reading in Chapter 7) precisely <u>how</u> it was said. The difficulties increased with the number of speakers, the degree of spontaneity involved, and in some instances the quality of the recording (for example, some parts of the data in Chapters 4 and 5). Any areas of uncertainty are discussed in the relevant chapter and/or indicated in the transcripts.

(e)   Accidental wiping of precious material is always a danger during the rewinding and replaying process. It is advisable, therefore, to remove the little plastic lugs at the top of the audiotape before starting to transcribe. There can then be no possibility of recording over any section. (Audiotape can be reused at a later date if adhesive tape is stuck over the gaps where the lugs have been removed, though it is advisable to retain all significant data for some time after any project has apparently been completed.)

(f)   All of the spoken data was recorded on, and transcribed from, audiotape. Videotapes of the television advertisements examined in Chapter 8 were used in conjunction with the transcripts in arriving at the 'plain' texts (with their visual descriptions) and the analyses. Videotapes of the political conference speeches for Chapter 6 were <u>not</u> examined.

The use of video (rather than audio alone) for the collection of spontaneous data can in some circumstances be of practical help in clarifying what seems to be going on, particularly where more than two participants are involved (see discussion in, for example, Chapter 5). For many researchers, however, video is not a realistic possibility. It can, in fact, have some <u>dis</u>advantages, proving a distraction, increasing participants' self-consciousness and reducing the chances of obtaining the desired relaxed conditions. Discreet note-taking as appropriate may well be a satisfactory alternative. Further complications are likely to arise, of course, if the researcher is <u>also</u> a participant (as in Chapters 4 and 5), with its further division of concerns and responsibilities.

1.2.3   Choice of text extracts

Individual text extracts have been kept as short as is both practicable and adequate for satisfactory demonstration of the principles involved. Judgements as to what is adequate will depend on the analytical approach and descriptive framework adopted, the numbers and types of feature/s involved and/or the rank of structure being examined. Some texts are therefore very short (for example those in Chapters 2 and 3) while some are comparatively long (those in Chapters 4 and 5). Comparability of length of text extracts within chapters has been maintained so far as is practicable, while allowing for other considerations to be admitted such as matching of content (see, too, Section 1.2.10). Decisions and strategies are explained at each point.

1.2.4 Presentation of text extracts

Each set of text extracts has been reproduced in more than one way – the first being an initial 'plain' text, with a subsequent version displaying the chosen analyses (see Section 1.2.9). Printed texts (Chapters 2, 3 and 7) have been presented in a word-processed form which reproduces the general format (for example paragraphing) of the original. Tape-recorded spoken texts (Chapters 4–7 and 8) have been transcribed (see Section 1.2.5). Each text has been assigned a relevant number and/or letter within each chapter to facilitate cross-referencing. Numbering of some kind has also been added within most texts at the analysis stage for reference purposes (see Section 1.2.9).

In a few instances short sections of material have been omitted or proper names disguised in the interests of confidentiality. Such instances are made clear within the particular extract.

1.2.5 Transcription conventions adopted for spoken material

The actual form in which transcriptions are presented and the degree of detail involved were to a large extent determined by the circumstances and needs of individual chapters. Extended monologues (the speeches in Chapter 6) are organised into paragraphs punctuated by audience applause. Conversational data (principally Chapters 4 and 5) is presented in a fairly conventional 'play'-type format, though with an attempt to give a visual indication of the sequencing and timing of some contributions/utterances.

'Contribution', when used to refer to elements within transcripts, is defined entirely in surface terms, that is, as a chunk of text marked off in the relevant transcript as being assigned to a particular speaker. 'Utterance' is a general, non-specific, functional term used to refer to a stretch of speech by a particular speaker which constitutes some kind of functionally identifiable contribution or part-contribution to the conversation (compare Hymes's 'speech act' – see Section 1.1.5). (More detailed explanations and/or definitions are given as necessary in the relevant chapter.)

The initial 'plain' transcripts were prepared using approximately standard orthography (though see the special strategy adopted in Chapter 7), including some conventional abbreviations such as *OK* and *MA* and 'spoken' forms such as *cos* and *Tefl*. There is limited use of conventional punctuation: for example capital letters are used for proper names, some of which are given in an edited form. In some instances hyphenations are used (*preparation-wise*). Hyphenations can of course be based on subjective judgements by the transcriber (Crystal, 1996: 226, remarks on the inconsistencies involved) and this has further implications in the context of 'word counts' (see discussion of the latter in Section 1.2.10). Decisions are explained at each stage, the overall aim being to arrive at as consistent a methodology as possible.

Full transcription conventions are set out below, using illustrative examples taken from the data. Conventions are developed from those used in Hillier (1992: 82–3), which in turn were adapted from Stubbs et al. (1979: 32–3).

–	brief pause
—	slightly longer pause
-(2)-	pause of a given number of seconds
. . .	tailing-off speech
[	overlapping or simultaneous speech
[. . .]	omitted material
does / advise *	stressed word or syllable
urr / oooh	lengthened word or sound
c-	incomplete word
(well)	transcription uncertain
( )	indecipherable
((laugh))	gloss
?	rising intonation
((reading from screen?))	interpretation uncertain ('gloss' plus 'rising intonation')

* It should be noted that italics are used to indicate stress only within transcripts. In the discursive material of each chapter stress (if needed) is shown by the use of underlining, with italics being used to cite quoted examples from the data.

1.2.6 Text evaluation

From time to time statements are made about the data which include some degree of evaluation. This may involve more or less explicit evaluations by others which informed the text collection itself (see, for example, Chapters 2 and 7) or the obtaining of views on particular texts presented to informants, the latter being solicited either formally via a simple questionnaire (Chapter 3) or informally (Chapter 6). Sometimes the judgements are my own (Chapters 4, 5 and 8). In each case evaluations are presented as fully as possible.

The use of independent informants is recommended where evaluative judgements are to be made about potentially controversial texts. This is particularly important where matters of 'political bias' (often a popular area with students) are involved. Stubbs (1999: 110–11) sounds a note of caution about the explicitly 'committed' approach adopted by the proponents of Critical Discourse Analysis, as exemplified by Fairclough, 2001, warning of the risk of 'circularity' in the identification – by the analyst alone – of ideological bias in contentious texts. Obtaining the judgements of independent informants in response to specific questions allows the analyst to then try to account for those judgements by interrogating the texts according to a particular linguistic framework, as this book aims to demonstrate (see Section 1.2.7).

Such independent informants may well be ordinary, 'naïve', members of the public – that is, with no special knowledge of, or inside information about, the particular topics or texts involved. Alternatively, they may be deliberately chosen to represent specific, and contrasting, sectional interests, whether of a political or other nature. The informants used for the studies in this book were, in fact, 'naïve' students in each case, but the aims of the particular study will tend to determine the kinds of informants chosen and the actual approach adopted. (Berry, 1987: 27–32, discusses some of the factors to be considered when setting up 'informant tests'.)

The method of approach to informants is similarly likely to vary. It may take a quantitative or qualitative stance; it may involve the construction and completion of formal questionnaires (as in Chapter 3) (Wray et al., 1998: 167–81, contains a useful chapter on the design and purpose of questionnaires) or informal and discursive conversations (as in Chapter 6). Whatever the method of approach, it is often valuable to include an informally expressed rider asking whether informants can pinpoint any particular bits of the text/s which they feel might have made them respond in the ways they did. Their comments can then be drawn on at an appropriate point, either in suggesting particular areas of investigation or in throwing light on aspects of the findings.

Collection, collation and eventual presentation of the results of the different approaches to informants will be determined by the method of the approach itself. Both will, however, involve the obtaining and careful noting of some specific information which can then be used in a more or less concrete manner (see the relevant chapters).

1.2.7 Intuitions about and/or questions to be asked of the data

Analytical approaches have been decided within each chapter according to the kinds of questions which seemed appropriate to the particular data. Ideas and theories in each chapter are introduced first under the heading 'general expectations', which draws selectively from existing literature on others' theories and findings about approximately comparable texts, and then under the heading 'specific areas of enquiry', which identifies the specific linguistic features to be examined and/or approaches to be adopted.

Such areas of enquiry may be regarded as specific questions to be asked of the data or as informally expressed hypotheses. It was not felt necessary to formulate absolutely precise hypotheses at each stage (of the kind recommended by, for example, Berry, 1987: 36–47; Butler in Wray et al., 1998: 258–60). Formally expressed hypotheses could, however, be developed by students and their tutors if desired. Linguistic features to be investigated (and the appropriate framework/s to be applied) were arrived at by a combination of reference to others' work and my own intuitions about and initial explorations of the particular data. These features are various in terms of level of language (some, for example, are syntactic, some semantic) and type and size of linguistic unit. The latter range from the conversational contribution (Chapter 4) to the individual phoneme (Chapter 7). A summary of chosen features appears in Table 1.2.

1.2.8 Descriptive frameworks

Given the diversity of linguistic features examined it has been necessary to draw on an eclectic range of descriptive frameworks. Grammatical frameworks include those of both 'traditional' grammar and systemic functional grammar. Conversational data draws on the insights of conversation analysis, ethnomethodology and discourse analysis as appropriate. Accent and dialect data requires a broad sociolinguistic perspective. Analysis of the television advertising data takes a classic account of the advertising situation and builds on that basic framework by incorporating selected aspects of frameworks introduced in other chapters.

Analysis and discussion of lexical choices assumes a rather lower profile in these studies than those of grammatical and other choices. No specific lexical frameworks are therefore used, though the insights and suggestions of, for example, Carter (1998) are drawn upon as appropriate. Dictionary definitions are also quoted from time to time. This is not to suggest that a dictionary (any dictionary) can be cited as an ultimate authority. Readers and hearers will inevitably interpret particular meanings and contexts in the light of their own existing knowledge and social associations – drawing on what Fairclough (2001: 8–9, 20) characterises as their individual 'members' resources'. Dictionary definitions are therefore offered as further evaluative support for intuitive judgements of different kinds including (and especially) my own. (Groups of informants can, in fact, perform a valuable service in providing independent evidence of the likely connotations of particular lexical choices and/or patterns – see, for example, Carter, 1998: 257–62, in a 'literary' context, and also Section 1.2.6.)

Accounts of the different frameworks are given in the earliest relevant chapter, and cross-reference is made as appropriate in subsequent chapters. The frameworks are expounded in summary form, the aim being to provide adequate – though inevitably only very basic – criteria for reliable identification of the significant feature/s and thus a basis for replicable analyses. If the chosen framework appeared not to account completely satisfactorily for all of the data, or was insufficiently precise in providing reliable criteria for identifying (some of) the features being investigated, modifications were made. If necessary and/or possible, potentially useful tests have been devised in an attempt to fulfil the basic aim of arriving at frameworks with a maximum degree of replicability. Cited supporting examples are given from time to time, including those which are considered questionable or impossible. Such examples are signalled by the use of the following conventions: ?*example* for questionable ones and **example* for impossible ones. Explanations are given at each stage.

In addition, and where appropriate and/or necessary, the displayed analyses (see Section 1.2.9) are supplemented by annotations making more detailed reference to points from relevant framework/s in order to justify particular

Table 1.2 Summary of linguistic features examined and principal frameworks applied within each chapter

	Linguistic features	**Frameworks**
Chapter 2 Literary narrative	Sentence and clause Noun phrase Adverbial	Crystal (1996); Quirk et al. (1985)
Chapter 3 Newspaper reports	Clause Transitivity Voice	Crystal (1996) Halliday (1970); Bloor and Bloor (1995) Berry (1989); Crystal (1996)
Chapter 4 Women's talk	Minimal responses Hedges Hesitations	Coates (1994, 1996); Stubbs (1983a) Coates 1996; Crystal (1996) Crystal and Davy (1969)
Chapter 5 Children's talk	Deixis Participant roles	Halliday and Hasan (1976); Quirk et al. (1985) Hymes (1994); Goffman (1981); Bell (1984, 1997)
Chapter 6 Political speeches	Personal pronouns Lexical repetition Grammatical repetition	Crystal (1996) Halliday (1989b, 1994b) Crystal (1996)
Chapter 7 Dialect narrative	Selected dialect features Selected accent features	Hughes and Trudgill (1996); Edwards et al. (1984) Hughes and Trudgill (1996)
Chapter 8 Television advertisements	Direct v. Indirect Address Participant roles	Leech (1966) Leech (1966); Cook (2001); Hymes (1994); Bell (1984, 1997, 1991)

analytical decisions. It is expected that readers will make full use of the cited sources to clarify any remaining areas of uncertainty – indeed they are urged to do so. They should thus be able to both widen and deepen their linguistic knowledge. Table 1.2 summarises the features and the principal frameworks chosen for each set of text extracts in each chapter.

It will, I hope, have become apparent that I do not regard the use of different theoretical approaches (and therefore different frameworks) as a problem – rather the reverse. Different kinds of text are likely to respond best to different kinds of treatment. Different approaches, too, can potentially offer complementary perspectives on the nature of particular texts, and an attempt has been made to point out where differences occur and make connections between them where possible. Indeed, many differences are those of terminology – arising at the level of notation only – and it should be valuable to observe how different analytical methods may achieve common goals. Notational conventions adopted in this book are given in the relevant chapters.

1.2.9 Analytical procedures and methods of presentation

Analysis of each text in each chapter was carried out systematically, taking each feature separately and in turn, using the appropriate (part of the) chosen framework. Analyses have been displayed as clearly as possible on each text, thus providing explicit illustration of the claims being made. Line or contribution or sentence numbers have been added for reference purposes, according to the analytical approach adopted. (The needs of Chapter 4, for example, differ from those of Chapter 5, hence the different conventions adopted.) Annotations give support for individual analytical decisions as appropriate, since alternative analyses may be possible in a number of instances.

The combination of a systematic approach, clear display and scrupulous annotation is good practice in applying any descriptive framework, and I strongly recommend it to students. I would also advocate the use of colour-coding, where possible, in order to distinguish different ranks of structure and different types of feature being investigated, since it can provide the reader with a very clear, and instantly accessible, visual demonstration of analytical decisions. This is particularly valuable where two or more different features are being displayed on the same text – a procedure followed (for reasons of economy of space) in this book.

The use of colour-coding has not in fact been a practicable strategy here. Instead, a mixed system of display has been adopted, including underlinings, contrasting font styles and/or superscripts involving numbers and letters. These are all, however, used to the same end: to provide transparent and readily checkable evidence of the analytical decisions made.

All analysed texts are presented together in Appendix 1.

1.2.10 Calculation of results

Results have been calculated on a quantitative basis in line with the particular analytical approach adopted. Quantitative methods were considered adequate for present purposes, and it was not felt necessary to adopt a fully statistical approach (see, however, Butler's recommendation in Wray et al. 1998: 255–64). Results were arrived at via calculation of the total number of occurrences of a chosen feature in proportion to a given set of features or stretch of text. Such an approach allows direct comparison of results based on texts of unequal length (for example those in Chapters 2 and 4). The relevant calculations are explained at each stage, since it is obviously necessary to make clear, and to justify, exactly what is being calculated in proportion to what, and why.

Several chapters use the total number of words in a text as the basis for calculations. This required that decisions be made about what was to count as a word – and any definition had to be applicable to both written and spoken language. There is no very simple answer to this question, as Carter, for example, acknowledges (1998: 4). It was decided to start with Halliday's (1989b: 64) basic formal definition of 'running words . . . in the sense of what is treated as a word in the writing system, being written with a space on either side' and then tighten it up sufficiently to fit the overall needs of the book. The different kinds of data required different kinds of decisions to be made: for example how to deal with hyphenated words in written language, how to apply the same criteria to transcribed spoken language and so on. These kinds of question are considered in individual chapters, and decisions are arrived at which together enable the application of a consistent definition of 'word' across all chapters. The basic principles adopted are:

- contractions (*it's, travelling's*) count as <u>one</u> word;

- <u>all</u> repeated words (*it's it's, do do*) are counted;

- 'noises' (*urr, um*) count as words;

- actually 'spoken' abbreviations (*OK, RSA*) are counted as <u>one</u> word;

- conventionally amalgamated words (*postgrad*) are counted as <u>one</u> word;

- words presented in brackets in transcripts (indicating uncertainty) have <u>not</u> been counted at all;

- an incomplete word (for example *mobil-*) <u>has</u> been counted – and as one word;

- hyphenated words have been counted as <u>two</u> words if each could, in theory, stand alone (*part-time, rock-solid, line-dried*) and <u>one</u> word if one of the two (*non* in *non-bio*) could not easily stand alone.

The value of the computer function 'Word Count' should be realistically assessed, especially for transcribed spontaneous speech involving designation of different speakers. There may be no satisfactory alternative to laborious 'hand' counting.

1.2.11 Presentation of results

Results are presented where possible via quantitative tables (supported by qualitative assessment and interpretation as appropriate – see Section 1.2.12), since these (together with bar graphs, pie charts and so on) can give numerical information in a concise and readily assimilable visual form to support the discursive discussion of findings. Tables have been presented 'progressively' so far as possible, in order to take the reader step by step through the different stages of the argument.

Tabulated figures (showing the number and proportion of a particular unit to a particular group of features) have been given in percentages of up to one decimal place where appropriate. This was felt to be useful in presenting comparative results based on short texts with relatively few instances of a chosen feature. It is important, however, to be aware of the limits of such calculations and to be wary of conveying an impression of scientific precision, which may in fact be spurious. These are all very small studies, intended principally to illustrate particular approaches to some interesting texts and to stimulate comparable endeavours. Quantitative results should therefore be regarded as a means to an end, showing possible differences to be accounted for and prompting exploration of how and why such differences might occur. They can only provide working hypotheses prompting further investigation.

In the context of 'scientific precision', it may be appropriate to comment here that calculators and/or computers are only as good as their users – and the material at their disposal. The most impressive percentages and visual displays of results will prove vacuous if the figures which are fed in to the calculator are unjustifiable and/or inaccurate in terms of the overall approach and the actual analysis.

1.2.12   Discussion of findings

Results are discussed stage by stage, according to the different features investigated, and then brought together. Overall findings are assessed and likely interpretation/s considered and connections made, where possible and appropriate, with original expectations and/or with informants' judgements. Any surprising, or apparently anomalous, findings are examined in some detail and some possible reasons suggested. Overall implications of the findings are explored, always acknowledging the small amount of data examined and consequently the necessary limitations of the individual study.

1.2.13   Suggestions for further work

Each chapter ends with a range of suggestions for further work, for example:

- other features in that particular data which might be examined;
- comparable texts to which the same framework, or a modification of it, might be applied;
- potential application of the same or adapted framework to <u>different</u> type/s of text.

Cross-references to frameworks and/or texts presented in other chapters are made where appropriate.

CHAPTER 2

Literary Narrative

2.1   Introduction

The language studied in this chapter is that of 'literary' narrative. Its place within the overall framework of the book will be under Gregory and Carroll's 'writing intended to be read' (see Figure 1.1). It will be concerned specifically with comparing a short extract from two different versions of the same novel, *Bleak House* by Charles Dickens. The first will be from the original nineteenth-century text, as published by Oxford University Press, and the second from a simplified Guided Reader, written by Margaret Tarner, published in the twentieth century by Heinemann and intended for learners of English.

The broad aim of the study is to compare the different linguistic choices made when expressing the same basic content and at the same time to gain some insight into what might constitute a 'literary' text.

2.2   Identifying the variables

2.2.1   The controlled variables

The variables to be controlled are:

- **Mode**:   The language is **written** in each case and is intended to be processed by the eye (the graphic channel is used). It is being regarded as an 'unmarked' instance of written language, that is, there is congruence and consistency across the principal factors identified in Section 1.1.6.3: the communication is entirely one-way (the reader comes to the text as a finished product and cannot share in text creation) and writer and reader inhabit separate environments (there is no visual contact between them).

- **Field**:   The **purposeful activity** engaged in is the consumption by the reader of (an extract from) a fictional narrative, a story intended to delight, divert and entertain its audience. The basic **content** of the story is essentially the same: each text represents paragraphs taken from the opening pages of the respective books, and these paragraphs provide an atmospheric description of the London setting for the story which is to follow.

2.2.2   The varying variables

The Heinemann Guided Reader contains the following preamble:

> The Heinemann Guided Readers provide a choice of enjoyable reading material for learners of English. The series is published at five levels – Starter, Beginner, Elementary, Intermediate and Upper. Readers at **Upper Level** are intended as an aid to students which will start them on the road to reading unsimplified books in the whole range of English literature.

On the basis of this preamble, therefore, the deliberately varying variable relates to aspects of:

- **Tenor**:   The **participants** in each case are the respective writers and readers of the particular texts, Dickens and his intended readers compared with Tarner and her intended readers. The Heinemann text is a version of the original Dickens text adapted to meet the needs of a specifically targeted readership – those who are learners of English 'at Upper Level' – principally non-native speakers of English. The adapted text can therefore be regarded as having some degree of educational purpose in addition to its overall one of diversion and entertainment as specified under Field, and this may be linked to Gregory and Carroll's 'functional tenor' (see Section 1.1.6.2).

The centuries in which the different texts were actually produced, the identity of the writer in each case and his/her gender are possible additional factors which could be regarded as determining Tenor relations (specifically under 'personal tenor'). These, however, have not been regarded as of primary significance in the current study. The overriding concern under Tenor has been the <u>addressee</u> relationship, the relative status differences as these affect the writer's interaction with the reader (Gregory and Carroll 1978: 49–50). In the original text the relationship may be presumed to be one of approximate equality: Dickens is writing for an audience very like himself. In contrast, the declared aim of the Tarner text is to modify the original in recognition of the (lower) ability in English of the target audience. This has therefore been the principal focus of attention in designing the study.

2.3   Description of the data

The texts chosen for analysis are as follows:

Text 2.1:   The fourth and fifth paragraphs (108 words) from the beginning of Chapter 1 of *Bleak House* by Charles Dickens, as they appear on p. 12 of the edition published by Oxford World's Classics (1998).

The raw afternoon is rawest, and the dense fog is densest, and the muddy streets are muddiest, near that leaden-headed old obstruction, appropriate ornament for the threshold of a leaden-headed old corporation: Temple Bar. And hard by Temple Bar, in Lincoln's Inn Hall, at the very heart of the fog sits the Lord High Chancellor in his High Court of Chancery.

Never can there come fog too thick, never can there come mud and mire too deep, to assort with the groping and floundering condition which this High Court of Chancery, most pestilent of hoary sinners, holds, this day, in the sight of heaven and earth.

Text 2.2:   The third and fourth paragraphs (70 words) from the beginning of Chapter 1 of *Bleak House* by Charles Dickens as retold by Margaret Tarner for Heinemann Guided Readers, as they appear on p. 4 of the edition published by Heinemann English Language Teaching (1992).

Cold, mud and fog filled the streets of London. And the fog was thickest and the mud was deepest near Lincoln's Inn, the very heart of London. The Lord High Chancellor was there, sitting in his High Court of Chancery.

Some of the fog had got into the courtroom too. Perhaps a little fog and mud had got into the minds of the people in the High Court of Chancery.

Two short paragraphs (four and five) have thus been chosen as the basis for Text 2.1 and for the comparative analysis. Identifying directly comparable paragraphs in the Tarner version of the book was not in fact entirely straightforward: simplification could not easily be done on a sentence for sentence, or even perhaps paragraph for paragraph, basis. It is arguable in fact that the first sentence of the first paragraph and at least part of the second paragraph of Text 2.2 are close in content and spirit to parts of the very extensive paragraphs in Dickens which immediately precede and follow the extract in Text 2.1. For reasons of economy of scope, however, it was decided to focus on just these two selected pairs of paragraphs and to regard them as constituting suitable texts for current purposes.

2.4   General expectations re the varying variables

As Carter states (1982a: 4): 'As readers of literature we are involved first and foremost in a response to language.' That response frequently stays at the intuitive level, however, and even if attempts are made to locate it in particular features of the language the process can often be both impressionistic and selective. Carter argues that a principled and systematic analytical approach based on a detailed knowledge of the workings of the language system has the capacity to provide 'insightful awareness of the effects produced by literary texts'.

The language of Dickens has long been popular with linguists for precisely this purpose (see, for example, Leech and Short 1983; Mason 1982; Page 1988; Fowler 1989; Weber 1989; Simpson 1993; Carter et al. 2001). Indeed, the opening paragraphs of *Bleak House* are celebrated in both literary and linguistic circles, being a favourite text selected by university teachers for demonstrating how linguistic analysis can enhance awareness of and admiration for Dickens's creation of atmosphere. A recent instance is an insightful discussion of paragraphs one to four by Carter et al. (2001: 139–43), which focuses principally on the effects of the use of verbs, particularly non-finite verbs.

A comparison of original and deliberately simplified versions of particular literary texts has already been shown to be a useful strategy in pursuit of comparable goals. Freeborn et al. (1993: 209–12), for example, analyse two versions of an extract from a Sherlock Holmes story, suggesting that the simplified version would be easier to read for a learner of English and adequate to convey the basic narrative. However, they conclude that Conan Doyle's more complex style is an inseparable part of his creation of highly plausible characters in Holmes and Watson: the simplified version was 'quite inadequate for a convincing rendering of place, character and dialogue' (1993: 212).

It is not, of course, suggested that 'complexity' is, in itself, a necessary concomitant of a 'literary text', still less that complex effects can be created only by complex grammatical structures (however these might be defined). Indeed, the work of Ernest Hemingway, for example, is famous for its 'simple style' and the way that that style may be used for highly complex ends (Carter

1982b: 67–8). Nevertheless, for some writers – Dickens among them – a close and detailed 'complex v. simple' comparison would seem likely to be illuminating. In pursuit of this aim, therefore, this study asks the following broad questions:

- How might these particular texts differ in terms of their relative complexity/simplicity?

- What do the differences suggest about the way Dickens appears to create some of his literary effects?

- What do the findings of this study suggest about what might constitute a 'literary' text?

2.5 Specific areas of enquiry

It is expected that the status of the target audience will be the overriding factor in influencing linguistic choices in the two texts, in particular the goal of simplification in Text 2.2. The Heinemann preamble already quoted in fact continues as follows:

> the content and language of the Readers at **Upper Level** is carefully controlled with the following main features:
>
> **Information Control**
> As at other levels in the series, information which is vital to the development of a story is carefully presented in the text and then reinforced through the Points for Understanding section. Some background references may be unfamiliar to students, but these are explained in the text and in notes in the Glossary. Care is taken with pronoun reference.
>
> **Structure Control**
> Students can expect to meet those structures covered in any basic English course. Particularly difficult structures, such as complex nominal groups and embedded clauses, are used sparingly. Clauses and phrases within sentences are carefully balanced and sentence length is limited to a maximum of four clauses in nearly all cases.
>
> **Vocabulary Control**
> At **Upper Level**, there is a basic vocabulary of approximately 2,200 words. At the same time, students are given the opportunity to meet new words, including some simple idiomatic and figurative English usages which are clearly explained in the Glossary.

This preamble suggests that it would be most fruitful to explore contrasts in structural choices made within sentences (and clauses), and within nominal groups/noun phrases. It is expected, therefore, that Text 2.1 will display greater complexity than Text 2.2 in both of these areas.

It will be noted that the preamble uses the term 'nominal group' (from systemic functional linguistics) for what some linguists (for example, Crystal

1996) call a noun phrase. The latter term will be used in this chapter for what is in fact the same rank of structure. (See the discussion in Section 1.2.8 of possible differences of terminology and the extent of comparability of different analytical approaches.)

2.6 The frameworks for this study

The frameworks summarised here are intended to assist in reliable identification of the relevant features which are to form the basis for analysis – in this case sentences, clauses and noun phrases. The frameworks are inevitably highly condensed and over-simplified, and can only provide signposts to full explication of the relevant areas. Readers are urged to follow up specific points at each stage.

The frameworks have been adapted from parts of Crystal (1996), and cited page references are to that source unless otherwise stated. Supplementary reference is made at the analysis and commentary stage to the work and insights of others as appropriate, particularly Quirk et al. (1985, 'Q et al.'). Again, readers are recommended to follow up these references.

2.6.1 Sentences

For the purposes of this specific analysis (of written-down literary texts) the simplest criterion for identifying the **sentence** will be regarded as being adequate: a stretch of language which begins with a capital letter and ends with a full stop. (See pp. 30–1 for Crystal's discussion of the limitations of this definition for <u>some</u> texts.) A sentence can be broken down into one or more sets or clusters of patterned elements (**clauses** – see Section 2.6.2), so that a **simple sentence** will consist of one clause and a **multiple sentence** of more than one clause (pp. 32–3).

Clauses within a multiple sentence can have either equal or unequal status. In a relationship of coordination clauses have equal and potentially independent status (thus forming a **compound** sentence), and these clauses are usually linked by a coordinating conjunction such as *and, or, but* (pp. 196–7). In **complex** sentences the relationship is one of subordination, where one clause (the subordinate, dependent or embedded clause) relies grammatically on – or is embedded within – another clause (the main, or superordinate, clause). (For Crystal 'subordinate', 'dependent' and 'embedded' are alternative labels for the subordinated clause, having the same basic meaning, though this is not necessarily so for others – see, for example, Bloor and Bloor, 1995: 153–74.) That relationship may be signalled via a range of markers having a range of meanings (pp. 200 ff.), examples being subordinating conjunctions such as *although, if, when*. Subordinate clauses can be embedded within other clauses (including another subordinate clause), either by replacing, and acting as, an <u>entire</u> clause element or by appearing as <u>part</u> of a clause element (see following subsections).

2.6.2 Clauses

There are five basic elements which go to make up a clause, and each element tends to express a particular kind of meaning (pp. 36 ff.):

- **Subject (S):** usually identifies who or what as the 'topic' of the clause, usually appearing before the verb (V); it controls the form of the verb (V) when in the present tense. S elements can be realised by **noun phrases** (including pronouns – see Section 6.6.1) and some subordinate clauses (pp. 52–3).

- **Verb (V):** the most obligatory of all the clause elements; it expresses some kind of action or process; it can be realised only by a verb phrase. All the other elements can be related to the V element in some way, often in terms of form as well as meaning (pp. 48–51).

- **Object (O):** identifies who or what has been directly affected by the process realised by the verb, usually appearing after the V element. Realised by **noun phrases** (including pronouns) and some subordinate clauses (pp. 54–5).

- **Complement (C):** adds information about another clause element (S or C). Realised by **noun phrases** (including pronouns), adjective phrases, some subordinate clauses (pp. 56–9) and some prepositional phrases. (Note: systemic functional linguistics (see Bloor and Bloor 1995: 47–8) uses the term 'Complement' for what Crystal and traditional grammar call 'Object'.)

- **Adverbial (A):** expresses a wide range of meanings, most frequently acting as 'adjunct' in the clause and relating directly to the process realised by the verb, such as where, when, how, why. Most are optional, though some verbs – for example *put* – require an A element to complete their meaning. Given their role in contributing a wide range of information to the clause, more than one A element can occur in a clause. They can appear in different positions within the clause, though some are more restricted than others and/or have different relationships with other clause elements. Realised by adverb phrases, prepositional phrases, some **noun phrases**, some subordinate clauses (pp. 60–1, 172–9; see also Section 4.8).

It will be seen from the above that subordinate clauses can realise the whole of any clause element except the verb (V). It is important to note, too, that they can also occur as part of a clause element, for example as postmodifier within a **noun phrase** (see following subsection).

2.6.3 Noun phrases

Noun phrases appear in all shapes and sizes (pp. 104 ff.), and it will be apparent from the preceding subsection that they can realise a wide range of clause elements. Each noun phrase consists essentially of a noun or noun-like word (it can be a pronoun) which acts as centre or **head** of the phrase, and while it can occur on its own it is more often accompanied by other constituents which cluster around the head. Noun phrase structure can be characterised as follows:

- The **head**:   the obligatory item; most frequently a noun, traditionally regarded as naming some entity, whether concrete or abstract, count or non-count (pp. 108–27). The head controls the concord, or agreement, with other parts of the clause – compare the S element above.

- One or more of a set of **determiners**:   appearing before the head, the principal one being the central determiner (for example definite article *the* or indefinite article *a(n)*). A range of other words can, however, act as predeterminers, appearing before the central determiner (for example *all, both*), and postdeterminers, appearing after the central determiner (for example cardinal and ordinal numerals like *three, third*) (pp. 128–35).

- The **premodification**:   appearing between the determiner and the head; frequently adjectives, though other word classes are possible, including participles (*–ing* and *–ed* forms) and nouns (pp. 136–7).

- The **postmodification**:   appearing after the head, but still within the noun phrase; usually prepositional phrases or clauses (clauses may be finite or non-finite) (pp. 138–43).

2.7   Method and presentation of analysis

Each extract was analysed according to the frameworks outlined in Section 2.6, first identifying sentences, clauses and noun phrases (Texts 2.1A and 2.2A) and then analysing the structure of each individual noun phrase (Tables 2.1 and 2.2). The analyses are presented as set out below. (Complete analyses will be found in Appendix (1.1.)

2.7.1   Identification of sentences, clauses and noun phrases

Sentences within each text are numbered and set out in sequence.

Clauses within each sentence are indicated by a system of double vertical lines; individual clause elements are indicated by single vertical lines and designated S V A and so on. Square brackets indicate embedded clauses and/or clause elements; superscripts S^1, S^2 'match' grammatical and notional subjects; round brackets indicate where S elements occur within V elements.

The displayed sentence and clause analysis is then summarised in linear form. (The chosen system of display has been adapted from that of Berry, 1996.)

Noun phrases (including all embedded noun phrases) are individually identified and placed between curly brackets. Each 'first stratum' noun phrase is, in addition, underlined.

The analysis is displayed in Texts 2.1A and 2.2A, respectively. Annotations give support for various analytical decisions.

2.7.2 Noun phrase structures

Each of the noun phrases identified in Texts 2.1A and 2.2A has been analysed and categorised as either simple (**S**) or complex (**C**). The analysis follows Crystal (1996: 107) in classifying determiner plus head (or head alone) as a simple noun phrase. If other constituents are present, this has been categorised as a complex noun phrase.

Tables 2.1 and 2.2 display the structures of all the noun phrases in Texts 2.1A (Dickens) and 2.2A (Tarner) respectively, including all embedded noun phrases. Square brackets indicate second and third strata noun phrases. As before, annotations support particular analytical decisions. (Tables 2.1 and 2.2 will be found with Texts 2.1A and 2.2A in Appendix 1.1.)

2.8 Presentation of results: sentences and clauses

Table 2.3 presents a comparison of results for the two texts.

It shows that the most notable differences between the two texts at sentence and clause ranks of structure occur in the number of words per sentence (Dickens's sentences are almost three times as long as Tarner's) and the number of clauses per sentence (Dickens has almost twice as many as Tarner). Three of Tarner's five sentences are in fact simple sentences (see Section 2.6.1) compared with only one of Dickens's three sentences. Differences in number of elements per clause are less pronounced, though still notable: 4.3 in the Dickens compared with 3.4 in the Tarner. The simplification aimed at by Tarner's publishers would thus seem to have been successfully achieved at both sentence and clause rank.

Moving beyond the quantitative results, Texts 2.1A and 2.2A show that the similarities and differences between the two extracts are at their clearest when sentence 2 of Tarner is compared with sentence 1 of Dickens. Tarner parallels Dickens's approach when she uses a compound sentence which consists of

Table 2.3 Comparison of results for sentence and clause analysis

	Dickens	Tarner
Number of running words	108	70
Number of paragraphs	2	2
Number of sentences	3	5
Number of clauses	8	7
main	6	6
embedded	2	1
Number of clause elements	34	24
Number of words per sentence	36	14
Number of clauses per sentence	2.7	1.4
Number of elements per clause	4.3	3.4

'interpolated coordination' of SVC clauses (see note **1** to Text 2.1A) with a postponed A element, the latter realised by a prepositional phrase governed by *near*. Tarner, however, uses only <u>two</u> interpolated coordinate clauses compared with Dickens's three, and – crucially – the delayed A element contains relatively simple noun phrase structures compared with the multiple embeddings in the Dickens (see further discussion in Section 2.9). The cumulative effect created by Dickens in this first sentence is inevitably somewhat dissipated in the Tarner version and this has consequences for the overall impact of the passage (see Section 2.10).

Tarner's sentence 3, with its supplementive VA clause (see note **3** to Text 2.2A), is on the face of it more complex than Dickens's simple sentence 2. However, for her main clause she chooses an 'unmarked' (SVAA) ordering of clause elements which contrasts with Dickens's 'marked' sequence of A elements which initiate the clause and act to constantly postpone the appearance of the necessary S element *the Lord High Chancellor*. Dickens's effect is compounded by the similarly unusual placing of the V element *sits* <u>before</u> the S element (see, too, Carter et al.'s discussion of this sentence (2001: 142–3)).

The most complex sentence of all in the Dickens extract is clearly sentence 3, and it is notable, though perhaps not surprising, that this time Tarner makes no attempt to reproduce in a simpler form the multiply complex structures and effects created in the original. Instead she gives us two simple sentences which to some extent (see Section 2.3) aim to reproduce the content in Dickens's sentence 3. The displayed summary analysis in Text 2.1A gives a clear indication of Dickens's densely packed constructions in this one sentence, both <u>between</u> clauses and <u>within</u> clauses (more interpolated coordinate clauses, each having a parallel marked structure of its own) leading (or perhaps *groping and floundering*) towards the extended, equally densely packed, final Adverbial element. All of this works cumulatively to create an accretion of highly complex obfuscating structures which appear deliberately to mimic, even embody, the obscure – indeed almost impenetrable – legal processes.

As indicated above, Dickens uses slightly more elements per clause than Tarner, and it is on the face of it noteworthy that both texts have a fairly high number of A elements (11 and 8 respectively). In terms of numbers alone, however, this might not in fact be regarded as unusual, especially given the descriptive, scene-setting function of each extract. Indeed, Q et al. (p. 478) note that 'in the Survey of English Usage corpus there are on average 15 adverbials in every 100 running words of material, spoken and written alike'. As already indicated, however, Dickens does use his A elements in particularly striking ways within individual sentences. The functions, realisations and deployment of A elements in both texts are re-examined in Section 2.10.

2.9 Presentation of results: noun phrases

Tables 2.4 to 2.6 show comparisons of simple versus complex noun phrases for each text – at first stratum (Table 2.4), second and subsequent strata (unpacked embedded noun phrases) (Table 2.5) and finally a comparison over all (Table 2.6). Totals of simple and complex noun phrases respectively are shown as a percentage of total noun phrases for each extract.

It will be seen from Table 2.4 that at primary level of structure the actual number of noun phrases is the same (15) in each extract. However, Table 2.5 shows that Dickens has a further ten embedded noun phrases (twice as many as Tarner), and these in fact involve four third-stratum embeddings (see displayed noun phrase structures in Table 2.1). In terms of complexity, the Dickens extract has a higher percentage of complex noun phrases at each stratum, and overall – at 48 per cent compared with 25 per cent – it has almost twice as many as the Tarner (see Table 2.6). Once again, Tarner has fulfilled the publishers' aims in using a higher proportion of simple noun phrases overall (75 per cent of all noun phrases compared with 52 per cent for the Dickens extract) and in general avoiding complexity at this rank of structure.

A notable feature of Dickens's use of the noun phrase is the recurrence of noun phrases in apposition (see note **a** to Text 2.1A). A series of three occurs in sentence 1 within the final Adverbial which provides the required, but postponed, completion of the three preceding coordinated clauses (see Section 2.8). The first two of these appositional noun phrases are complex (with the second involving yet more embedded noun phrases), thus compounding the delay in reaching the final goal: *Temple Bar*. A second series of appositional noun phrases, this time of two, occurs in sentence 3 (see note **b** to Text 2.1A). This is the very long and complex sentence already discussed in Section 2.8, and again the sequence of appositional noun phrases occurs within the final

Table 2.4 Comparison of simple v. complex noun phrases at first stratum

	Total first stratum NPs	Simple	%	Complex	%
Dickens	15	8	53.3	7	46.7
Tarner	15	11	73.3	4	26.7

Table 2.5 Comparison of simple v. complex embedded noun phrases, at second and subsequent strata

	Total embedded NPs	Simple	%	Complex	%
Dickens	10	5	50.0	5	50.0
Tarner	5	4	80.0	1	20.0

Table 2.6 Comparison of all simple v. complex noun phrases

	Total NPs	Simple	%	Complex	%
Dickens	25	13	52.0	12	48.0
Tarner	20	15	75.0	5	25.0

Adverbial. The second of these is a complex and particularly unusual (marked) noun phrase which involves cataphoric ellipsis of the (usually obligatory) head and postponement of interpretation of the ellipted head until the postmodification (see note 4 to Table 2.1). We thus find, as with the clause elements discussed in Section 2.8, both linear placement and structural complexity of noun phrases combining to create the very delay, difficulty and potential confusion conveyed by the <u>content</u> of the Dickens extract.

The analysed noun phrase structures displayed in Table 2.1 show that the Dickens text uses both pre- and postmodification, and the latter is, of course, the potential source of more complexity – especially more embedded noun phrases. Most of the postmodification is via prepositional phrases, with many of the prepositional complements being additional complex noun phrases. There is just one embedded clause (*which this High Court* . . . , in sentence 3), the only postmodifying embedded clause in either of the extracts.

As Table 2.2 shows, Tarner's noun phrase complexity is virtually all via postmodification (she has just one premodifying *very*) and, further, most of the postmodifiers are prepositional phrases. However, only one of the prepositional complements is a complex noun phrase. The Tarner extract cannot therefore make use of heavily complex embeddings at noun phrase rank to suggest the difficulty and obscurity of the original.

2.10 Adverbials

Much of the complexity at noun phrase rank tends to occur within the Adverbial elements in both texts. In fact it would seem to be the <u>combined</u> effects of strategic positioning within the clause (see Section 2.8) and degree of complexity within the elements themselves (see Section 2.9) that are so striking. Tables 2.7 and 2.8 therefore list in numerical order each of the A elements identified in Texts 2.1A and 2.2A respectively, together with its basic function and formal realisation. (A elements occurring within embedded clauses are shown in square brackets within each table.)

It will be seen that the predominant function of the A elements in the clauses of both extracts is that of adjunct, specifically space adjunct. This would be in keeping with the scene-setting role of these early paragraphs within the whole work in each case – that is, the A elements are answering the question '<u>where</u> is this happening' (and, to a lesser extent, '<u>when</u>'). Six of the eleven A elements in the Dickens extract and five (or possibly six) of the eight in the Tarner are space adjuncts. All of the space adjuncts in the Dickens are realised by prepositional phrases, several of which have further layers of complexity, such as complementation by a complex noun phrase and/or noun phrases in apposition (see Section 2.9).

The most complex A elements of all, however, are not space adjuncts but time+result and manner adjuncts (numbers 8 and 9 in Table 2.7). The second of these is embedded within the first, and, in addition, itself embeds two further Adverbials, a time adjunct and a space adjunct (numbers 10 and 11 in Table 2.7). All of this occurs, significantly, within the highly complex, increasingly obfuscating, sentence 3.

Table 2.7 Adverbial elements extracted from Text 2.1A (Dickens)

No.	Sentence	Adverbial element	Acting as	Realisation
1	1	near that leaden-headed old obstruction, appropriate ornament for the threshold of a leaden-headed old corporation: Temple Bar	space adjunct	prepP
2	2	hard* by Temple Bar	space adjunct	prepP*
3	2	in Lincoln's Inn Hall	space adjunct	prepP
4	2	at the very heart of the fog	space adjunct	prepP
5	2	in his High Court of Chancery	space adjunct	prepP
6	3	Never	time adjunct	adverb
7	3	never	time adjunct	adverb
8	3	to assort with the groping and floundering condition which this High Court of Chancery, most pestilent of hoary sinners, holds, this day, in the sight of heaven and earth	time + result adjunct	non-finite clause
9	3	[with the groping and floundering condition which this High Court of Chancery, most pestilent of hoary sinners, holds, this day, in the sight of heaven and earth]	process (manner) adjunct	prepP
10	3	[this day]	time adjunct	nounP
11	3	[in the sight of heaven and earth]	space adjunct	prepP

* *hard* has been regarded as an adverb meaning 'close' (Cassell 1998: 673) modifying *by* and thus forming a complex preposition (Crystal 1996: 182).

Table 2.8 Adverbial elements extracted from Text 2.2A (Tarner)

No.	Sentence	Adverbial element	Acting as	Realisation
1	2	near Lincoln's Inn, the very heart of London	space adjunct	prepP
2	3	there*	space adjunct	adverb
3	3	sitting in his High Court of Chancery	space? time? adjunct	non-finite clause
4	3	[in his High Court of Chancery]	space adjunct	prepP
5	4	into the courtroom	space adjunct	prepP
6	4	too	additive subjunct	adverb
7	5	Perhaps	content disjunct	adverb
8	5	into the minds of the people in the High Court of Chancery	space adjunct	prepP

* *there* is being used here as an adverb of place, and is therefore different from the instances of existential *there* which occur in sentence 3 of Text 2.1 (see note **3** to Text 2.1A).

In the Tarner extract the main area of complexity overall also lies within the A elements. The most significant instance is the space/time adjunct (number 3 in Table 2.8) realised by the non-finite supplementive (VA) clause of rather indeterminate meaning (see note **3** to Text 2.2A). This clause has its own embedded A element, the space adjunct *in his High Court of Chancery*, realised by a prepositional phrase whose complementation is a simple noun phrase. The degree of complexity is, however, much less notable than in the Dickens and this, together with the relatively unmarked placing of the A elements (see Section 2.8) tends to preclude the creation of the kinds of effects achieved by Dickens.

2.11   Summary and overall comparison of findings

We now return to consider the findings of this small study in the context of the broad questions set out in Section 2.4.

It will be apparent that the Dickens extract does indeed display greater grammatical complexity than the Tarner extract, and that this greater complexity is found at several different ranks of structure:

- **in sentences** (overall length; numbers of clauses; sequencing of clauses)
- **in clauses** (both numbers of elements and marked ordering of elements)
- **in specific clause elements** (both sequencing of Adverbials and their realisations)
- **in noun phrases** (sequencing via use of apposition; multiple embedding; marked structural choices)

The cumulative effect of all of these varied instances of grammatical complexity contributes to the difficulty of the Dickens text even for a native speaker of English – and of course prompts Tarner's admirable attempt at simplification for the benefit of learners of the language.

The analysis has demonstrated, however, that the Dickens text is not just complex and 'difficult' in an abstract way. Its difficulty is an intrinsic part of its literary quality: its complexities and their strategic manipulation are all working in the same direction, that is, to keep readers waiting, to make us struggle through the multiple complexities, to cloak in fog-like obscurity the ultimate goal, which is justice. The multiply embedded and swirling grammatical structures create the very confusion which is inherent in the delay, difficulty and duplicity of the legal process. The linguistic form here is the narrative content.

Has this small contrastive study brought us any closer to saying what might constitute a 'literary' text? Tarner's aim is to make the basic content of a famous and well-loved text accessible to learners of English and at the same time to use the text as a teaching and learning tool. In pursuit of these aims she appears to be making a modest attempt to mirror some aspects of Dickens's style, but presumably she would not make a strong claim to 'literary' quality. The act of carrying out this study has enabled us to:

identify and describe some very specific areas of complexity in the linguistic choices made in the original which are thrown into relief precisely because they are not found in the simplified version;

suggest some likely explanations for those choices and the effects they appear to create.

It is hoped that in a small way the study has confirmed what was probably already known: that a 'literary' narrative goes beyond the telling of an entertaining, intriguing or even life-enhancing story. On this very limited evidence, the 'literary' quality of a text would seem to consist in its chosen <u>means</u> as much as its ends, its <u>form</u> as much as its meaningful content.

2.12   Conclusion

This chapter has explored texts representing contrasting versions (original and simplified) of an extract from an established instance of literary narrative. It has identified areas of grammatical difference between the two texts at the rank of sentence, clause and noun phrase, and has used those differences to explore how some of Dickens's effects appear to be created. The overall findings of the study confirm that the <u>form</u> in which a 'literary' text is expressed is an essential element of its constitution, a union of content <u>and</u> form.

2.13   Suggestions for further work

(a)   Other valuable work might be done on these particular texts, especially if more extended extracts were to be used, for example:

  ● exploration of the relationship between perceived literary effects and linguistic choice (both grammatical and lexical), via use of independent informants (see Section 1.2.6) followed by detailed analysis to try to account for their judgements (compare Section 3.4.2).

  ● contrasts in specific lexical choices (see 'vocabulary control' in Section 2.5), for example of 'non-core' versus 'core' choices (Carter 1998) in relation to the grammatical patterning identified. This might also serve to foreground what appears to be Dickens's disgust at the stupidity and obduracy (*leaden-headed old obstruction*) and the potential for corruption (*hoary sinners*) inherent in the legal process.

(b)   Comparable texts to which a version of the approach adopted in this chapter could be applied include other works by Dickens and, of course, other writers – whether or not directly comparable modified versions are available. Hemingway and Conan Doyle have already been referred to (see Section 2.4). Other writers whose grammatical choices would repay investigation in terms of their literary effects include Henry James and, especially, e e cummings. The final stanzas of cummings's poem 'anyone lived in a pretty how town' (1963: 44) show him contravening expectations of grammatical, lexical and graphological choice to moving effect:

> all by all and deep by deep
> and more by more they dream their sleep
> noone and anyone earth by april
> wish by spirit and if by yes
>
> Women and men (both dong and ding)
> summer autumn winter spring
> reaped their sowing and went their came
> sun moon stars rain

(c)   The framework and principles expounded in this chapter might be applied to other, non-literary, kinds of text, for example academic text books on a given subject aimed at different age groups. Alternatively, a chosen text might be deliberately manipulated to make it more or less 'complex' or 'literary' (perhaps focusing on some of the features specified in the Heinemann preamble quoted in Section 2.5). Informants could be asked to judge the different versions in terms of their perceived degrees of 'difficulty' or 'literariness' (Carter and Nash 1990: 30–5).

Newspaper Reports

3.1 Introduction

This chapter will continue with 'writing intended to be read' (see Figure 1.1), but this time with the language of print media: news as it appears in newspapers. It will compare very short extracts from reports of the same incident: the first sentence of the report appearing in six different British daily newspapers (three each of broadsheet and tabloid) published on the same date.

It will examine how the different texts appear to be interpreted by readers and will try to account for those interpretations by analysing aspects of the form in which the incident is presented.

3.2 Identifying the variables

3.2.1 The controlled variables

The variables to be controlled are:

- **Mode**: The language is 'written' in each case. As in Chapter 2, it is being regarded as an 'unmarked' instance of written language, in that there is consistency across the principal factors identified in Section 1.1.6.3: communication is via the graphic channel (intended to be processed by the eye), is entirely one-way (the reader cannot share in the process of text creation) and there is no visual contact between writer and reader.

- **Field**: The **purposeful activity** involved is the reporting of what is regarded as a significant incident for the benefit of the paper's readership (see, however, Section 3.2.2 below). The **content** of each report as represented by the extracts is essentially the same. The incident occurred during a visit made in February 1984 by Ian MacGregor, the then chairman of the National Coal Board (later British Coal), to Ellington Colliery, Northumberland, England. It was a time of some unrest in the coal industry and in fact the miners' strike followed later in the year – beginning a period of serious industrial and political conflict in Britain. During the Ellington visit the chairman was surrounded by miners, and at some point he hit the ground.

3.2.2 The varying variables

As Fowler (1991: 11–12) notes, all news is inevitably mediated and no news medium can be completely 'neutral' or 'unbiased'. In fact events only <u>become</u> 'news' when selected for inclusion in news reports, and different newspapers will report differently in both content and presentation, showing disaffections and also affiliations in their treatment of particular topics: 'The world of the Press is not the real world, but a world skewed and judged.'

Fairclough (2001: 41, 128) goes further, claiming that mass-media discourse involves hidden relations of power: text producers in mass communication address an 'ideal subject', constructing their own notion of their 'ideal reader', and by this means may succeed in manipulating audiences to accept their view of particular events.

Significantly-varying variables are therefore likely to arise under:

- **Tenor**:   The **participants** here are the writers/copy-editors of each of the selected newspapers and their presumed readership in each case (that is, the reader/addressee). There is likely to be some evidence of the particular newspaper's views of a given industrial/political situation and a corresponding assumption about its readership's views – particularly at a time of industrial and political unrest. There are also likely to be differences in the degree to which those assumptions are actually made manifest via specific linguistic choices (perhaps in order to 'manipulate' the reader, as claimed by Fairclough). These separate presumptions can be related to Gregory and Carroll's (1978) distinctions within Tenor relations, that is, to personal and functional tenor respectively.

3.3   Description of the data

Each of the extracts chosen for analysis is the first sentence of a report of the incident as it was published on 23 February 1984. The six chosen newspapers are *The Times*, the *Guardian*, the *Daily Telegraph* (all broadsheet – that is, large format – papers), the *Sun*, the *Daily Mail* and the *Daily Star* (all tabloid – smaller format – papers. (It should be noted that the terms 'broadsheet' and 'tabloid' are used here as purely physical descriptions, with no implied evaluation.) For reasons of simplicity and economy the extracts have been presented as Extracts A to F within a single text, **Text 3.1**, and in the following order: *The Times*, the *Sun*, the *Daily Mail*, the *Guardian*, the *Daily Star* and the *Daily Telegraph*.

Text 3.1   Extracts from six newspapers dated 23 February 1984

Extract A from *The Times* (broadsheet):
Mr Ian MacGregor, the National Coal Board chairman, was knocked to the ground as angry miners surged round him at the Ellington Colliery, Northumberland, yesterday.

Extract B from the *Sun* (tabloid):
Coal chief Ian MacGregor, 71, was flattened yesterday by a mob of rampaging miners.

Extract C from the *Daily Mail* (tabloid):
Coal Board chief Ian MacGregor was knocked to the ground unconscious yesterday when mob fury erupted during a pit visit.

Extract D from the *Guardian* (broadsheet):
The chairman of the National Coal Board, Mr Ian MacGregor, said last night that he was fit and well after being knocked to the ground earlier in the day by protesting pitmen.

Extract E from the *Daily Star* (tabloid):
Coal Board chief Ian MacGregor was battered to the ground yesterday by a mob of angry miners.

Extract F from the *Daily Telegraph* (broadsheet):
Mr Ian MacGregor, National Coal Board chairman, was knocked stunned to the ground by a surging mob of 400 miners who had thrown eggs and slices of bread, at Ellington Colliery, Northumberland, yesterday.

This incident took place some time ago and it is possible that the extracts might therefore be considered somewhat out of date. They are, however, exemplary illustrations of contrasting reports of a readily comprehensible incident occurring in a politico-industrial conflict situation – and one, moreover, which is usefully indeterminate in terms of 'what really happened'. For whatever reason in the context of the wider political climate, fewer comparable situations have arisen in recent years. The extracts themselves are admirably succinct, lending themselves readily to analytical comparison, and they have proved invaluable for teaching purposes over the years. They provide a ready model for potential adaptation and application to more recent texts (see Section 3.16 below).

3.4   Expectations re the varying variables

3.4.1   General expectations

Fowler et al. (1979: 1–4) and others (for example, Fairclough 1995, 2001; Fowler 1991; Hodge and Kress 1993; Simpson 1993) claim that the assumptions referred to in Section 3.2.2 are 'ideological' assumptions. These assumptions are considered to be implicit in the reporting of news, particularly when situations of conflict in a directly political context are being reported. As Simpson comments (1993: 5): '[there is] a proliferation of definitions available for the term *ideology*, and many of these are contingent on the political framework favoured by the analyst.' For present purposes, therefore, Hodge and Kress's very simple definition of 'ideology' will be adopted: 'a systematic body of ideas, organized from a particular point of view' (1993: 6).

Trew (1979a, 1979b) explored the ideological implications of particular linguistic choices in newspaper reporting, focusing specifically on 'transitivity' choices (Halliday 1970). He examined a number of different conflict situations, for example in Rhodesia (now Zimbabwe) and the UK, and looked in particular at how events were represented in terms of what was happening, who was responsible for particular actions, how both actions and those responsible were described, and so on. He related his areas of interest to the kinds of processes which were represented, the degree of specification of agency involved in those processes, and the ways in which participants within each reported situation were identified and described. Trew, therefore, offers a potentially valuable model to draw on in analysing the current data, particularly since his ideas have proved to be fertile ground for a number of subsequent linguists interested in comparable approaches to media language (for example, Fairclough 2001; Fowler 1991; Freeborn et al. 1993; Simpson 1993).

3.4.2 Evaluative responses

Evaluative responses to specific texts are essentially subjective, and it is therefore advisable to obtain, where possible, independent views of particular kinds of evaluation – independent, that is, from those of the analyst. This is likely to be particularly important where political stances may be involved and where claims about ideological implications of language use are being investigated (see warnings about the dangers of 'circularity' in Section 1.2.6).

These extracts have been used for teaching purposes over several years, and an essential part of the pedagogic process has been a prior evaluation by each group of students (regarded as 'naïve' informants) as to what they perceive to be the degree of 'bias' (if any) in each text. In order to arrive at such an evaluation groups of students (undergraduates, adult education students, in-service teachers) have been presented with the set of (uniformly reproduced and unattributed) text extracts and asked to assess them. They were specifically asked to rank the texts according to their perceived bias against the miners, that is, to place the texts in order from most to least biased in a specific direction.

Results have been remarkably consistent overall (see Section 3.12 for discussion of a few anomalies), with Extract D (*Guardian*) being always ranked last (that is, regarded as being <u>least</u> biased against the miners), and Extracts B (*Sun*) and E (*Daily Star*) alternating as first or second (that is, as <u>most</u> biased against the miners). The remaining three extracts were ranked more or less consistently between these two as follows (from more biased to less biased): Extract C (*Daily Mail*), Extract F (*Daily Telegraph*) and Extract A (*The Times*). There was clearly something to be accounted for here via detailed linguistic analysis.

3.5 Specific areas of enquiry

During the informant test a general supplementary question was asked as to what it was in the extracts that informants thought might be influencing them. Their comments focused mainly on vocabulary choices, for example *a mob of rampaging miners* versus *protesting pitmen*, and *battered to the ground* versus *knocked to the ground*. These comments in fact can be related to Trew's 'terms for the "principal" participants' and 'terms for the "focal" process' respectively (1979b: 151), and it was therefore decided to carry out a systematic comparison of such choices across the six extracts.

The analysis was also broadened to include other potentially significant features identified by Trew (1979a: 98–9). These were the choice of passive rather than active voice, with its consequent option of specification or non-specification of 'agency' (who or what is represented as being responsible for the carrying out of the significant action – the 'focal' process), and how far the option of <u>non</u>-specification is chosen. It was felt that informants would be responding to a range of these features, whether consciously or unconsciously.

Trew was drawing on the semantic concept of Transitivity as set out in Halliday (1970) and subsequently developed and further explicated by him (for example, Halliday 1994a). Frameworks for identifying the components of the Transitivity system and their possible realisations are therefore outlined in Section 3.7.

3.6   The frameworks: structural elements – clauses

Choices from within the Transitivity system are made within the clause, and it is therefore necessary first to identify all clauses in the extracts. Decisions about Voice also require prior identification of clauses and their individual structural elements. The latter can then be related to the different meaning components being realised: that is, the 'performer' and/or 'undergoer' of an action or happening can be related to the clause element/s which may realise those meaning components (see following sections).

A framework for identifying sentences and clauses has been set out in Section 2.6, based mainly on Crystal (1996), and this has been regarded as suitable for present purposes. Halliday's own grammatical categories and labels may differ in places from Crystal's but these differences are not significant at this particular point. Most importantly, Crystal's categories connect quite satisfactorily with the most salient features of Halliday's theory of Transitivity.

3.7   The frameworks: Transitivity

A number of linguists have given valuable accounts of Halliday's theory, for example Berry (1989), Eggins (1994), Bloor and Bloor (1995), Davidse (1999), and some of these are drawn on as necessary and/or appropriate in what follows. Particular use is made of Bloor and Bloor (1995) ('B&B'), and page references cited are to that work unless otherwise indicated.

Halliday (1970: 145–50) begins from the basic premise that language is used to represent a speaker's experience of the world (its 'ideational' function). The expression of that experience involves the configuration of particular 'meaning components', or semantic 'roles' (1970: 146) to communicate about happenings (termed 'Processes'), persons, objects, entities involved in those happenings ('Participants'), and different aspects of those happenings ('Circumstances'). Further, these components are made manifest via particular lexicogrammatical choices, with Processes most usually being realised in English by verbal groups/verb phrases, Participants by nominal groups/noun phrases and Circumstances by adverbials. (Less expected realisations of, for example, Processes can also be found, and these may have interesting implications - see discussion in Fairclough (2001: 43, 103), Fowler (1991: 79–80), Hodge and Kress (1993: 187–9) of instances of 'nominalisation', that is, where Processes are realised by <u>nouns</u> rather than verb phrases.)

In the account which follows the model outlined will be the most usual, or 'unmarked', choice – the one which is 'congruent', less metaphorical (Halliday 1994a: 342). It also represents a highly simplified account of the principal types of Process (and the Participant roles associated with those processes) which are most directly relevant to this particular study. (Readers are urged to go to more extensive accounts in pursuit of important detail.)

Processes are the happenings or 'goings-on' (B&B: 110) as represented in a clause: they are something to which aspects of time may be applied. The goings-on may be actual physical actions (for example *knocked* in Extract A) or something less directly physical (for example *was* in Extract D), and these different kinds of Process are associated with different Participant roles.

3.7.1 Material Processes and associated Participants

Material Processes involve action, the 'doing words' of traditional grammars, typically answering the question 'what did he do?' (B&B: 116–17). Verbal realisations cited by B&B are *took, picked up, strolled* (p. 111) and examples from the extracts are *surged* (Extract A) and *had thrown* (Extract F).

The principal Participant roles associated with Material Processes are Actor, Goal and Beneficiary (pp. 111–14). Actor is the performer of the relevant action (*angry miners* in Extract A; *who* [*a surging mob of 400 miners*] in Extract F). Goal is the undergoer of the action (the person or thing being acted upon) (*Coal Board chief Ian MacGregor* in Extracts C and E). Beneficiary is the receiver (as distinct from the undergoer) of the action. In B&B's example (p. 114) *He gave no money to Thaler, Thaler* is Beneficiary and *no money* is Goal. As B&B comment, the role is that of Beneficiary whether or not the action may be regarded as 'beneficial'. (There are no instances of a specified Beneficiary in the six extracts being examined.)

B&B also describe (pp. 114–16) what they acknowledge is a rather difficult component to identify – Range – in such constructions as *He took a bath*. This is brought about by the tendency of English to realise some Processes (e.g. *bathe*) as nouns (*bath*) (a particular type of 'nominalisation'), where in semantic terms Process and Participant are blended together. The Participant role for *a bath* in such constructions would be Range. B&B illustrate the distinction between that meaning and the formally identical, though hypothetical, report of a domestic burglary *He took a bath*, where *took* would be Material Process and *a bath* would be Goal. (There are no instances of Range in the six extracts.)

Goal and Range are typically realised by noun phrases and Beneficiary by noun phrases or prepositional phrases.

3.7.2 Mental Processes and associated Participants

Mental Processes 'involve phenomena best described as states of mind or psychological events' (B&B: 116). Realisations cited by B&B include *think, feel, see, hear*. Participant roles here would be Senser (the one experiencing the Process) and Phenomenon (that which is experienced). B&B give the examples *he knew what speed was* and *I heard the shots*.

Phenomenon is typically realised by noun phrases and some subordinate clauses. (There are no instances of B&B's Mental Processes in the six extracts.)

3.7.3 Relational Processes and associated Participants

B&B (pp. 120–22) acknowledge that the semantics of Relational Processes are very complicated (see Davidse 1999: 166–289, for an extensive exposition), and in fact they begin their account by citing how these Processes are typically realised. Realisations tend to be by *be* or other copular verbs such as *seem* and *become*, and sometimes by verbs such as *have, possess* and so on. B&B subclassify Relational Processes as follows:

- **Attributive** Processes: These ascribe 'an attribute to some entity', and Participant roles are Attribute (what is attributed) and Carrier (the person or thing bearing what is attributed). An example is *he was fit and well* in Extract D.
- **Identifying** Processes: These relate an Identified with an Identifier and B&B cite the examples *His name is Quint* and the disambiguating *Carpenter is his name* (rather than his profession) (pp. 121–2), adding that the precise allocation of Participant roles can be highly dependent on context.

Attributes and Identifiers are typically expressed by clause Complements and realised by noun phrases and adjective phrases.

3.7.4 Verbal Processes and associated Participants

As B&B acknowledge (pp. 122–5), Verbal Processes have some features of both Material and Mental Processes, since speaking can be regarded as the action of verbalising thought. (Berry (1989: 152) in fact categorises speaking as an 'externalised mental process'.) B&B, however, argue for Verbal Processes as a separate category. Typical realisations are *said* (as in Extract D), *ask, exclaim, tell*.

The main Participant role is Sayer (the person producing the utterance – *The chairman of the National Coal Board, Mr Ian MacGregor* in Extract D), with other Participants categorised according to the representation of what is verbalised. If the latter is presented as being identical to the Sayer's utterance (that is, as Direct Speech) it is labelled Quoted. If it is presented as being reported through the perspective of the writer or speaker (Indirect or Reported Speech) it is labelled Reported. An example of Reported is the embedded clause beginning *that he was fit and well . . .* in Extract D.

B&B identify two other potential Participants in the Verbal Process – Verbiage and Target. Verbiage represents some kind of classification or interpretation of what the Sayer said (*I told her <u>the truth</u>; He told me <u>what I wanted</u>*

to know). Target is 'a fairly peripheral Participant' (p. 125) which tends not to occur with direct or indirect speech; B&B's example is _Former party officials criticised party leadership_.

It will be apparent that Quoted, Reported, Verbiage and Target are typically realised by clauses (main and subordinate) and noun phrases.

3.7.5   Other Processes

B&B identify two other, minor, Processes – Existential and Behavioural. Existential bears some resemblance to Relational Process, but it has only one Participant, the Existent, and it appears in two main forms. The first is with a copular verb and existential _there_ as Subject (see note **3** to Text 2.1A) – _There were ten of us in the party_ (i.e. group); the second is with a copular verb, the Existent as Subject and usually a Circumstantial Adjunct – _Ten of us were in the party_ (p. 125).

Behavioural Process is apparently 'the bottom of the barrel' (p. 125), being a grey area between Material and Mental Processes. As with Existential Process, only one Participant is normally required – the Behaver. B&B cite a (non-finite) clause as a 'straightforward' example of Behavioural Process – . . . _its police department number plate vanishing around a corner,_ and also offer as a possible further example _the car slid away._ They acknowledge, however, that the latter could equally be argued to be a Material Process.

3.7.6   Circumstance

Circumstance is in some respects a more peripheral 'role' than Participant (p. 126). It adds information such as location (both spatial and temporal) of the Process (where, when) and/or manner of the Process (how) (see Section 2.10). There may therefore be more than one instance of Circumstance within the same clause.

Circumstances are typically expressed by Adverbial elements, which may be realised by adverbs, prepositional phrases, some noun phrases or some subordinate clauses (see also Section 2.6.2). Examples of temporal Circumstances are _yesterday_ in Extract B (realised by a noun phrase) and _when mob fury erupted._ . . . in Extract C (realised by a finite subordinate clause).

3.8   The frameworks: Voice

The Voice system relates Transitivity choices to the way they are represented in the surface structure of the clause (Berry 1989: 153–61). The Participant in the role of Actor may be represented by the S element of a clause (_John kicked the ball_) or by the A element (_The ball was kicked by John_). The Participant in the role of Goal may be represented by the O element of a clause (_John kicked the ball_) or by the S element (_The ball was kicked by John_). Where the <u>Actor</u> of a Process is represented by the S element Active Voice has been chosen; where the <u>Goal</u> of a Process is represented by the S element Passive Voice has been chosen (Berry 1989: 154; emphasis added).

Crystal (1996: 88) describes the way Passives are formed from Actives in terms of surface manoeuvres:

> The subject of the active verb is moved to the end of the clause, and becomes the passive agent. *By* is added. The object of the active verb is moved to the front of the clause and becomes the passive subject. A passive verb phrase replaces the active – a form of the auxiliary verb *be* followed by the *–ed* participle.

In formal terms, most 'transitive' verbs (or rather those which are being used 'transitively' – that is, requiring an Object) can be either Active or Passive, though there are some exceptions (see Crystal 1996: 89). It will be apparent that verbs being used 'intransitively' (not requiring an Object) cannot form Passives (Quirk et al. 1985: 162). In semantic terms (that is, in terms of the account of Transitivity outlined in Section 3.7), this means that Passives can occur with (most) Material Processes, some Mental Processes (B&B's *I was seen; shots were heard*; p. 117); and some Verbal Processes, for example some of those involving Verbiage (*questions were asked*) or Target (*The party leadership was criticised*) (B&B: 124–5). Relational Processes, where, for example, Attribute is expressed by a Complement, cannot form Passives.

A consequence of the choice of Passive is the potential for non-specification of the Participant responsible for the Process (B&B: 41). Crystal (1996: 90–1) makes the same point, using the generalised 'agent' to include all the roles indicated by B&B's Actor, Senser and Sayer. Non-specification of responsibility for the Process may be because the addition of an agent would be 'to state the obvious' (Crystal 1996: 90) or for flexibility in organising information (Halliday 1994b: 68–9), but there may be other – ideological – implications, as suggested by Trew (1979a: 98–9) and others (see Section 3.4.1).

3.9 Method and presentation of analysis

The following describes the analytical methods adopted for identifying each of the linguistic features specified in Sections 3.6 to 3.8. The full displayed analyses will be found in Appendix 1.

- **Stage one:** Each extract was analysed in terms of its sentence and clause structure, using the framework and system of notation outlined in Sections 2.6 and 2.7, with the full analysis displayed as Text 3.1A. Notes give support for various analytical decisions.

- **Stage two:** Each clause in each extract was analysed using the frameworks outlined in Section 3.7. Meaning components were listed in terms of Processes (and kinds of Process), Participants (and their relationships to the relevant Processes), and Circumstances (and their relationship to the relevant Processes). Any clause acting as an element of a main clause was accorded its status as a component of that main clause (for example, temporal Circumstances in Clause 1 of Extract A and Clause 2 of Extract D). Each of these subordinate clauses was then separately analysed in terms of its own Processes, Participants and Circumstances.

Ian MacGregor was designated 'Participant 1' throughout and the miners 'Participant 2'. Minor Participants were designated 3, 4 and 5. Again, annotations explain analytical decisions.

- **Stage three**: Each clause was designated Active or Passive (see framework in Section 3.8) by conflating the S element of the clause and the relevant meaning component. Thus if S expresses Goal (as in Clause 1 of Extract A) then the clause was designated Passive; if it expresses Actor (as in Clause 2 of Extract A) the clause was designated Active.

Stages two and three of the analysis are displayed as Text 3.1B.

3.10   Presentation of results: Voice, Agency, Process

Table 3.1 summarises the findings for Voice, Agency (whether specified) and Process for each clause in each extract, as set out in Text 3.1B.

The table shows that of the overall total of 11 clauses in the six extracts, six are in the Passive form (one in each extract) and five in the Active. All of the extracts choose Passive clauses to express what may be called 'the focal incident', that is, the meeting of Ian MacGregor (Participant 1) with the ground and the part which may or may not have been played by the miners (Participant 2) in this. The Passive clauses express Material Processes and these are realised by forms of the verbs *knock*, *flatten* and *batter* (see below). Five of the Passive clauses are main clauses and either constitute the whole of the sen-

Table 3.1   Comparison of Voice, Agency and Process for each extract

Extract	Voice	Agency	Type and Realisation of Process
A Clause I	Passive		Material *knock*
Clause 2	Active	Specified	Material *surge*
B Clause I	Passive	Specified	Material *flatten*
C Clause I	Passive		Material *knock*
Clause 2	Active	Specified	Material? *erupt*
D Clause I	Active	Specified	Verbal *say*
Clause 2	Active	Specified	Relational *be*
Clause 3	Passive	Specified	Material *knock*
E Clause I	Passive	Specified	Material *batter*
F Clause I	Passive	Specified	Material *knock*
Clause 2	Active	Specified	Material *throw*

tence (Extracts B and E) or occupy first position in the sentence (Extracts A, C and F). The remaining Passive clause is a subordinate clause (Clause 3 of Extract D) which is doubly embedded within two preceding Active clauses.

Of the six Passive clauses, four (Extracts B, D, E and F) assign specific agency to the miners (that is, there is a designated Actor, realised by a *by* . . . phrase – see Text 3.1B). The Passive clauses in Extracts A and C have no specific assignment of agency. These two extracts choose to report events from the position that something happened to Ian MacGregor when something else happened, and they therefore leave the reader to make any relevant connections and possible assignment of responsibility. (Simpson (1993: 107), for example, notes that 'temporal contiguity' may be used to imply causation.) They each do this by using an embedded clause to express a temporal Circumstance: *as angry miners surged round him* . . . (Extract A) and *when mob fury erupted* . . . (Extract C).

The lexical realisations of the Material Processes involved in the focal incident differ notably. Extracts A, C, D and F choose the relatively neutral *knocked* (*to the ground*). This could imply an accident, though C and F add the Circumstance *unconscious* and *stunned* respectively to convey the effect on Ian MacGregor. Extract B chooses *flattened* and E chooses *battered* (*to the ground*), both of which have strongly negative implications, with *battered* also implying intentional action by the miners.

The five Active clauses of necessity specify agency (see Section 3.8). However, only two of these (Extracts A and F) involve Material Processes which have the miners as Actor, and neither of these represents the focal incident nor does the latter have Ian MacGregor as Goal. *Surge* in Clause 2 of Extract A is an intransitive verb and thus has no Goal. The verb itself has the denotation 'swell, heave (of waves) . . . move with a sudden rushing or swelling motion' (Cassell 1998: 1482). The Goal of *throw* in Clause 2 of Extract F is *eggs and slices of bread* (Participant 5). (No Beneficiary of the Process is specified.) The two Active clauses in Extract D express Verbal and Relational Processes respectively, in which Ian MacGregor himself is either Sayer or Carrier.

The remaining Active clause is that involving the slightly problematic Material/Behavioural Process (Clause 2 of Extract C) (shown as Material? in Table 3.1). The verb realising the process is *erupt*, which denotes a sudden and violent bursting out (Cassell 1998: 490) with connotations of uncontrollability (volcanoes 'erupt'). The agent here is *mob fury* (Participant 3) – whether labelled Actor or Behaver – that is, it is realised by a noun phrase which has an abstract (and therefore inanimate) noun as head (Crystal 1996: 112). The lexical realisation of that noun (*fury*), denotes 'vehement, uncontrollable anger, rage . . . uncontrolled violence' (Cassell 1998: 594). Its noun premodifier (*mob*) has (human) animate connotations which are similarly negative and this violent happening is presented as occurring at the same time as the focal incident. It should be noted that there is no explicit mention <u>at all</u> of the miners (Participant 2) in extract C (see Table 3.2). However, the conjunction of *mob fury* and the *pit visit* element of the temporal Circumstance may serve to create an association of 'miners' with that *mob*.

3.11   Presentation of results: Participants I and 2

Table 3.2 compares the realisations in each extract of the principal Participants for this study: Participant 1 (Ian MacGregor) and Participant 2 (the miners).

The various choices for each Participant will first be considered from the perspective of the type and structure of noun phrase used in each case, and then in lexical terms.

3.11.1   Structural choices

It will be clear from Table 3.2 that the numbers of first stratum (that is, non-embedded) noun phrases realising Participant 1 (11) greatly exceeds those for Participant 2 (six). This is a consequence, first, of the lack of any explicit mention of Participant 2 in Extract C and, second, of the different patterns of structural choices made for the different Participants: broadly, apposition for Ian MacGregor and postmodification for the miners. These are made clear when the structures of each of the noun phrases used to realise each Participant are displayed in Tables 3.3 and 3.4. (The analytical and display procedures adopted are as outlined in Sections 2.6.3 and 2.7.2.)

Extracts A, D and F each choose to use two noun phrases in apposition (see note 1 to Text 3.1A) to identify Participant 1 (Ian MacGregor). Each extract states his full name, and in addition accords him his official status. The former is realised by the same simple noun phrase, and the latter by complex noun phrases involving either premodification (Extracts A and F) or postmodification (Extract D). There are two realisations by pronouns (*him* in Clause 2 of

Table 3.2   Realisations of Participants 1 and 2 in each extract

Extract	Participant I – Ian MacGregor	Participant 2 – the miners
A	Mr Ian MacGregor the National Coal Board chairman him	angry miners
B	Coal chief Ian MacGregor, 71	a mob of rampaging miners
C	Coal Board chief Ian MacGregor	0
D	The chairman of the National Coal Board Mr Ian MacGregor he	protesting pitmen
E	Coal Board chief Ian MacGregor	a mob of angry miners
F	Mr Ian MacGregor National Coal Board chairman	a surging mob of 400 miners who

Table 3.3 Structure of each noun phrase used to realise Participant I (Ian MacGregor) in each extract

Extract/ NP	Determiner	Premodification	Head	Postmodification
A.I	—	—	Mr Ian MacGregor	—
A.2	the	National Coal Board	chairman	—
A.3			him	
B.I	—	Coal chief	Ian MacGregor	71
C.I	—	Coal Board chief	Ian MacGregor	—
D.I	The		chairman	of the National Coal Board
D.2	—	—	Mr Ian MacGregor	—
D.3	—	—	he	—
E.I	—	Coal Board chief	Ian MacGregor	—
F.I	—	—	Mr Ian MacGregor	—
F.2	—	National Coal Board	chairman	—

Extract A and *he* in Clause 3 of Extract D). Extracts B, C and E each choose a single, complex, noun phrase consisting of name as head with only slightly different forms of premodification. Extract B also chooses to add *71* after the head, here analysed as a postmodifying element within the relevant noun phrase (see discussion of its possible status in note **2** to Text 3.1A).

When we turn to Participant 2 (the miners) we see from Table 3.4 that although there are only six 'first stratum' explicit realisations of the miners, three additional realisations appear in postmodifying elements. The embedded status of the latter is indicated by the use of square brackets in Table 3.4.

Table 3.4 shows that all realisations (apart from *who*) are complex noun phrases having a variety of structures. Extracts A and D choose premodification alone. Extracts B, E choose postmodification alone, while Extract F chooses both pre- and postmodification. Each choice of postmodification in fact contains a further, embedded, noun phrase also realising Participant 2. There are thus eight lexical realisations in total and one grammatical realisation (by the pronoun *who*).

Table 3.4 Structure of each noun phrase used to realise Participant 2 (the miners) in each extract

Extract/NP	Determiner	Premodification	Head	Postmodification
A.1	—	angry	miners	—
B.1	a	—	mob	of rampaging miners
B.2	—	[rampaging	miners]	—
D.1	—	protesting	pitmen	—
E.1	a	—	mob	of angry miners
E.2	—	[angry	miners]	—
F.1	a	surging	mob	of 400 miners
F.2	[400	—	miners]	—
F.3	—	—	who	—

3.11.2   Lexical choices

As with structural choices, the lexical choices for Participant 1 fall into the same two broadly similar groups: Extracts A, D and F and Extracts B, C and E. (These groups are in fact the broadsheet versus the tabloid newspapers – see Section 3.14 below.) Extracts A, D and F each identify Participant 1 by stating his full name *Ian MacGregor* and, in addition, each precedes that with the formal title *Mr*. Each also separately states his official position (a concomitant of the choice of appositional structures), and in very similar terms. Extract F has *chairman* as headword premodified by *Coal Board* and Extract A has the same with an added determiner *the*. Extract D has *The chairman* as determiner and headword, with *of the National Coal Board* as postmodifier. (It may be significant that in Extract D Participant 1's official status precedes his full name – see Section 3.12.)

Extracts B, C and E each make very similar choices for Participant 1. The headword is his full name in each case (but <u>without</u> the formal title *Mr*), and this is premodified by either *Coal Board chief* (Extracts C and E) or the even more informal *Coal chief* (Extract B). Extract B not only omits to mention the *Board* which Participant 1 represents but also increases the emphasis on the personal element by adding his age after his name. Given that his age is stated to be *71* it is likely to have even greater significance in overall evaluative terms (see Section 3.12).

Lexical choices for Participant 2 are rather more various than for Participant 1. Four of the overall total of eight fully lexicalised noun phrases include the potentially 'neutral' item *miners* (Extracts A, B, E and F), but they are modified in rather different ways. Two (Extracts A and E) choose the premodifier *angry*, one (Extract B) the premodifier *rampaging*, and one (extract F) a post-determiner and cardinal numeral *400*. It is arguable that *angry* is a fairly low-key item in this context when used alone as in Extract A. However, as part of the postmodification of *mob* (Extract E) it acquires some of the latter's negative connotations (see below). The *rampaging* in Extract B has pejorative connotations of violence and extreme loss of control. The choice of the substantial numeral *400* in Extract F emphasises the disparity between the very large number of miners and the lone individual, particularly in conjunction with the headword *mob*.

In only one instance (Extract A), is *miners* used as the headword of its first stratum noun phrase, and thus given maximum focus. In the remaining three instances (Extracts B, E and F) the headword in each case is – perhaps significantly – *mob*, with *miners* appearing as part of the postmodification. Cassell (1998: 936) offers several definitions of *mob*, including 'a gang of criminals engaged in organized crime; a disorderly or riotous crowd, a rabble; a group or class (of people of a specified kind)', all of which are more or less derogatory. The choice of such an item as (first stratum) headword was very striking in terms of overall evaluations – see further discussion in Section 3.12.

Only one extract premodifies *mob* (Extract F) and the choice here is *surging*. The use of the verb *surge*, in Extract A, was discussed in Section 3.10, where it was felt to have relatively 'neutral' connotations. Its 'neutrality' is, however, compromised to some extent in Extract F when its *–ing* form is placed in close premodifiying association with *mob*.

The remaining lexical item used to refer directly to the miners is *pitmen* in Extract D, where it appears as headword of its first stratum noun phrase. This is an interesting choice, in that it may be regarded as potentially 'neutral', perhaps even having positive connotations for some readers. Its premodifier *protesting* appears to be even more low-key than *angry*, with its suggestions of moderation and reasonableness, even possible justification. The effects of these choices are considered below in the context of the overall findings.

3.12 Overall comparison of findings in relation to general expectations and evaluative judgements

Section 3.5 has suggested that informants will have responded to a range of specific linguistic features in arriving at their evaluative judgements of the different extracts. Further, it is expected that the relative salience of particular features for a particular informant, and the ways in which they cluster together in a particular extract, will tend to determine the ratings position accorded to it.

Table 3.5, therefore, brings together the main findings for each of the linguistic features for each extract in turn which were separately presented in Tables 3.1 and 3.2, that is, for Voice, specification of Agency, realisations of Processes and realisations of Participants 1 and 2.

Table 3.6 then presents essentially the same information but this time reorders the extracts in line with the overall evaluative judgements of bias against the miners described in Section 3.4.2. The findings are therefore presented in the following order: Extract B (*Sun*), Extract E (*Daily Star*), Extract C (*Daily Mail*), Extract F (*Daily Telegraph*), Extract A (*The Times*) and Extract D (*Guardian*). Table 3.6 also highlights in bold those features which have been identified in Sections 3.10 and 3.11 as having potentially negative

Table 3.5 Overall comparison of findings for each clause of each extract

Extract/ Clause	Voice	Agency Specified	Realisation of Process	Realisation of Participant 1	Realisation of Participant 2
A.1	Passive	No	knock	Mr Ian MacGregor the National Coal Board chairman	
A.2	Active	Yes	surge	him	angry miners
B	Passive	Yes	flatten	Coal chief Ian MacGregor, 71	a mob of rampaging miners
C.1	Passive	No	knock	Coal Board chief Ian MacGregor	
C.2	Active	Yes	erupt		
D.1	Active	Yes	say	The chairman of the National Coal Board Mr Ian MacGregor	
D.2	Active	Yes	be	he	
D.3	Passive	Yes	knock		protesting pitmen
E	Passive	Yes	batter	Coal Board chief Ian MacGregor	a mob of angry miners
F.1	Passive	Yes	knock	Mr Ian MacGregor National Coal Board chairman	a surging mob of 400 miners
F.2	Active	Yes	throw		who

connotations so far as the representation of the miners' role in the focal incident is concerned, and which might have influenced informants.

It would seem from Table 3.6 that there is <u>some</u> degree of correspondence between the number of potentially negative features in each extract and its place in the table. Extract B, which alternated with E in being evaluated as 'most biased', has five highlighted features (which might, in very broad terms, be represented as 'B: –5'), and Extract D ('least biased') has only one (D: –1). However, it is clear that such simple (even crude) quantitative figures based on the highlighted features are not sufficient to account for overall judgements. For example, Extracts A and C have no highlighted features at all yet both were rated as more biased than extract D. Further, Extract C was rated as more biased than both Extracts A and F, the latter having three (F: –3). This suggests that some features may carry more 'negative weight' than others, and/or that some other features or factors have to be considered, which were identified in Text 3.1B but which do not appear in Table 3.6.

Some of the latter ('other') features have in fact already been mentioned in

Table 3.6 Overall comparison of findings for each clause of each extract in order of perceived bias

Extract/ Clause	Voice	Agency Specified	Realisation of Process	Realisation of Participant 1	Realisation of Participant 2
B	Passive	**Yes**	*flatten*	*Coal chief Ian MacGregor, 71*	*a **mob** of **rampaging** miners*
E	Passive	**Yes**	***batter***	*Coal Board chief Ian MacGregor*	*a **mob** of angry miners*
C.1	Passive	No	*knock*	*Coal Board chief Ian MacGregor*	
C.2	Active	Yes	*erupt*		
F.1	Passive	**Yes**	*knock*	*Mr Ian MacGregor National Coal Board chairman*	*a surging **mob** of **400** miners*
F.2	Active	Yes	*throw*		*who*
A.1	Passive	No	*knock*	*Mr Ian MacGregor the National Coal Board chairman*	
A.2	Active	Yes	*surge*	*him*	*angry miners*
D.1	Active	Yes	*say*	*The chairman of the National Coal Board Mr Ian MacGregor*	
D.2	Active	Yes	*be*	*he*	
D.3	Passive	**Yes**	*knock*		*protesting pitmen*

Sections 3.10 and 3.11, and some indeed were commented on during discussions with groups of informants (see Section 3.4.2). They are re-examined here:

- Neither Extract A nor Extract C specifies Agency in connection with the focal incident, though each one could be regarded as implying some degree of responsibility via the use of a subordinate clause to express temporal Circumstance (see reference to Simpson, 1993: 107, in Section 3.10, and also a comparable comment by Trew, 1979a: 98–9). Clause A.2, however, has the relatively neutral *angry* and *miners* and *surged*, while Clause C.2 has the negative *mob* and *fury* (together realising an apparently separate Participant) and also *erupted*. It is possible that these lexical choices in Extract C work by further implication to designate the miners (who are not actually mentioned at all in the extracted sentence) as a furious and violent mob associated with an uncontrollable action (see Note **1** to Text 3.1B and discussion in Section 3.10) and thus 'confirm' and reinforce their implied responsibility. Extract C could in fact be regarded as having potentially three negative features (C: –3).

- The Circumstances *unconscious* (Clause C.1) and *stunned* (Clause F.1) may be further negative factors (thus C: –3 –1 = –4; F: –3 –1 = –4).

  There could, in fact, be <u>positive</u> connotations attaching to some features and these too should be taken into account:

- The use of the word *pitmen* for Participant 2 in Clause D.3 has already been mentioned, together with the possibility of its having positive connotations for some readers and therefore informants. (At least one informant also commented approvingly on the alliterative effects of *protesting pitmen*.) (D: –1 +1 = 0)

- It is also notable (and received positive comment from some informants) that Extract D postpones the account of the focal incident until the third clause of the sentence, that is, after two clauses in which Participant 1 is reported as saying he is *fit and well*. (D: 0 +1 = +1)

- It <u>may</u> be significant that Extract D identifies Participant 1 first by his official position (*chairman* being chosen as headword of the first noun phrase) and only then by his name. This may therefore place greater emphasis on his 'role' in the specific industrial context rather than his 'person' (contrast the approach of, for example, Extract B). (D: +1 +1? = +2?)

- The non-restrictive clause in extract F.2 is particularly interesting. A substantial number of informants over the years have commented on the humorous – even bizarre – effect created by the reference to *eggs* and (in particular) *slices of bread* as being missiles thrown by the miners. Many felt that the humour (whether intentional or not) might have served to mitigate, at least to some extent, the negative effects of *mob* and *400*. (F: –4 +1 = –3) On the other hand, it should be mentioned that in an informant test carried out with undergraduates in 2001, several felt the *eggs and slices of bread* reference could be interpreted as being contemptuous of the miners (especially in a mining area) and for them this <u>heightened</u> the negative effect of the extract as a whole. This particular group of informants gave Extract F a higher ('more biased') overall rating than Extract E, closer in fact to Extract B, the only real deviation from the general pattern described in Section 3.4.2 above.

An allocation of all the suggested 'negative' and 'positive' features along the lines of the above would give overall 'scores' for the bias-rated extracts as follows: Extract B –5; Extract E –3; Extract C –4; Extract F –3; Extract A zero; Extract D +2. Adopting this perspective, the only remaining anomaly would be the placing of Extract E in comparison with Extract C and, possibly, Extract B. This is considered in Section 3.13.

3.13   Discussion and summary

The findings so far suggest that some linguistic choices may carry more 'negative weight' than others in the six extracts. Specification of Agency, and the question of explicit (or indeed implicit) responsibility in the focal incident, may be of less significance or salience for informants than the clustering of various <u>lexical</u> choices realising both the Processes and Participants involved. (Informants did appear to focus on vocabulary choices in their comments on their judgements, though it is possible that they found it easier to be explicit in that particular area.) For Processes, both the degree of intention involved (see note 1 to Text 3.1B) and the force implied appear to be highly significant. Thus:

- *batter* (Extract E) brings with it both intention (**He battered him accidentally* would require a <u>very</u> carefully explained context to be an acceptable construction) and great force;

- *flatten* (Extract B) <u>could</u> be unintentional, but in any case suggests great force or impact;

- *knock* (Extracts C, F, A and D) could indicate both lack of intention and minimal force, especially when used alone. However, when used in conjunction with certain Circumstances of manner – *unconscious* (Extract C) and *stunned* (Extract F) – that force is notably increased.

The degrees of both intention and force in Processes (whether inherent or implied) are increased when those lexical choices are allied with comparably significant lexical realisations of the Participants involved in those Processes. Thus:

- the *flatten*ing of one *71*-year-old (and therefore potentially vulnerable) man by *a mob of rampaging miners* (Extract B);

- the even more deliberate and forceful *batter*ing of one man by *a mob of angry miners* (Extract E);

- the *knock*ing (*stunned*) to the ground of one man by *a surging mob of 400 miners* (Extract F)

all work together to reinforce the negative effects of the relevant extracts. It is possible, in fact, that it is the extra negative weight of inherent <u>intention</u> in the choice of *batter* which accounts for Extract E's approximately equal overall rating with Extract B (see Section 3.4.2 and the attempt at crude quantitative comparisons made in Section 3.12). Extract C suggests that, even without explicit specification of either Agency or Participant 2, carefully chosen lexical items (*mob* and *fury* in close proximity to *a pit visit*) can suggest both a negative representation of the miners and, by extension, the violence involved in the focal incident (*knocked unconscious* and, especially, *erupted*).

In contrast, the omission of specification of Agency in Extract A – on the face of it comparable to that in Extract C – in conjunction, this time, with relatively neutral lexical choices (*knocked* and *angry*) appears to create the overall 'neutral' impression suggested by its 'zero' score. The 'least biased', even positive, rating of Extract D appears to be enhanced by its lexical choices for both Process (*knocked*) and Participant 2 (*protesting* and *pitmen*).

In all, therefore, the findings appear to confirm that naïve informants are not just most consciously responsive to lexical choices (items of vocabulary) when intuitively evaluating text extracts. They also appear to be highly sensitive to both shades of meaning in and particular <u>clusters</u> of those lexical choices. These are likely to work together to influence them in arriving at judgements and ratings of, in this case, degrees of perceived bias against the miners.

3.14 Ideological positions and the tabloid/broadsheet dimension

What, finally, might this very small study have to say about the ideological positions suggested by the chosen extracts? Some tentative connection may be made between the apparent perspective on the miners as represented here and the presumed political stance of the relevant newspaper. For example, in a situation of industrial and political conflict in the UK most of the selected newspapers might be expected to incline towards the 'establishment' and therefore be less than sympathetic to any challenge to that establishment. The *Guardian*, stereotypically, might be expected to take up a more 'liberal' position on industrial and political matters. Its editorial stance is therefore likely, in principle, to be more ready to consider the pros and cons of an establishment challenge. The findings of the study do tend to bear this out to some extent, even, in the case of The *Guardian,* showing some degree of sympathy for the protagonists of that challenge. (It should be emphasised that informants' judgements were based on unattributed text extracts and they were <u>not</u>, therefore, automatically coloured by stereotypical preconceptions.) The findings do, moreover, provide some support for Fowler's claim (1991: 11) that both 'disaffections <u>and</u> affiliations are obvious when one starts reading carefully' (emphasis added).

What is also of great interest is the fact that the findings show a notable tabloid versus broadsheet dichotomy: the three 'most biased' extracts (Extracts B, E and C) are all tabloids and the remainder (Extracts F, A and D) are all broadsheets. Many writers (for example, Crystal and Davy 1969: 174; Hodge 1979: 157–8; Fowler 1991: 39–40; Freeborn et al. 1993: 175–6) have found differences in degrees of formality in the styles of tabloid versus broadsheet newspapers, which they relate to expectations about and of their presumed readerships. Hodge, in particular, linked a particular format of newspaper with its readership's social class background – a broadsheet with a middle-class readership and a tabloid with a working-class one – though, given the increasing popularity of the tabloid format generally, that theory may now be less tenable. This, in any case, introduces an additional ideological dimension concerned with social class which would not necessarily correlate with that concerned with political ideology.

An examination of the data from a specifically tabloid/broadsheet perspective is beyond the scope of this particular study (see Section 3.16) but one or two relevant points may be illuminating.

- A few informants reacted favourably to the longer, more 'wordy', extracts, tending to regard the shorter extracts as expressing a more negative view of the miners. (There is, in fact, an approximate correlation of word length with tabloid/broadsheet format and also with evaluative ratings. The respective figures are: Extract B (*Sun*) 14 words, E (*Star*) 17 words, C (*Mail*) 20 words, F (*Telegraph*) 33 words, A (*Times*) 24 words, D (*Guardian*) 32 words.)

- The shorter (tabloid) extracts tend to make the most informal and emotive – and negatively-associated – lexical choices (see Sections 3.10 and 3.11), and it may be significant that the 'most biased' of the broadsheet extracts (Extract F) makes one notably emotive lexical choice. The *Daily Telegraph*'s use of *mob* to characterise the miners contrasts strongly with its much more formal and dignified representation of Ian MacGregor, according him his full name and official position. Indeed, in some later and more delicate informant tests (involving individual 'scores' for each extract rather than mere placing in order) Extract F's total score brought it much closer to the three tabloids, with a notable gap before Extracts A and D.

3.15   Conclusion

This chapter has analysed brief extracts (indeed fragments) from six newspapers and has used these as a basis for an exploration of newspaper reporting from a particular ideological perspective.

It has considered the way that specific linguistic choices within the sentence and the clause may represent different views of essentially the same reported incident, and it has attempted to account for independent judgements of perceived bias in the different text extracts by applying a detailed Transitivity and Voice analysis to each extract. Informants' judgements of relative 'bias' have been found to be related to significant clusters of lexical choices used to represent both the Processes and the Participants involved in the reported incident.

3.16   Suggestions for further work

(a)   Other features which might be systematically investigated in these particular texts, especially if longer extracts were used (including headlines), include:

- specific vocabulary choices, to be explicitly evaluated by informants as part of their general assessment of the different extracts (see, for example, Carter 1998) thus providing external evidence to complement interpretations here;

- degrees and types of grammatical complexity within the noun phrase (building on Section 3.11.1), adopting an explicit tabloid-versus-broadsheet perspective (see Crystal and Davy 1969: 173–92; Freeborn et al. 1993: 175–6).

(b) The precise framework adopted for this study could be used to good effect with more recent news stories. Reports published in Britain on 17 May 2001 confirm that the same kind of reporting can still be found and of virtually the same kind of event – including the egg-throwing!

> The deputy prime minister, John Prescott, was manhandled and attacked by protesters yesterday while campaigning in north Wales. *(Guardian)*

> John Prescott punched a protester who hurled an egg at him in an astonishing election brawl last night. *(Mirror)*

> Contrasting viewpoints of contentious events (whether in a political or other context) will of course be found in other English-speaking cultural environments. Potentially fruitful comparisons could therefore be made between newspapers which might be expected to take up different ideological positions on a particular national or regional issue or event. Alternatively, the local equivalents of broadsheet and tabloid newspapers could be analysed in terms of their formal or informal treatments of a specific story (and see below).

(c) A modification of the framework could be devised which identified some of the features of the 'oral model' of print news reporting noted by Fowler (1991: 59–65). In terms of Figure 1.1 this could perhaps be characterised as 'writing which is intended to be read as if heard'. Brief illustrations of such writing are the headlines of two British tabloids of 29 September 2002 (which, coincidentally, throw an unexpected light on the John Major who features in Chapter 6):

> YES, YES, YES PRIME MINISTER
> EDWINA: MY 3-HOUR SEX ROMPS WITH MAJOR
> > *(News of the World)*

> (Parody of *Private Eye* cover: photograph of John Major and Edwina Currie, with speech bubble emanating from latter)
> *Back to basics at my place tonight John?*
> SEX, STRAWBERRIES, CREAM . . . AND WHIPS
> > *(Sunday Mirror)*

An additional example would be the headline of Figure 7.1, though features of 'spoken' style can extend beyond news headlines, as Fowler suggests (1991: 39–40), and indeed into other types of journalism. The chosen analytical approach could be based on (elements of) the frameworks presented in this chapter, augmented by approaches and/or findings throughout the book, for example reproduction in writing of characteristic features and patterns of speech such as: informal, often punning, lexical choices (Chapter 8); 'conversational' utterances (Chapters 4 and 5); particular personal pronouns (Chapter 6); contracted and reduced forms as described by Quirk et al. (1985: 1595–7), whether as indicators of non-standard pronunciation (Chapter 7) or not (Chapter 8).

(d) A further development of (c) could be a study which explicitly incorporated broader Mode variation, for example by comparing reports of the same news story in print with those broadcast on particular television or radio channels, that is, with texts which have been written expressly to be spoken (with or without visual support). What kinds of 'spoken' features might be identifiable? How far might these differ between the different texts?

4.1　Introduction

This chapter explores aspects of talk between women friends. Its place within the framework presented in Figure 1.1 will be under 'speaking (conversing) spontaneously'. It will compare an extract from a telephone conversation with one from a face-to-face conversation between the same two women.

The broad aim of the study will be to investigate how far conversational characteristics which have been stereotypically ascribed to women are used during the two conversations and how far their use may differ between the two situations.

4.2　Identifying the variables

4.2.1　The controlled variables

- **Mode**:　The participants are 'speaking spontaneously' and 'conversing'. That is, the speaking and hearing are simultaneous. Communication is via the phonic channel, the role of the language is constitutive, and the participants are sharing in the process of text creation (see Section 1.1.6.3).

- **Field**:　The **purposeful activity** involved in each case is an informal conversation which is re-establishing friendly links and enabling the two friends to get up to date news after a time lapse since their last conversation. In each conversation, therefore, they are 'catching up' on interactive gaps, a conversational activity which plays a particularly important role in women's friendships (Coates 1996: 50–1). The chosen extracts involve approximately similar **content** in each case: details of one (the same) participant's new job, travelling arrangements, feelings involved and so on. (The content is outlined in more detail in Section 4.3.) In the extracts transcribed, therefore, participant R does most of the talking (see Section 4.10).

- **Tenor**:　The participants are two women, R and H, who are former colleagues and friends of long standing, having been fellow postgraduate students in Nottingham, England. Both are sociolinguists. At the time of the first conversation, in 1986, R had completed her PhD and H was still working on hers; they were both teaching in Higher Education but in different parts of Britain. Both were teaching on a part-time basis, but H's contract was on a year-to-year, hourly paid, basis, whereas R's was a permanent 'proportional' post. By the time of the second conversation, in 1998, R had a full-time permanent post with a different institution and with a different kind of teaching role. H had completed her PhD and was still teaching in Higher Education and still on an hourly paid basis, but within a different institution.

4.2.2　The varying variables

The deliberately varying variable between the two text extracts relates to aspects of **Mode** – specifically **spatial Setting** (see discussion in Sections

1.1.6.3 and 1.1.6.4). In the telephone extract the participants are in physically separate places and there is no visual contact between them; in the face-to-face extract there is, of course, visual contact.

4.2.3 'Uncontrolled' variables

The telephone extract is part of a spontaneous conversation which was accidentally recorded by a telephone answering machine, that is, there was no awareness at the time – on either side – that it was being recorded.

The later recording of the face-to-face data was carried out with the full awareness of both participants that it was taking place and also that it was to be used specifically for this book. It is possible that this knowledge could have had an influence of some kind on the linguistic behaviour of one or other participant. The focus of the content was to some extent decided in advance by me, in that I wished to emulate aspects of the content of the telephone extract (see Field). However, I would regard the actual detailed interaction which emerged as 'spontaneous' in terms of its specific form, certainly so far as R was concerned. R had received a copy of the telephone tape when she originally gave permission for its use for teaching purposes (see Section 4.3 below), but she had no knowledge of precisely <u>how</u> it had actually been used. Similarly, while she was fully aware of the supplementary and 'comparative' element behind the later recording, she did not know what particular approach to the data would be adopted, nor precisely what was to be compared with what. These had not, in any event, been fully determined at the time of the later recording.

Two other 'uncontrolled' factors will be apparent, both of which relate to Setting and both arising under Mode. The telephone and face-to-face data differ in their temporal Settings, since the former was recorded in 1986 and the latter in 1998. They also differ in their spatial Settings, although along a different (and less significant) dimension from that identified in Section 4.2.2. At the time of the telephone conversation the participants were both in Nottingham (though at separate locations), whereas for the face-to-face conversation the participants were in Beckenham, Kent (and, of course, at the same location).

The temporal and spatial Setting differences are not felt likely to be significant in terms of their effect on the precise linguistic choices made, and this is particularly so for the spatial Setting factor. I have no intuitions at all about the possibility of increased or decreased use of the types of linguistic feature to be investigated as a consequence of the time lapse between the two conversations, the professional changes which had occurred for both women, or the kinds of job discussed. The effect of a Nottingham versus Beckenham context is likely to be negligible. The degree of planning for the second conversation, and its possible influence on H's choices, will be considered again in Section 4.14.3. In the meantime, the findings of the analyses will merely be noted and any potential effects arising under the 'uncontrolled' variables will be assessed, where appropriate, at a later stage.

4.3 Description of the data

Text 4.1 is a transcribed extract from a recording of a long telephone conversation between R and H, which took place on 30 October 1986. The recording was made accidentally via a telephone answering machine. It was not realised until some time afterwards that the conversation had actually been recorded, at which point the audiotape was put aside as being potentially interesting and useful linguistic data. It was indeed used subsequently for teaching purposes (during the late 1980s and early 1990s) with groups of international diploma students and also with some native-English-speaking undergraduates, principally to illustrate the kinds of features which had been claimed to be characteristic of spontaneous speech by women in English.

The extract is taken from the early part of the conversation and progresses through two broad phases: an account of the time devoted to R's part-time job in London, including the travelling time; and an extended discussion of the possibilities around Teaching English as a Foreign Language (Tefl), particularly in relation to her current post and her feelings about it. The extract runs for approximately two and three-quarter minutes and consists of 555 words in total.

Text 4.1   Phone

[…]
H: [h- how's it going
R: [oh
H: [I gather you're having a bit of a tiring time
R: well – yeah – it's um – it's almost like a full – teaching load in a way I mean sort of preparation-wise I'm spending a long time – preparing – lectures and seminars and things
H: yeah
R: um – the travelling's not very nice
H: no I gathered you've got a lot of travelling
R: oh yes
H: [urr
R: [( ) well nearly two hours a day – well two hours there and sort of two hours back
H: oh
R: in actual fact it does take me two hours when I walk up to the station
H: oh dear
R: ( ) very good – oh to be in Nottingham – (this is) what I keep saying to myself
H: oh really – do you miss it a bit
R: well – yes I do – um London's not really – to me not all it's cracked up to be or I haven't found it yet but maybe it just takes a few months to settle into it

H: mm

R: um I'm actually applying H for a Tefl course postgrad at Birmingham

H: *are* you

R: yeah — well — this job would be OK if it was full time really

H: yeah

R: you know I – at first I I was getting a bit bored sort of staying at home and –
I mean I'd quite like to go into Tefl I think ( ) well I was talking to C about it
and she thinks it's good to get some kind of Tefl qualification anyway

H: mm

R: so I'm
um applying to do um the RSA preparatory course in Tefl at English
International House – that's um – a part-time course in the evenings
two evenings a week – hopefully if I get on that that'll be sort of next
term Tuesdays and Thursdays so then I'll be able to teach Tefl in the summer
holidays   [( )

H: oh [that that's in London you mean or

R: well I'll do the course in London yeah

H: yeah

R: you've got to pay for it but – I
thought it was worth it (well) you know

H: mm

R: and then if I liked it I could either stay on at D and – do the RSA – Diploma
course which is the higher course

H: mm

R: um and just sort of carry on like that
or else – if I get on Birmingham postgrad do do that and then do it permanently

H: mm — [mm

R: [yeah – yeah

H: [oh

R: [it's difficult because I don't really want to give up a a a job I've got you know
that's sort of permanent and it's not badly paid

H: [no

R: [so it'd be silly to sort of give it up without something – else

H: yeah of course – and it'll be good experience won't it – for you I mean – [for
for a year or so

R: [yeah – yeah –
[yeah

H: [I mean presumably that would mean you'd be there for a year wouldn't it

R: well yes (and I'd) yeah I'd I'd be there till – July

H: [yeah yeah

R: [yeah yeah – and the teaching's quite nice

H: [is it

R: [apart from the bloody phonetics

H: yeah I gathered you were doing phonetics – B said

R: [yeah

H: [so that's a bit of a pain

R: well I'll I'll have to do a course in it for next year – I mean – when I do the Tefl course hopefully – I mean that will cover the phonetics anyway

H: yes

R: um so I'll probably feel a bit better about it

H: yeah – [well it's

R: [but this year's not been very good at all

H: oh

[…]

Text 4.2 is a transcribed extract from a recording of a face-to-face conversation which took place on 22 November 1998 during a visit made by H to R's home in Beckenham, Kent. The visit was a social one, but it was also explicitly intended to collect some possibly comparable recorded material. R (as a sociolinguist) was familiar with the whole procedure of tape recording for research purposes, so she was unfazed by the presence of the tape recorder, which was placed on the floor in front of the two women – the apex of a triangle. The quality of the recording is rather poor, certainly in comparison to that of the telephone extract, but it was sufficiently clear to enable a serviceable transcript to be prepared. In terms of content, R was asked to talk about her work and in generally comparable terms.

The extract is taken from the early part of the conversation and consists of an account of what her new job entails and some of the difficulties encountered. Text 4.2 is slightly longer than Text 4.1, running for approximately three and one-quarter minutes and consisting of 591 words in total.

Text 4.2 Face

[…]

R: I think part of the problem's been that I've been so tired basically – and I hadn't really taken on board what the job involved

H: what *does* it involve

R: oh right

H: I mean cos I'm not really sure

R: yeah yeah well it's taken me quite a while to sort of find out but a lot of it is to do is working with newly arrived refugees that have been in that have come into the country within the last two years – and it's really to help them with the resettlement process in schools to make sure that they adjust the adjustment process is as smooth as possible – and it's to try and um – help with the the schools with their induction and admission procedures so it's making sure that the schools – create that very – comfortable and warm secure environment cos a lot of these children are quite you know trauma-tised and they might not have been in school for several years or they've had a (disruptive) education and er so it's really to make them feel welcomed into the school environment

H: but it's they're all – actually in your school all the time

R: yeah yeah well the the (other) difficulty with refugee children is that a lot of them are placed in temporary accommodation because of their – asylum status and er there's a very high – is it transition rate you know a high mobil- is it mobility movement problem you know the refugee population is always shifting so it's often very hard for schools to keep tabs on where the children go cos they might start at the school and a couple of months later just disappear and nobody knows where they've gone to – cos there's no [tabs being kept on them

H: [oh   oh   mm

R: very often – so another part of the job is to make sure that the the right questions are actually asked at the interview because obviously we need to find out more information than if you're working if it's just like a monolingual child – so like have they had – formal education before – um – have they had schooling perhaps in another country – I mean cos some of the children like – ones that come from Somalia some of them have now c- just come to this country from Holland – for example we've got two families who've lived in Holland for the last six years

H: oh

R: and – goodness knows how they've done it but they've come here – I don't know if they're going to be sent back I don't know but they could be because it's that third country rule you see – anyway so it's questions like that and er what sort of accommodation they're living in – do they have a social worker are they on income support – all these other questions need to be asked you know – are they registered with doctors are they having emotional behaviour problems that we need to know about the child and you might not get it all at interview it might come in dribs and drabs   [and things

H: [(oh oh) but – (   )

you have to do that

R: well no no

H: (oh)

R: but my my role is to sort of – kind of —— not advise the schools but er to make sure that the right questions (   ) or to put those sort of questions down for the schools to consider – um – cos a lot of teachers don't feel comfortable in asking a refugee child what their refugee status is – you see they think it's a bit of a thorny – issue and one that can make (   ) problems but I I personally don't see a problem (with it myself)

[…]

4.4   General expectations

4.4.1   Some features of women's talk in general

Many claims have been made about the characteristic features of women's conversational behaviour since the ideas originally put forward by Lakoff in the 1970s, particularly in her seminal 1975 book *Language and Woman's Place*. Working from introspective data, Lakoff claimed that women make frequent use of a range of varied phenomena such as tag questions, modal auxiliaries, so-called 'empty adjectives' (*divine, adorable*), 'minimal responses', 'hedges' (*I think, sort of, well*) and so on. The use of such phenomena was presented as evidence of women's general compliance and lack of assertiveness – their implicit acceptance of their (inferior) 'woman's place'. Others working in the area of women's language sought to challenge and/or test her theories over the years. Such work tended to focus mainly on whether women did indeed show a higher preference than men for using certain forms, and how far such preferences might support (or not) some of Lakoff's claims about 'lack of assertiveness' and 'powerlessness'. (Useful accounts of the kinds of issues involved can be found in Preisler (1986), Coates and Cameron (1989), Cameron (1990), Coates (1993), Holmes (1995), Crawford (1995).)

The most significant point to be emphasised here, however, is that the majority of studies in this area compared women's use of particular forms with men's; indeed, men's language appeared to be regarded, at least implicitly, as some kind of 'norm' against which women's language was to be measured. Some linguists, however, chose to re-examine some of the basic premises. Coates in particular (for example, 1989, 1994, 1996) adopted a different perspective. She carried out in-depth investigations of conversations entirely between women, discovering how far, and in what circumstances, women do make use of features of so-called 'women's language' and then, crucially, reconceptualising these in positive rather than negative terms. She found that women friends did indeed use many such features, but far from regarding 'hedges', for example, as evidence of unassertiveness or weakness she suggested that their use demonstrates the strength of women's conversational and personal skills. She claimed that hedges can be deployed for a range of very positive functions (1996: 152–73):

- to introduce and explore potentially sensitive and uncomfortable topics;
- to engage in mutual self-disclosure;
- to show awareness of addressee's feelings;
- to help in the struggle for accurate self-expression;
- to show solidarity and avoid 'playing the expert' on a particular topic.

Her data shows her women subjects allowing space for such explorations and struggles, at the same time giving appropriate, encouraging and carefully timed indications of their close involvement in the talk (for example 1996: 117–45).

In the current study, therefore, women's talk – and the linguistic choices women make – will be taken as the norm. It will follow Coates's approach by investigating women's talk on its own terms, with no attempt being made to compare it with, or measure it against, men's talk.

4.4.2 The telephone factor

The telephone data extract obtained in 1986 had proved to be fertile ground for considering the frequency of use of some of the phenomena referred to: it had always generated lively discussion amongst students – international students in particular. When I came to prepare material for this book I wanted to continue to explore the frequency element but also to look more closely at what such use might indicate. In addition, I wanted to expand the database a little and at the same time introduce some element of contrast in line with the underlying comparative principle of the book, as presented in Section 1.1.2.

It has been claimed (for example, by Crystal and Davy 1969: 116–21) that telephone conversations can give rise to distinctive linguistic choices, and some of those choices appear to overlap with the phenomena ascribed to 'women's language'. It was therefore decided to examine a face-to-face conversation involving the same two participants. This would make it possible to investigate the extent to which selected phenomena were used in <u>both</u> situations, how they seemed to be functioning within the different contexts, and how far both kinds of data might provide support for Coates's claims about the positive strengths of women's conversational interactions – including the wider discourse function of, for example, hedges.

Crystal and Davy (1969: 119–20) make the following significant observations about telephone talk:

> The telephone situation is quite unique, being the only frequently occurring case of a conversation in which the participants (and of course the contexts in which they speak) are not visible to each other. As a result, certain differences between this kind of conversation and [face-to-face conversation] become immediately apparent. A different range of situational pressures is exerted upon the participants. . . . visual feedback being absent, auditory cues become all-important . . . there is a tendency to avoid long utterances without introducing pauses which allow one's listener <u>to confirm his</u> (sic) <u>continued interest, and his continued auditory 'presence'</u>. (1969: 119–20; emphasis added)

The 'situational pressures' brought about by the lack of visual contact between participants will lead speakers to both expect and give regular signals that the line is still open, that aural contact is being maintained, that they are 'still there' in the conversation. Contributions which perform this kind of function generally (that is, in face-to-face conversations too) have received a variety of labels in the linguistic literature, examples being 'back-channel cues' (Graddol, Cheshire and Swann 1994: 169–70) 'reinforcers' (Carter et al. 2001: 286), and, the term most commonly used, 'minimal responses' (Holmes 1995: 56; Coates 1996: 142–5). Minimal responses, and the signalling of continued 'presence' in the conversation, are among the features which are claimed to be characteristic of women's general conversational behaviour. It is possible that these will be even more prevalent in the telephone extract than in the face-to-face extract.

Crystal and Davy also suggest other distinctive features of telephone conversations, such as the use of a range of hesitation phenomena intended essentially to fill anything other than a very brief pause. The pauses which allow confirmation of 'presence' <u>have</u> to be brief, since 'anything approaching a silence on the part of one of the speakers is either interpreted as a breakdown of communication . . . or as an opportunity for interruption which may not have been desired' (1969: 120). Voiced hesitations which serve to 'fill the gap' include false starts to, and repetitions of, words (1969: 120) and also so-called 'voiced pauses'. Voiced pauses usually have the quality of the central vowel in English [ə] (1969: 35) (also referred to as a 'schwa'; see Section 7.9.1), and are frequently represented in standard orthography via forms such as *um, erm* and *er.*

Hesitations are, of course, also evident in conversations and speech of all kinds: that is, they are not confined to telephone conversations. Carter et al. (2001: 96) characterise *er* and *um* (which they term 'fillers') in a similar way: they serve to 'keep the turn in speaking'. Halliday (1994b: 65) claims hesitations, changes of direction and similar features tend to arise when 'attention is being paid to the process of text production' – that is, when there is a degree of self-monitoring of language choices as they are being made. It was likely to be fruitful, therefore, to examine both the extent of the use of hesitations by the two women and their apparent functions in the different contexts.

4.5 Specific areas of enquiry

It was decided to select three features from the phenomena referred to in Section 4.4 and investigate whether – and how far – the telephone and face-to-face data might differ in the use of:

- **Minimal responses:** Since women have been found to make frequent use of these in general, are they even more likely to occur in the telephone data? How do they appear to be used?

- **Hesitation phenomena:** Are these indeed used more frequently in the telephone data? What functions do they appear to serve for the women in either context?

- **Hedges:** Are these likely to be more frequent in the telephone data? What functions do they appear to serve for the women in either context?

4.6 The frameworks for the study: the overall approach

All of the phenomena to be investigated tend to be defined in the literature in mainly functional terms, illustrated by citation of typical realisations. This is not entirely satisfactory, since the characteristic functions in each case seem to be many and various in both type and actual description, and the significant subjective element involved can inevitably make them difficult to identify on a reliable basis when analysing specific data. The difficulty is exacerbated by the fact that:

- some differently <u>labelled</u> phenomena can appear to serve similar functions;
- similar functions appear to be served by different specific <u>forms;</u>
- the same <u>form</u> can be used for a slightly, or indeed very, different <u>function</u> in a given context.

Others have, of course, noted such difficulties, for example Swann (1989: 125) and Holmes (1995: 78–9). This section, therefore, tries to draw up an overall framework or set of frameworks into which the different phenomena can be slotted.

The phenomena can be found at different ranks of structure – from discourse contribution (minimal response) down to word fragment (hesitation). Frameworks – and analyses – will therefore move from largest to smallest unit; each will try to establish identification criteria in both functional and grammatical terms (suggesting tests where possible) and will also indicate typical formal realisations. The aim is to arrive at a set of frameworks which might be used by others to carry out replicable analyses of comparable data. The reader is urged to seek any necessary clarification from the original source/s cited.

4.7   The frameworks: minimal responses

4.7.1   The discourse background

The framework for identifying and describing 'minimal responses' must be placed against a background of attempts to describe and account for the overall structure of conversation generally. The following, therefore, sketches in those aspects which seem to be most relevant for the purposes of the current study. Parts of this section draw heavily on Chapter 6 of Levinson (1983), and readers are directed to that book (and the further references cited there) for fuller explication.

Two broadly differing attempts have been made to characterise the patterns and structures of conversation. The first to be discussed here is Conversation Analysis (CA), the main elements of which were initially described by Sacks et al. (1974) and subsequently built on by others. CA is essentially an ethnographic account of the flow of natural conversation, one which tries to ascertain, from the inductive study of empirical data, patterns of occurring and recurring language behaviour between participants. Phenomena which were observed and described included:

- the negotiation of 'turn-taking' by participants at appropriate points in the conversation;

- the strategies and timing evident in such negotiation, with minimal 'gaps', 'overlaps' and so on;

- the 'rules' by which successful turn-taking might be brought about;

- so-called 'adjacency pairs' – pairs of connected utterances consisting of a first part (for example a question) and an 'expectable' or 'preferred' second part (an appropriate response);

- 'preference' organisation, a preferred second being 'unmarked' and a 'dis-preferred' second being linguistically 'marked' in some way.

The second approach to the patterning of discourse is that adopted by Discourse Analysis (DA). This attempt to describe the patterning of interactive spoken discourse was developed by Sinclair and Coulthard (1975) and the so-called 'Birmingham school' (see, for example, Coulthard and Montgomery 1981; Stubbs 1983a). This is a much more structured and linguistically for-malised account of what was to be regarded as the 'predicted' patterning of spoken interactions. The particular situations investigated tended in the main to be relatively formal, socially structured and asymmetrical settings such as classrooms (Sinclair and Coulthard 1975), doctor surgeries (Coulthard and Ashby 1975) magistrates' courts (Harris 1987) and so on. On the evidence of the talk found there, discourse analysts identified a broadly hierarchical overall discourse structure consisting of:

- 'transactions' (the largest identifiable element), made up of a series of:

- 'exchanges', typically made up of:

- two or more 'moves', in turn made up of:

- one or more 'acts' (the smallest element in the overall structure).

A (very) approximate correspondence can be made at the organisational level between CA's 'adjacency pairs' and DA's 'exchanges', and between CA's 'first and second parts' and DA's 'opening and answering moves'. This remains, however, an oversimplification. (Further characterisation of some aspects of the DA approach appears in Section 4.7.2.)

Both models have illuminated important areas of naturally occurring dis-course, but both have been felt to show limitations in accounting for some specific types of data. For example, the highly structured DA has been found to be much less readily applicable to informal and spontaneous conversation (see Burton's (1981: 61–81) attempt to address some of the difficulties involved). This becomes especially apparent when more than two participants are involved, as Hillier found when attempting to devise a framework for her investigation of the spontaneous talk of three children (1992: 97–101).

Of more direct relevance to this aspect of the current study, Coates (1994) found even the CA model too constraining in some areas, particularly when more than two participants were involved. Specifically, she found CA's model of turn-taking (with its particular definitions of 'turn', 'overlap' and 'interruption') to be inappropriate for women's conversations. She preferred to regard talk as jointly constructed, with her women subjects sharing in the building-up of units at a range of levels, producing overlapping speech, and completing each other's utterances ('duetting') (1994: 181). (Coates's difficulties were highlighted when she attempted to set out her transcribed data (1994: 182 and 1996: x–xi). The layout of transcripts for the current study is, in fact, an imperfect attempt to represent comparable phenomena for just <u>two</u> participants.)

Both CA and DA give valuable insights into the nature of conversational interaction, and while I have not attempted to make full and detailed analytical use of either model the insights of both have informed the framework outlined in Section 4.7.2. Some of DA's concepts and terms have also been borrowed and applied, very loosely, in the discussion of findings in Section 4.11.2.

For the purposes of this framework (and subsequent analysis and discussion) discourse terms will be used as defined below. Illustrative examples from the data are shown by use of the name of the relevant analysed text extract followed by the appropriate line number/s.

- the terms 'conversation' and 'discourse' may be used interchangeably to indicate connected stretches of speech from contributing participants;
- 'contribution' is defined entirely in <u>surface</u> terms, that is, as a chunk of text marked off in the relevant transcript as being assigned to a particular speaker;
- 'utterance' will be a general <u>functional</u> term to refer to a stretch of speech by a particular speaker which constitutes some kind of functionally identifiable contribution or part-contribution to the conversation;
- a 'contribution' can express one or more functional 'utterances' – for example two (or more) 'minimal responses' (MRs) (for example Phone **49**, Face **24**);
- an MR can be expressed by a complete 'contribution' to the overall structure of a conversation (for example Phone **14,** Face **33**);
- several 'contributions' can express a single continuous and ongoing 'utterance' (for example Face **17–42**, where R's utterance is represented in the transcript as spanning three of her contributions).

4.7.2 Defining a 'minimal response'

The following are the defining features of an MR for the purposes of this study:

1   The term 'response' is crucial – that is, it can be seen to be responding in some way to a preceding, or ongoing, utterance by another participant. It does not initiate any stage of a particular conversation, that is, it <u>cannot</u>

act as a 'first part' (CA) (Levinson 1983: 303–4) or as the 'Opening' move of an Exchange (DA) (Sinclair and Coulthard 1975: 44–9). It is 'minus-initial' (Stubbs 1983a: 135–40). It <u>can</u> act as a 'second part' (CA), or as an 'Answering' move (DA) in a two-part exchange, and also as what Sinclair and Coulthard would, in their very different context, regard as a 'Follow-up' move in a <u>three</u>-part exchange. Significantly, however, in <u>any</u> of these cases it is <u>optional</u> in discourse structure; that is, it is not actually required or predicted by the immediately preceding utterance: it is 'minus-predicted' (Stubbs 1983a: 135–40). (A question, for example, would be regarded as <u>requiring</u> some kind of response, whether or not it actually received one. A response to a question would thus be 'plus-predicted' (Stubbs 1983a: 137), as would a response to a command/directive.)

2. The term 'minimal' is also crucial. The meaningful content of an MR is very low indeed: it adds nothing to the substantive progress of the talk or to the content of the conversation (Fishman 1990: 240). It functions to give an indication that the hearer acknowledges and accepts another speaker's contribution ('I'm listening and I support your right to hold the floor'; Coates 1993: 189) and to provide an 'appropriate' reaction, for example it may imply agreement with or approval of the content of that utterance (to 'endorse and accredit' a speaker's contribution; Giles and Coupland 1991: 88). In DA terms, an MR would appear to subsume both the categories 'acknowledge' and 'accept' identified by Sinclair and Coulthard (1975: 42–3) as discourse 'acts' in their classroom data.

3. MRs <u>may</u> follow utterances expressed as statements (which are being regarded as typically 'minus-predicting' and are typically realised by declarative or moodless clauses), but may <u>not</u> follow questions or commands/directives/requests (which are 'plus-predicting' and are typically realised by interrogatives and/or imperatives) (see Sinclair and Coulthard (1975: 27–9) for the relationship between their discourse acts and the grammatical form in which they may be realised). Tag questions appear to fall somewhere in between statements and questions or commands, since tag questions may or may not be interpreted as actually requiring a response. (Coates cites a data sample (1996: 144) which has an MR following a tag question.) Some individual instances of tag questions will be considered at appropriate points in the analysis.

    Significantly, an MR <u>must</u> follow the polarity of the relevant clause/s realising the preceding utterance (Stubbs 1983a: 139). Thus, *no* may signal acceptance or agreement as well as *yes*, depending on the relevant polarity (see, for example, Phone **54**, where H's *no* appears to indicate acceptance and agreement with R's preceding . . . *I don't really want to give up a a a job I've got . . .*).

4. Typical realisations of MRs are *mm, mhm, yes, yeah, right, no, oh,* and non-verbal noises such as laughter. Gestures such as nods (Brown and Yule 1983: 92) and smiles (Coates 1993: 112) can also act as MRs, though inevitably these are largely non-retrievable from audio-recorded data.

5. Intonation is typically neutral (Graddol, Cheshire and Swann 1994: 169–70).

4.8 The frameworks: hedges

Of the three phenomena being investigated in this particular study the identification of 'hedges' is the one which seems to be most dependent on functional definitions, with their inevitable introduction of the subjective element. Hedges tend to be presented in terms of a list of typical realisations represented by a range of grammatical forms. This can, however, introduce uncertainty over precise identification of an item as a 'hedge'.

An attempt has been made in what follows to arrive at an overall functional definition of a Hedge for current purposes, but to support it by admitting other criteria, including their grammatical expression and surface form. For the purposes of this analysis, therefore, and in approximate line with the approach adopted for MRs in Section 4.7.2, I propose to outline distinct steps, in identifying:

- the kinds of items which it is claimed can function as 'hedges';
- the underlying function/meaning in context of such items;
- the syntactic status which such items typically appear to have when functioning as 'hedges' in a given context;
- possible tests which can be used to tighten up the identification process.

Modal auxiliaries and tag questions have been excluded from this study and this analysis since they appear to be on the periphery of the items classed as 'hedges' and not all writers in the area bring them under that specific umbrella label. It is possible that modal auxiliaries and tag questions have functional links with hedges in particular instances of discourse, but these are beyond the scope of this study. Tag questions have in any case been the object of much attention over the years in connection with gender issues (see, for example, extensive references in Holmes 1995).

This framework therefore concentrates on a range of very specific items, or groups of items, all of which have been cited by others as realising 'hedges' in their analysed texts. These have been organised into approximate groupings according to, first, perceived similarities in their meaning in context and, second, their grammatical status. (Crystal 1996 and Quirk et al. 1985 have been drawn on in the latter connection.)

The following are the groups of formal items which have formed the basis of the analysis of hedges:

Group I
I think, I mean, I suppose, I feel: These items give an indication or implication of the speaker's attitude or degree of commitment to a given proposition expressed by an utterance.

you know, you see: These items imply that the speaker takes for granted the hearer's confirmation of attendance to and/or understanding of a given proposition.

Group I items are classed by Crystal (1996: 206–7) as 'comment clauses'; they are apparently complete clauses in themselves, but they lack the other elements normally required by the verbs used. They display great freedom of movement within and between clauses.

Group II

We then have a very wide range of formal items which can be used as Hedges. These include the following:

maybe, perhaps, possibly, probably, hopefully, really, actually, in actual fact, apparently, basically, in a way, anyway, well, just, like, almost, sort of, kind of, quite, a bit, a bit of

The principal 'hedging' meanings expressed by these forms are:

- to indicate the attitude of the speaker to the proposition expressed

- to moderate or mitigate the degree of intensity of some part of the proposition

- to make a qualified observation about the truth of the proposition or a value judgement about its content

(Crystal 1996: 170–9)

The forms cited are all acting as adverbials when realising these 'hedging' meanings, and they can function in different ways and with different degrees of integration into the particular clause involved (see Section 2.6.2). They can appear as:

- **subjuncts**, playing a subordinate role to one of the other clause elements, or to the whole clause (Crystal 1996: 174–5);

- **disjuncts**, playing a superior role to other elements in the clause, as if they were outside it and thus in a position to comment on some aspect of its expression or content (Crystal 1996: 176–7);

- **conjuncts**, linking – 'conjoining' – independent units such as clauses and, for current purposes, utterances (Crystal 1996: 178–9).

Many of the items appear to be readily identifiable as Hedges in given stretches of data. Some, however, are potentially more difficult to categorise, perhaps because the same form can perform very different functions in particular contexts, and these functions have to be ascertained. For example, **really, actually** and **quite** can be used to serve a heightening and emphasising/boosting function in some contexts rather than the diminishing and therefore 'hedging' function we are concerned with. These are among the individual items now considered:

- **Really** can add emphasis when it modifies an adjective, adverb or verb, so that in the following: *it's really nice, it goes really well, I really like it*, the *really* (as defined above and by most writers) would <u>not</u> be regarded as a Hedge. One useful test for reaching a decision seems to be the degree of mobility allowed. (Crystal, 1996: 168, refers to mobility and its possible effect on meaning.) *Really* could not be moved in any of the above examples without changing the meaning radically: *I really like it* versus *I like it really*. The latter would, I suggest, be incontestably a Hedge. Another test might involve substituting alternative items: successful substitution of *very (much)* for *really* in each instance would confirm it as a 'booster'. As a further point, it would be possible to regard a boosting *really* as having been 'converted' into a Hedge if it comes within the negative scope of a clause – *I don't really like it*. (Q et al.: 485 emphasise the central role of the negative in the semantics of truth value or force.) It will be apparent from this brief account that *really* is a many-faceted item.

- **Actually** raises similar questions to *really*. In some contexts *actually* can function as a Hedge – *I'm actually applying H for a Tefl course postgrad at Birmingham* (Phone **24**), while in others it can be used to modify and add emphasis to specific clause elements, usually the one or ones immediately following, which also receive notable stress – *make sure that the right questions are <u>actually asked</u>* (Face **26–7**). As with *really*, one test might be to try moving the item and inspecting for possible change of meaning (*actually I'm applying H . . .*) since flexibility of movement appears to be characteristic of this kind of Hedge. The hedging function of *actually* would seem in fact to be at its clearest when it appears in End position. (Q et al.: 490–501 draw attention to the likely significance of the positioning of A elements in the clause.) There is no very obvious substitutable item for testing purposes which could correspond to the '*very*' test. It would appear in fact that the 'hedging' *really* and *actually* would be more or less interchangeable, while *really* would seem to substitute less easily for an 'emphasising' *actually* (*?make sure that the right questions are really asked*). It will be apparent that arriving at a replicable framework can have its difficulties, and individual instances will be considered at the appropriate time.

- **Quite** is an acknowledged area of difficulty of interpretation, since it can be used – and in the same environment – <u>both</u> to 'maximise' the force of an utterance or part-utterance (Q et al.: 590–1) <u>and</u> to 'compromise' or 'diminish' that force (Q et al.: 597–9). (Only in the latter case would *quite* be regarded as a Hedge.) In broad terms, *quite* appears to maximise when it modifies a verb, adjective or adverb that is either non-gradable or at the end of a notional scale. Thus, in the following: *I quite forgot, it's quite perfect/horrible, it goes quite splendidly/appallingly, quite* would <u>not</u> be regarded as a Hedge. In other contexts, however, it would tend to act as a compromiser or diminisher (and thus as a Hedge): *I quite like him, it's quite nice, it goes quite well*. In case of doubt, a possible test for reaching a decision could involve substituting alternative items. For example, the substitution of *absolutely* or *completely* might decide the likelihood of its being a maximiser, while the substitution of *fairly* or *reasonably* might confirm its Hedge status.

- **Anyway** appears to act as a Hedge only when it is 'outside' the relevant clause and is commenting or reflecting on the content of the whole clause. Its hedging function would seem to be clearest when it appears in Initial or End position (compare *actually* above).

- **Just** can act in some contexts as a 'time' adverbial (Crystal 1996: 170, 175) rather than as an informal 'attitude diminisher' (Q et al.: 598). Only in the latter context would *just* be regarded as a Hedge. Mobility does not appear to be a useful disambiguating test here (the potential movement of *just* is in any case limited), but substitution of *recently* (or perhaps *at this moment* in some contexts) versus *simply* might be illuminating. A further complication arises with *just* in that it is possible for it to act as an emphasiser/booster (rather than a diminisher/Hedge) in some contexts. A substitution test here might involve *absolutely* to decide a booster, and perhaps something like *merely* to decide a Hedge.

- **Like** presents some classification difficulties in general terms, as Q et al. acknowledge (pp. 661–2). For present (disambiguating) purposes it can act as a preposition (Crystal 1996: 185), in which case it appears to be <u>non</u>-hedging, or it can act as a conjunct, occupying Initial position in a clause, and indicating a relationship of some kind between two linguistic units (Q et al.: 631–4) – for present purposes, utterances or parts of utterances. In the latter case it <u>may</u> be used to realise a Hedge. It thus bears some degree of resemblance to the conjunct *well*. Individual instances of *like* will be considered at the relevant point, where appropriate.

4.9   The frameworks: hesitations

There seem to be areas of overlap in function between some 'hesitations' and some of the forms classified as Hedges in Section 4.8. For example, items like *you know* and *I mean* have been regarded as also functioning like 'fillers' – and thus like hesitations – to keep the turn in a conversation (see Section 4.4.2). For the purposes of this study, however, the identification criteria for Hesitations have been drawn up in a very restricted and narrowly defined form. An examination of any potential functional overlap between the two categories has been left to a later stage (see Section 4.13.2).

The following phenomena will be regarded as Hesitations for this study. They are taken in order of size, with the largest elements first.

- **Repetition of words:** complete words or incomplete groups of words, none of which can constitute a potentially independent functional utterance. Examples of repeated complete words are: *that that's in London* . . . (Phone **37–8**) and *I I personally* . . . (Face **50–1**). (Repetition of complete potential utterances such as *yeah yeah* (Face **17**) and *no no* (Face **44**) will <u>not</u> be regarded as Hesitations for the purposes of this analysis.)

- **False starts to words:** for example *h-* (Phone **1**) and *mobil-* (Face **19**). (Changes of syntactic direction, which might be regarded as false starts to clauses, will <u>not</u> be regarded as Hesitations for the purposes of this analysis.

An example of a change of direction would be *a lot of it is to do is working with* . . . (Face **6–7**).)

- **Voiced pauses:** represented in the text extracts as *um, er* and so on (Phone **4**; Face **19**).

4.10   Method and display of analysis and calculation of results

The selected groups of features were taken separately, and in turn, using the frameworks outlined in Sections 4.7 to 4.9, and identified on each text extract. Each analysis has been annotated where appropriate, referring to the relevant item and its particular line number and explaining the analytical decision taken. Material appearing in round brackets in the extracts – indicating uncertainties in transcription – was not included as either potential material for analysis or in the total word count for each extract.

For reasons of economy of space, the three separate analyses are all displayed on the same text in each case (though see Section 1.2.9 for generally recommended practice), with the full analyses presented as Text 4.1A: Phone and Text 4.2A: Face respectively (see Appendix 1.3). Cited examples in the discussion will refer to line numbers in the relevant analysed text. The display methods adopted are:

- **Minimal Responses** are underlined, for example mm (Phone **31**), and annotated via superscripts [1, 2] and so on;

- **Hedges** are in bold and annotated via superscripts [a, b] (where two – or more – Hedges immediately follow each other they are separated by a single vertical line, for example **in a way | I mean | sort of** (Phone **4–5**));

- **Hesitations** are in bold and underlined, for example **um** (Face **48**), and annotated via superscripts [i, ii].

Calculations of results for each feature (see Sections 4.11 to 4.13) have been made as proportions of total words in the relevant extract rather than, say, total contributions, or utterances (or 'turns'), which might, on the face of it, have been considered appropriate in the case of MRs. The word-count method was chosen for two reasons.

- It avoided having to make any pre-emptive decision about what constitutes a 'turn' and where a speaker's particular 'turn' might end and another begin – see, for example, Face **23–5**, where H's MRs fit seamlessly into R's continuing utterance. (The difficulties mentioned by Coates in identifying a basic 'turn' unit occur in two-party as well as multi-party talk, and such decisions have important implications when quantitative results are to be prepared – see Section 1.2.10.)

- It also allowed more readily for the comparison of texts of different lengths and involving different amounts of talk by the two speakers.

Table 4.1   Words spoken by R and H in proportion to total words used in the two extracts

	Total words	R number of words	R's % of total words	H number of words	H's % of total words
Phone	555	440	79.3	115	20.7
Face	591	559	94.6	32	5.4
Total	**1,146**	**999**	**87.2**	**147**	**12.8**

This decision has consequences for the actual form of presentation of both texts and quantitative results. First, the analysed texts are presented as sequences of chronologically numbered lines rather than as separate and individually numbered speaker contributions (contrast the method adopted in Chapter 5). Second, the calculation of occurrences of the different phenomena in proportion to total numbers of words (rather than any larger unit) means that the percentages to be compared are inevitably small. This does not, however, obscure notable differences, as will be seen.

The procedure for arriving at total word counts is set out in Section 1.2.10, basically that a 'word' is regarded as that which is presented in the transcript as having a space on either side. Thus, *mm — mm* (Phone **49**) is counted as two words, and *er* and *mobil-* (Face **19**) are similarly counted as two words.

The chosen extracts differ slightly in overall length and, more significantly, in the amount of speech by each participant. R does much more of the talking than H in both extracts, since both at this point concern R's recent work experiences. Her talk thus becomes the main focus of attention. Table 4.1 sets out the numbers of words spoken by each participant in each extract.

It will be seen that R contributes almost seven times as many words to the talk as H overall. There is an even greater disparity between them in the Face text, with almost 95 per cent of the words being spoken by R. This disparity underlines the importance of calculations being made on a proportional basis in arriving at quantitative results – in order to compare like with like – and of its being made clear at each stage exactly what is being calculated in proportion to what. Appropriate word counts for each individual speaker in each text are therefore used in the following sections in calculating the results for the phenomena being investigated, both for each speaker and for each text.

4.11   Presentation and discussion of results: Minimal Responses

4.11.1   Frequency

Table 4.2 compares the total number of Minimal Responses occurring in the two text extracts as a proportion of the total word count in each case.

The individual percentage figures here are all very small. Nevertheless Table 4.2 shows some interesting differences between the two texts. The Phone text has a frequency of occurrence of 4.5 per cent MRs, which is more than six times the 0.7 per cent for the Face text – a very notable difference indeed.

Table 4.2 Minimal Responses in proportion to total word count for each extract

	Number of MRs	**Total word count**	**% of MRs to total word count**
Phone	25	555	4.5
Face	4	591	0.7
Total	**29**	**1,146**	**2.5**

Table 4.3 Minimal Responses used by each speaker in each extract in proportion to their respective word counts

	Phone			**Face**			**Total**		
Speaker	**MRs**	**Words**	**%**	**MRs**	**Words**	**%**	**MRs**	**Words**	**%**
R	7	440	1.6	0	559	0	7	999	0.7
H	18	115	15.7	4	32	12.5	22	147	15.0
Total	**25**	**555**	**4.5**	**4**	**591**	**0.7**	**29**	**1,146**	**2.5**

This finding would thus accord with expectations regarding the difference between the two situations (see Section 4.4).

Individual speakers' uses of MRs show marked differences, as Table 4.3 shows. H uses a very high proportion of MRs overall in comparison to R: 15.0 per cent of her total word count compared with R's 0.7 per cent. This is, of course, consistent with her listening and responding to R's news in both texts. When we consider the texts separately we see that H uses a higher proportion of MRs in the Phone text than the Face text (15.7 per cent compared with 12.5 per cent of her respective word counts – a 25 per cent increase). R's use of MRs overall is low – only 0.7 per cent of her total word count – and all of her MRs occur in the Phone text, 1.6 per cent of her words in that text.

On the evidence of this limited amount of quantitative data, therefore, there is some support for claims about a greater use of verbal MRs in telephone conversations compared with face-to-face conversations, and this is so for both participants.

4.11.2   Patterns of occurrence

When we consider the way the MRs are actually used in each extract, the findings for the Face text (which includes R's extended account of her job), may bear some correspondence to Coates's finding that MRs occur much less frequently during a 'story' (1996: 145). H produces just four MRs in the Face extract, all of these acting to support and blend in with R's ongoing narrative thread (Face **24, 33**). H's three MRs in Face **24** in fact run simultaneously with parts of R's Face **23**, but without interrupting her syntactic flow: *cos there's no tabs being kept on them . . . very often. . . .* In approximate DA terms, all of the MRs realise, or form part of, second or 'Answering' moves.

The Phone data is more varied and interesting, and in a number of ways. First, it involves greater linguistic interaction between participants than does the Face data and there are notably more MRs from both speakers. Second, the 'minimal' semantic element of MRs – their relative emptiness in fact – is demonstrated in H's use of *mm*s to respond to R's various statements across a range of topics such as the shortcomings of London (Phone **21–2**), the virtues of a Tefl qualification (**29–30**), its likely cost (**41–2**) and so on.

What is most interesting, however, is the way the relative emptiness of the MRs combines with their patterning in the discourse structure of the Phone data. The 25 MRs overall realise 20 'moves', the vast majority of which (17) are supportive second/'Answering' moves. These are principally from H as she acknowledges and accepts R's various statements across the extract and encourages her to continue. There are two third/'Follow up' moves, one of which is realised by H's sympathetic *urr* (Phone **11**) following R's confirmation that she has to do a lot of (not very nice) travelling.

The other 'third move' comes with R's *yeah*s at Phone **50**. This in fact is followed by the only instance in either extract of an MR being used to realise a 'fourth move' in a sequence (H's *oh* at Phone **51**) It forms part of a sequence beginning at Phone **47** (partly reproduced below), which seems to mark a very significant stage in the conversation and thus merits closer investigation:

48   R: . . . *if I get on Birmingham postgrad do do that and then do it permanently*
49   H: *mm* — [*mm*
50   R: [*yeah* – *yeah*
51   H: [*oh*
52   R: [*it's difficult* . . .

There is a notable pause after the first of H's two *mm*s of her 'second move' as she seems to wait for R to continue with her recounting of her possible plans for Tefl courses. When this doesn't happen she produces her second *mm*, which is overlapped by the first *yeah* of R's 'third move' and this in turn is followed after a brief pause by R's second *yeah*. H produces yet another MR *oh* as a 'fourth move', which is overlapped when R continues at Phone **52** with *it's difficult because I don't really want to give up a a a job I've got*. . . .

In retrospect it would appear that R is expecting something rather more substantial from H's second move than a 'minimal' *mm*, that in fact she might be hoping for some more concrete reaction to – even advice on – the important news about the postgraduate Tefl course application (announced at Phone **24**) and its implications in job terms. When this is not forthcoming R voices explicitly her 'difficult' dilemma in terms of her current job. Thus the conversation moves into the next stage of the second phase of the extract, as she links aspects of the Tefl course to her job and reveals some of her negative feelings about the latter.

It is apparent, therefore, that Phone **49–51** constitutes some kind of hiatus in the smooth flow of the conversation, and that this is signalled by a series of only partially coordinated and relatively 'unsuccessful' MRs which contrast notably with the mainly supportive and facilitative ones evident elsewhere in both extracts. (International students, particularly male ones, frequently showed amused reactions when we reached this 'hiatus' sequence while listening to the tape recording.) The sequence is considered again in Sections 4.12.2 and 4.13.2.

4.12 Presentation and discussion of results: Hedges

4.12.1 Frequency

The overall results for Hedges are set out in Table 4.4. The respective figures are small, being 8.8 per cent and 4.7 per cent for Phone and Face texts respectively. Nevertheless the difference is notable, with the Phone text having almost twice as many Hedges as the Face text in proportion to numbers of words used. These broad differences are to some extent emphasised when differential use of Hedges by the two speakers is considered.

Table 4.5 shows that R and H use virtually the same proportion of Hedges overall: 6.7 and 6.8 per cent of their respective word counts. Differences between the two women arise, however, when the different texts are compared. In the Face text R uses 4.7 per cent Hedges compared with H's notably higher 6.3 per cent. However, the numbers for H are very small indeed – just two Hedges in only 32 words – and this minimises their significance. The Phone text results are a little more reliable, with H using eight Hedges in 115 words (a proportion of 7.0 per cent) compared with R's 41 in 440 words (9.3 per cent) – a difference between the two women of 33 per cent.

Both women do, however, use more Hedges in the Phone text than the Face text, with the percentage differences for R in particular (9.3 compared

Table 4.4 Hedges in proportion to total word count for each extract

	Number of Hedges	Word count for extract	% of Hedges to word count
Phone text	49	555	8.8
Face text	28	591	4.7
Total	**77**	**1,146**	**6.7**

Table 4.5 Hedges used by each speaker in each extract in proportion to their respective word counts

Speaker	Phone			Face			Total		
	Hedges	Word count	%	Hedges	Word count	%	Hedges	Word count	%
R	41	440	9.3	26	559	4.7	67	999	6.7
H	8	115	7.0	2	32	6.3	10	147	6.8
Total	**49**	**555**	**8.8**	**28**	**591**	**4.7**	**77**	**1,146**	**6.7**

with 4.7) being greater than the overall figures shown in Table 4.4. How far this might arise as a direct consequence of Mode variation is, however, uncertain (see Section 4.14.2).

4.12.2 Patterns of occurrence

When we consider the 'placing' of Hedges in the two texts we find that their distribution patterns also appear to differ. In the Phone data there are some notable clusters at particular points in the extract, especially for R, whereas in the Face data the Hedges are more evenly spread across the extract.

In the Phone data, R's Hedges tend to be most heavily concentrated in those areas where she begins talking about aspects of her job, first of all in the first phase of the extract when she discusses the disproportionate amount of time she has to spend overall. Phone **4–6** alone, in fact, contains a total of five Hedges: **well** – *yeah* – *it's um* – *it's* **almost** *like a full* – *teaching load* **in a way** | **I mean** | **sort of** *preparation-wise I'm spending a long time* – *preparing* – *lectures and seminars and things.*

In the first stage of phase two of the extract (Phone **24–51**) R expresses some of her uncertainties about what career moves she might consider next in the context of the two Tefl applications, the first announced at Phone **24**. This stage is substantially hedged in places, most notably in Phone **28–9**: R: **you know** *I — at first I I was getting* **a bit** *bored* **sort of** *staying at home and* – **I mean** *I'd* **quite** *like to go into Tefl* **I think** ( ) **well** *I was talking to C . . . .* In the second stage, from Phone **52**, R begins to explore some specific aspects of her current job, including some negative feelings about her teaching. Phone **52–3** comes immediately after the 'hiatus' identified in Section 4.11.2. This utterance makes explicit her dilemma about her possible change of direction and the risks involved, and it is substantially hedged: *it's difficult because I* **don't really** *want to give up a a a job I've got* **you know** *that's* **sort of** *permanent and it's not badly paid.* Clusters of Hedges also occur in Phone **70–3**, when R is linking speculation about the content of the Tefl course to her lack of confidence over the phonetics teaching: **well** *I'll I'll have to do a course in it for next year* – **I mean** – *when I do the Tefl course* **hopefully** – **I mean** *that will cover the phonetics anyway* and *um so I'll* **probably** *feel* **a bit** *better about it.*

The clusters of Hedges, therefore, seem to be most dense when R is exploring areas of uncertainty, difficulty or particular sensitivity involving her own (and possibly others') feelings. There is a notable contrast, for example, between her completely unhedged statement of two clear alternatives at Phone **44–5** (*and then if I liked it I could either stay on at D and* – *do the RSA* – *Diploma course which is the higher course*) which is immediately followed at **47–8** by the more speculative (and hedged) *um and* **just** | **sort of** *carry on like that. . . .* R's use of Hedges thus shows clear support for Coates's claims (see Section 4.4) regarding such sensitive use by the women she studied.

H's Hedges in the Phone extract are, of course, of much lower frequency than R's. They seem intended in the main to show empathy with R's difficulties and in particular her dilemma as expressed in Phone **52–3** and **55**. H acknowledges the risks involved in giving up a permanent job and appears to pick up and support R's apparent need for reassurance that it might be better to defer a decision. She expresses this in the form of (hedged) tag questions at Phone **56–7** (. . . *and it'll be good experience won't it – for you* **I mean** *– for a year or so*), and **60–1** (**I mean | presumably** *that would mean you'd be there for a year wouldn't it*). Tag questions can be regarded as being more or less 'conducive' (Cameron et al. 1989: 87), and H's use of Hedges here would appear to reinforce the 'non-conducive' interpretation (see Note **4** to Text 4.1A). H wants to express support for R's apparent inclination towards staying put for the time being, but at the same time she seems not to want to commit herself too far.

The Face data shows no comparable clustering for either woman. H's Hedges are minimal in quantity (two) and also, at least on the face of it, fairly unremarkable in function, *I mean* and *(not) really* in Face **5** appearing to be retrospective attempts to mitigate the force of her direct question at Face **3**. (This utterance is briefly re-examined in Section 4.14.3.)

R's Hedges in the Face extract are, on the other hand, more substantial in terms of numbers and they are fairly evenly spread across the text: there are no notably heavy concentrations comparable to those found in the Phone data. This may reflect the fact that the Face data is, in the main, a descriptive account of aspects of her new job and only to a lesser extent an exploration of her feelings about it.

The functions of R's Hedges do, however, have several interesting points of similarity with those in the Phone data. Her Hedges right across the Face data appear to have an 'exploratory' function which is similar in some respects to that in the Phone data. From Face **6** on she is trying to construct 'on the hoof' as coherent an account as possible of a multi-faceted job. The job is also one which is sensitive in both practical and political terms, involving the resettlement of refugee children and families of sometimes indeterminate origins and educational histories. (This sensitivity is particularly apparent from Face **34** onwards, especially from **46** to the end of the extract.) As an essential element of this exploration and careful construction, R's use of Hedges indicates that she is searching for precisely the right word or form of expression. Examples of this are found at Face **12–13** (*a lot of these children are* **quite | you know** *traumatised*) and **19–20** (*er there's a very high – is it transition rate* **you know** *a high mobil- is it mobility movement problem* **you know** *the refugee population is always shifting*). Face **46–51** demonstrate both the search for the right word and the reference to the feelings of the teachers involved, with its underlying implications of possible conflicts: . . . *my my role is to* **sort of** *–* **kind of** *– not ad*vise *the schools but er to make sure that the right questions (   ) or to put those sort of questions down for the schools to consider – um – cos a lot of the teachers don't feel comfortable in asking a refugee child what their refugee status is –* **you see** *they think it's* **a bit of** *a thorny issue and one that can make (   ) problems but I I personally don't see a problem (with it myself)*.

The Face data, therefore, provides further support for some of Coates's claims about the way women use Hedges, but it also serves to highlight the interesting patterning in the Phone data by showing some of the differences between the two extracts. How far these differences might stem directly from differences in Mode will be examined in Section 4.14 when all the findings are considered.

4.13 Presentation and discussion of results: Hesitations

4.13.1 Frequency

Table 4.6 shows the number of Hesitations in each text as a percentage of the relevant word count. Percentages are small (3.2 for the Phone text as against 2.4 for the Face text), but Table 4.6 shows that once again there is an appreciable difference between the two: the Phone text uses a third more Hesitations than the Face text. This data would seem, therefore, to provide some support for Crystal and Davy's (1969: 120–1) claims about the greater use in telephone conversations of such phenomena as voiced pauses, false starts and repetitions.

Table 4.7 shows the extent of Hesitation use by the individual speakers in the different extracts and differences between them. R's Hesitations are almost one and a half times those of H overall – 2.9 per cent of her individual word count compared with H's 2.0 per cent – and both women use more in the Phone text than the Face text. R's 3.4 per cent in the Phone text in fact represents an increase of 36 per cent on her 2.5 per cent in the Face text. H's use of Hesitations is very small indeed, even allowing for her smaller quantity of speech – only three in the Phone text and none at all in the Face text.

Table 4.6 Hesitations in proportion to word count for each extract

	Number of Hesitations	Word count for extract	% of Hesitations to total word count
Phone	18	555	3.2
Face	14	591	2.4
Total	**32**	**1,146**	**2.8**

Table 4.7 Hesitations used by each speaker in each extract in proportion to their respective word counts

	Phone			Face			Total		
Speaker	Hesitations	Words	%	Hesitations	Words	%	Hesitations	Words	%
R	15	440	3.4	14	559	2.5	29	999	2.9
H	3	115	2.6	0	32	0	3	147	2.0
Total	**18**	**555**	**3.2**	**14**	**591**	**2.4**	**32**	**1,146**	**2.8**

4.13.2   Patterns of occurrence

H's three Hesitations in the Phone data are repetitions or false starts to words, and all appear to be designed to repair mistimings and reinstate what has become simultaneous speech. In the first case R has been speaking immediately before the chosen extract begins and H's false start *h-* (Phone **1**) in fact overlaps a preceding *yeah* from R. In the second case H's repetition of *that* (Phone **37**) comes after her *oh* which has filled R's brief pause in **36**, following which both women continue speaking. (R seems to have interpreted the *oh* as being another in H's series of MRs at this stage of the conversation.) Her repetition of *for* (Phone **57**) repairs overlap by the first of R's three MRs at **58–9**. Such mistimings may well be a consequence of the lack of visual clues in a telephone conversation, that is, as a direct reflection of variation in Mode.

R's Hesitations in the Phone text all occur within ongoing extended contributions: that is, none has an interactive 'repair' function comparable to those produced by H. The placing of R's Hesitations, however, seems to be significant. They frequently coincide with her heavily hedged utterances (for example in Phone **4, 28–9, 52, 70–1, 73**), all of which have been discussed in Section 4.12.2. They thus appear to be reinforcing the hedging function. Their effect is particularly notable when two or more Hesitations occur in the same hedged utterance. Thus the utterance at the start of the second stage of phase two of the extract (Phone **52**) features two Hesitations in addition to the Hedges already discussed (. . . *I don't really want to give up a* **a a** *job I've got you know* . . .) and this, in fact, comes immediately after the 'hiatus' discussed in Section 4.11.2.

Hesitations do appear to be used for an additional function and to particular effect. The very significant announcement of the Tefl course postgraduate application at Phone **24**, which begins the second phase of the extract, is introduced by the use of a voiced pause *um*. This would in fact accord with Crystal and Davy's observation (1969: 120) that a 'voiced hesitation' – their examples are all *um*s – may be used to fill any gap before the introduction of a new topic. (It also links with Levinson's discussion (1983: 313) of the 'marked' way a 'topic jump' is signalled on the telephone. His cited 'marker of discontinuity, *Hey*' is immediately preceded by a marker of 'hesitancy', realised by *Er*.) R's use of a vocative, *H*, at this point is also notable, being the only use in either extract. In Phone **32–4** three *um*s are used to announce the second (RSA) Tefl application, and they precede the hedged **35** (with its *hopefully* and *sort of*) which moves into more speculative territory about future contingencies. All of these particular Hesitations, then, appear to be used as some kind of indicator of the importance of the decisions taken, while at the same time suggesting a degree of self-deprecation.

R's Hesitations in the Phone data thus appear to have many functions similar to those of her Hedges, in helping her to explore and articulate her own doubts and uncertainties via the sympathetic ear of a friend who shows some degree of fellow feeling (Phone **69**). She also uses Hesitations (specifically, voiced pauses) to mark the significance of announcements.

R's Hesitations in the Face text are distributed across the extract and, as in the Phone text, all occur within extended contributions. Again, as in the Phone text, they reinforce Hedges at particularly sensitive points, including those with potentially negative implications. This will be seen, for example, in Face **46–51** (already discussed in Section 4.12.2) where four Hesitations (. . . *my . . . er . . . um . . . I . . .*) join with four Hedges when R talks about her personal role in relation to schools and teachers and the kinds of questions to be asked of the refugee children.

Hesitations, therefore, appear to function approximately like the Hedges in the Face text: that is they help in the construction of a complex account in a number of ways.

- They can allow space for thought, for example in Face **10–11** (. . . *it's to try and* **um** *– help with the* **the** *schools with their induction and admission procedures . . .*) and **47–8** (. . . *to put those sort of questions down for the schools to consider –* **um** *– cos a lot of teachers . . .*).

- They can signal a change or reorganisation of syntactic direction within a clause, for example in Face **31** (. . . *some of them have now* **c** *– just come to this country from Holland . . .*).

- They can mark a search for the appropriate word or phrase, for example in Face **19–20** (. . . *and* **er** *there's a very high – is it transition rate you know a high* **mobil-** *is it mobility movement problem . . .*).

All of these examples (and the Hesitations in Face **10–11**, in fact, seem to realise all three functions) show how Hesitations are used in combination both to construct the complex ongoing account and to give explicit verbal signals to the listener that this act of construction is going on. R is implicitly requesting time and space to pursue her 'struggle' (Coates 1996: 159) and on the evidence of this extract she does receive it.

4.14   Overall comparison of findings

Individual findings have been discussed under the relevant sections above, and the principal aim of this section is to bring together and summarise as succinctly as possible the main points of the different findings.

4.14.1   Frequencies

Tables 4.8 to 4.10 bring together for overall comparison the quantitative findings for all three chosen phenomena across the two different situations and then for each participant separately. Individual percentages have already been considered under the relevant sections, and discussion here will therefore be in broad terms only.

It will be apparent from Table 4.8 that the Phone data shows greater use of all three phenomena than the Face data. This is particularly so for Minimal Responses, which may perhaps be regarded as approximately in accordance with differences in Mode and thus in line with expectations outlined in

Table 4.8 Overall use of Minimal Responses, Hedges and Hesitations in each extract

	Total Words	Minimal Responses		Hedges		Hesitations	
		No.	%	No.	%	No.	%
Phone	555	25	4.5	49	8.8	18	3.2
Face	591	4	0.7	28	4.7	14	2.4
Total	**1,146**	**29**	**2.5**	**77**	**6.7**	**32**	**2.8**

Section 4.4. Hedges and Hesitations too show comparable patterns, though the differences are not quite as great as those for MRs.

The separate findings for R (Table 4.9) and H (4.10) show comparable patterns to those overall, in that both women use a higher proportion of each phenomenon in the Phone than the Face data. The degrees of difference are not quite the same, however, partly because the extents of their uses of the phenomena differ. H is the principal user of MRs, but her use of Hedges and Hesitations is much lower than R's, and as a consequence her quantitative findings for these two phenomena have less significance.

The findings for R, however, do appear to be significant in that her use of Hesitations and, especially, Hedges is fairly substantial. Further, she uses notably more of <u>both</u> in the Phone than the Face data. The findings for Hesitations would seem on the face of it to be in accordance with general expectations as outlined in Section 4.4: that is, that these differences may be attributable to differences in Mode. Is this in fact likely to be so, especially in the light of the discussion in Section 4.13.2 and the comparable findings for Hedges? Are other factors likely to be equally significant? In order to pursue this question we have to bring together and try to synthesise the separate

Table 4.9 R's use of Minimal Responses, Hedges and Hesitations in each extract

	Words	Minimal Responses		Hedges		Hesitations	
		No.	%	No.	%	No.	%
Phone	440	7	1.6	41	9.3	15	3.4
Face	559	0	0	26	4.7	14	2.5
Total	**999**	**7**	**0.7**	**67**	**6.7**	**29**	**2.9**

Table 4.10 H's use of Minimal Responses, Hedges and Hesitations in each extract

	Words	Minimal Responses		Hedges		Hesitations	
		No.	%	No.	%	No.	%
Phone	115	18	15.7	8	7.0	3	2.6
Face	32	4	12.5	2	6.3	0	0
Total	**147**	**22**	**15.0**	**10**	**6.8**	**3**	**2.0**

observations on patterns of occurrence and their possible meanings made so far.

4.14.2   Patterns of occurrence and functions in context

When summarising the findings for Hedges and Hesitations those used by R will be the main focus of attention. Thus the following are the principal points which arise from the separate discussions:

● The close relationship between Hedges and Hesitations is shown by their complementary and/or reinforcing role in explicitly signalling that a complex act of construction is going on – a search for appropriate expression – and at the same time implicitly requesting H to 'bear with me' while this is happening.

● This act of construction – at whatever length – centres on the exploration of areas of uncertainty, doubt, reservation and sensitivity, all involving to a greater or lesser degree elements of self-disclosure and expression of self-doubt.

Realisations of these functions by Hedges and Hesitations have in fact been found in <u>both</u> extracts. The most significant differences between the two texts in terms of both frequency and patterns of occurrence appear to arise less from differences in Mode (the minus-visual element) than from differences within (the notionally controlled) Field (see Section 4.2.1), specifically the kinds of topic addressed. The Phone text explores particularly sensitive topics when compared with the Face text, especially some of R's self-doubts in relation to her job.

It may also be appropriate at this point to consider aspects of (again, notionally controlled) Tenor. Without wishing to over-interpret, retrospectively, the Phone extract in comparison to the Face extract, it is possible to speculate on the effect/s of some of the differences between the two women at the relevant times as outlined in Section 4.2.1, particularly in conjunction with specific topics. Briefly, in the Phone text R is considering a change of direction from a well-paid, permanent (albeit part-time) job, taking up a possibly costly Tefl course, and with no secure future prospects. She wants interested support and, possibly, advice from a fellow-linguist, but someone who was at the time in rather a limbo of her own, having as yet no PhD, no secure job prospects, little money and so on. All of these could have added to the uncertainty and sensitivity felt – and demonstrated – in the Phone data, and in fact by both participants. By the time of the Face text things have changed at least to some degree, and such interpersonal and topic-focused sensitivities may have slightly less significance.

When Minimal Responses are brought into consideration, it would seem that on the evidence of both Phone and Face extracts MRs are, in the main, used to provide appropriate acceptance of the other speaker's utterances and encouragement to continue. Most, therefore, appear to be 'successful' in giving the sensitive conversational support required. The analysis does suggest, however, that there may be times when MRs can be used 'unsuccessfully' – that in fact they provide rather less than is required for a wholly successful negotiation. The discussion of the perceived 'hiatus' (see Section 4.11.2) shows, in fact, that close attention to the results of a particular MR patterning can be very revealing in discourse terms. Indeed the significance of this point of the Phone data is confirmed by the closely related patterns of both Hedges and Hesitations (see subsequent discussions in Sections 4.12.2 and 4.13.2). The miscommunication may have been exacerbated by the fact that no visual clues were possible, therefore being a direct consequence of Mode differences. However, it is likely that the more salient factor is related to the particular topic (that is, within Field), and for the reasons suggested above. It would seem, therefore, that temporary lack of success at the local level can serve to confirm the greater achievement of success overall.

4.14.3   The influence of 'uncontrolled' variables

'Uncontrolled' variables have been briefly considered in Section 4.14.2, specifically potential differences within Tenor and – especially – within Field. These do, of course, interact with elements of Mode as outlined in Section 4.2.3 – specifically the temporal difference arising from the time lapse between the two conversations.

A further consideration is the degree of planning involved in the collection of the Face data. H's attempt to control the Field may, quite unwittingly, have affected the extent to which it becomes a 'narrative' account by R about aspects of her job. H's direct question at Face **3** *what* does *it involve* (briefly referred to in Section 4.12.2) may perhaps have diverted R from exploring some of her feelings about her job in the way she does in the Phone extract. This is in some ways unfortunate, but it does have the unexpected benefit of producing a text which contrasts in some notable ways with the Phone text and thus throws into relief some intriguing elements of the latter.

4.15   Conclusion

This investigation has involved three separate analyses of the same text extracts, and extensive – occasionally repetitive, even laboured – discussions of each phenomenon in turn. Such independent analyses and discussions have, however, allowed a clear perspective to be adopted for <u>each</u> phenomenon individually before examining and demonstrating the extent to which they may be interrelated.

The study has thrown an interesting light on aspects of talk between women friends, whether on the telephone or face-to-face, and such detailed analyses have in fact meant a salutary and necessary reappraisal of some apparently familiar data. Overall, the findings of this chapter support many of the claims made by Coates about the ways in which women friends can work towards achieving rewarding conversational goals.

4.16   Suggestions for further work

(a)   Other features which might be systematically explored in this or comparable data include tag questions (in their various combinations of polarity and intonation); modal auxiliaries, 'vague language' (Channell 1994), changes of syntactic direction, and 'silent pauses' (Crystal and Davy 1969: 120–1). Some or all of these may have some functional links with Hedges and/or Hesitations as investigated in this chapter (see, for example, Coates 1996: 162). A detailed breakdown of actual Hedges used could also be carried out, showing which type/s seem to be preferred by each participant.

(b)   The same framework could be applied to comparable conversational data, perhaps controlling Mode and Tenor but deliberately varying Field, for example a (small) group of the same women in a 'working' versus 'social' situation, or even a comparable group of men.

(c)   Aspects of the same framework, together with elements found elsewhere in the book, might be tried on data which builds in some of the more delicate kinds of Mode variation outlined in Section 1.1.6.3, for example telephone talk v. answerphone messages (both being –visual contact, but the former two-way and the latter one-way). A message I received in September 2002 from a (different) woman friend of very long standing contained, in just a few words, Hedges and even a Hesitation:

> have you gone to bed early or – are you on the town tonight ((laugh)) it's ages since we've spoken – I've just had an exciting evening on the er internet – logging my name on the XZ work site to see ((laugh)) what that brings out of the woodwork – (I) just thought it might be a bit of a giggle for you – so – I'll phone you again – some time – have fun – bye

Other notable features which might be incorporated into an expanded framework to account for such data include 'conversational' or 'interactive' utterances (Section 4.7), contractions, informal lexical choices (Chapter 8), exophoric choices, assumptions of shared knowledge (Chapter 5) and so on.

Children's Talk

5.1   Introduction

This chapter will compare aspects of the conversational language of children. As with the language studied in Chapter 4, its place within the overall framework presented in Figure 1.1 will be under 'speaking (conversing) spontaneously'. In the first instance (the 'Talk' text) the language itself is the main focus of attention while in the second instance (the 'Task' text) the language is an accompaniment to an activity. In each text the children are in conversation with a third, adult, participant.

The chapter will be concerned principally with the ways in which the children's language differs when it is being used for different purposes.

5.2   Identifying the variables

5.2.1   The controlled variables

The variables to be controlled are:

- **Mode:**   The participants are speaking 'spontaneously' and they are also 'conversing'; that is, the speaking and hearing are simultaneous. In each case the phonic channel is being used; the participants are sharing both the same physical environment (there is visual contact) and the process of text creation (see Section 1.1.6.3).

- **Tenor:**   The participants are the same two 11-year-old boys in each case, A and R, with the same third participant, the adult researcher H. The boys are in their final year of primary school and have known each other for some years. They have also become familiar with H during the preceding year (see Section 5.3).

- **Setting:**   The interactions took place in the same physical environment (the activity room at Devonshire Drive Junior School, Eastwood, Nottingham, England) and on the same day (30 June 1992).

5.2.2   The varying variables

The varying variables are:

- **Mode:**   The **role** of the language differs between the two situations (see Section 1.1.6.3). In the Talk text the production and interpretation of language itself is the main aim of the interaction: its role is 'constitutive'. In the Task text the language is principally an accompaniment to the main aim of the interaction, the carrying out of a shared activity: its role is 'ancillary'.

- **Field:**   Consistent with the variation in 'language role' under Mode, the overall **purposes** of the two situations differ. The first is a part of an ongoing conversation, its principal aim and purpose being the sharing of information, opinions and feelings about a particular topic. In the second the language accompanies, supports and comments on the playing of a game on the school computer.

The different purposes have consequences, of course, for the **content** of each text. The Talk text involves opinions of a particular swimming pool known to the children. The Task text shows the children working through different stages in the educationally orientated adventure game called Mapventure. It involves topographical and geographical detail of the territory being explored (the 'psychological setting'; see Section 1.1.6.4) as the participants confer about and comment on the different stages of the game, the landmarks to be reached and the appropriate directions to be followed.

- **Tenor:** Both the **purpose** and **content** aspects of Field are in turn likely to have some effect on **participant roles** and **relations between participants**, that is, for 'functional tenor relations' (see Section 1.1.6.2). Each extract involves three participants and they are the same three participants. However, the focus on the computer in the Task extract introduces an external element which must be taken into account. More significantly, perhaps, the three participants differ in the extent of their knowledge of particular topics discussed in the Talk extract and particular aspects of the computer game in the Task extract (see Sections 5.3 and 5.4).

5.3   Description of the data

The data consists of transcripts of two short extracts taken from extended audiotape recordings made on 30 June 1992 in the activity room of Devonshire Drive Junior School, Eastwood, Nottingham, England. The participants in each are A and R (both aged 11), and the author/researcher H. (H had, in fact, once been a pupil at the school.) These recordings were part of a series, involving a number of small groups of different schoolchildren, which were made in Eastwood over the period 1991 to 1993 at Devonshire Drive Primary School (both Junior and Infants) and also at Greasley Beauvale Primary School (Infants only). A and R were in the same class at Devonshire Drive and both had taken part in earlier recordings in the series. They were thus familiar with both the recording procedure and the researcher. (Many of the recordings in the series in fact centred on the playing of computer adventure games, which had been found to be highly suitable for generating a lot of talk (see Hillier 1992, and also Fisher 1993).)

The research was part of a pilot investigation of the dialect grammar of Eastwood schoolchildren (see Hillier 1993a, 1993b, 1994, 1995, 1998; and also Chapter 7), funded by Nottinghamshire County Council via a grant to the University of Nottingham in 1993–4. These particular text extracts were not, therefore, originally collected for the purpose of comparing 'talk-centred data' with 'task-centred data'. They were, however, felt to be highly suitable for exactly this kind of study. (Stubbs, 1983a: 21, reports a comparably happy outcome when he found potentially rich data in what was 'an unplanned interlude' coming after his main interview with two 12-year-old boys at a school in Edinburgh.) The text extracts do, in fact, show the children using many examples of the non-standard grammar of the local, Erewash Valley, area. These are thus consistent with what Hymes would presumably categorise as the children's particular linguistic 'provenance' (part of his component 13; see Section 1.1.5).

Text 5.1 consists of 336 words, lasting approximately two minutes, occurring about one-fifth of the way through the recording of an informal 'interview/conversation' I conducted with the two boys. This was essentially designed to allow them to talk informally to me (and to each other) on a range of topics and thus to give me the chance to collect more evidence of their use of non-standard dialect features. The extract centres on a particular local swimming pool, swimming being a topic which the boys themselves had selected. (Previous and subsequent topics – also self-selected – included golf and music lessons.)

Text 5.1   Talk

[…]

A   I like Ilkeston baths

R   yeah I

H   Ilkeston – where's Ilkeston baths

R   er – I don't know – next to Victoria Park

A   yeah

R   right next to Victoria Park

H   oh yes (   )

R   it's got a big sl- it's got a slide what goes about – twenty metres – down — it goes like this oooh

A   no about fifty metres – it's big

R   yeah big

A   R you know that shower at the end of it

R   ((laugh)) there's a shower just as you come in

A   well when we went with Scouts last Wednesday

R   yeah

A   we blocked the end of it near that shower and everyone kept barging into us – then you know the man up at top who watches you go down – the one (on net) – he come down blowing whistle – down slide — with his shorts and T-shirt on ((laugh))

R   yeah there's like a sprinkler what comes down right in your face at end but then you go into a big – erm (   )

A   (right) it's only about that deep

R   yeah and then you go into water and it splashes right up all in your [face

A   [yeah

H   and that's before you go in is it

A   no that's after you that's [when you're coming out

R   [it's just like – you go right into a (pool/puddle) of water about this (   )

A   there's a dead dark park and you – dead dark part

R   yeah and then

A   and you get stuck there if you don't push hard enough cos there's like a bar at the beginning and you have to swing on that to get down

R   yeah and if you don't go down

A   on your back

R   flat on your back

A   then you [stop

R   [you stop half way through — and then you have to keep pushing yourself off

A   and there's disco lights

H   (so) if you sit up – you slow up

R   yeah

A   yeah

R   but if you lie on your back you come to this dark part and then next thing you're still in dark part and all water's sprinkling in your face

A   I know – you go down on your back and you go down dead fast

R   I know

A   you do it in about ten seconds

[…]

Text 5.2 consists of 174 words, lasting approximately one and a half minutes, occurring close to the end of the Mapventure recording. The recording was made later in the same afternoon and in the same room as that for Text 5.1. During the playing of the Mapventure game the boys are progressing through a particular territory represented by a map on the computer screen. They progress by operating the computer keyboard (which can be clearly heard on the tape recording) and they have to interpret clues and avoid traps as they make their way towards various targets. Their main aim during this particular extract is to try to find their way to the lifeboat station.

Text 5.2   Task

[…]

R   camping is here   ((reading from screen))

A   west

R   come on (A)

H   west

R   I'm staying over a couple of minutes – I am ((i.e. after school))

A   what to complete this

R   yeah

H   have you only got to get one more

R   yeah

```
H   oh well (     )
A   when we've found this clue it's the last clue
H   oh
R   we're nearly...
A   hang on where we got to go to – lifeboat (   )
R   yeah we're there at the moment – so  [(if I was   )
H                                            yes
A                                            [we're here
R   yeah – so (      ) go right up there – to the castle
H   can you get round to the lifeboat station that way
A   yeah —— it's the only way you *can* get
H   (you haven't got any ... )
A   that's the only way you *can* get
H   (there aren't any devils) [(      devils there)
R                             [I've found a I've found a route by em
H   oh
A   west – that's that way now we need to look (   )
H   (   )          ((reading from screen?))
A   I wish this computer was faster      ((banging keyboard))
    -(6)-
R   (     Lord) what you doing (              )
H   (     north)      ((reading from screen?))
    [(     north)      ((rising intonation))
A   [I can't see – R —— yeah – now we need to go west
H   where are you now
A   just there
H   oh —— oh I see —— oh I see you've got to go round that um- (no no no) –
    west
A   he keeps marking where we are and I keep thinking [they're traps ((ie on
    written map))
H                                                     [yes – it's very
    confusing R
    ((laugh))
[...]
```

The two extracts were chosen largely on the basis of manageability and approximate comparability in terms of length, relative compactness in being identifiable and fairly 'contained' sections of the respective ongoing interactions, and – in the case of Text 5.2 – being reasonably comprehensible and transcribable. For the latter text, occasional background 'activity room' noise on the one hand and a requirement for at least a minimal acquaintance with the principles of the computer game on the other together imposed notable strains on the transcription process – and thus on the transcriber (me). Such difficulty has to be acknowledged as a fact of life when researching spontaneous spoken language in a natural setting (see also Section 1.2.2). I feel, however, that this very difficulty might have had some positive outcomes – see discussion in Section 5.9.3.

5.4   General expectations re the varying variables

Work on children's language has shown children of different ages growing in competence in manipulating the basic material of language to successfully match particular linguistic choices to their desired function. For example, empirical studies of the language use of:

- one child at 19 months (Halliday 1973, 1999);
- nursery children of ages ranging from 3 years 6 months to 5 years 7 months (Garvey 1975, 1984);
- two children from 3 years 8 months to 5 years 5 months and, later, at 8 years (McTear 1985);
- three children aged 7 years 10 months, 11 years 6 months and 12 years 5 months (Hillier 1992);
- two children aged 12 years (Stubbs 1983a);
- six children aged 8 years and two aged 12 years (Fisher 1993)

have all demonstrated children's increasing competence in adapting to the specific linguistic needs of a given situation and in taking account of the degree of shared knowledge of their interlocutors. Thus children become adept at assessing all aspects of the immediate situation in deciding how much needs to be said ('what needs to be told'; Brazil 1995: 15) and to whom, adapting their language accordingly.

The studies by Stubbs (1983a), McTear (1985), Hillier (1992) and Fisher (1993) have been found to be of most direct relevance to the current investigation in terms of approximate age of the children involved and/or the kinds of approach adopted. These are considered in more detail below.

It is expected that the combination of Mode and Field/Purpose of the language will be the principal factors in influencing the linguistic choices made. Language which is accompanying or commenting on a particular purposeful activity and contributing to the achievement of that activity (language which is intended to <u>do</u> something, as in the Task extract) is likely to differ in its choices from that which is transmitting content (language which is principally <u>about</u> something, as in the Talk extract). The fact that the purposeful activity is centred on an entity in the immediate environment (the computer) is likely to affect the form of the overall interaction. There are frequent references to that specific entity in the Task extract and to many different aspects of the activity the children are engaged in. Further, the computer (signalled via the manifestations from time to time of the stages in the computer game) assumes to some extent the status of a quasi-participant. The human participants 'interact' with it in various ways, including reading verbal and visual messages from the screen, noting the different places reached on the map (within the different 'scenes'), and, of course, operating the computer keyboard. (Hillier, 1992: 65–70, and Fisher, 1993: 99–104, discuss some of the factors which may be involved.)

The presence of the computer will also affect aspects of relations between participants (the 'functional tenor'). In the Talk extract the three participants will have, at least potentially, equal access to the alternating roles of speaker, addressee and so on. In the Task extract, however, the advent of a potential fourth 'participant' is likely to have repercussions both for the role relationships which are realised and the degree to which individual participants occupy those roles. The computer clearly does not have the same autonomous status as the human participants, but the effects of its presence are likely to be significant.

5.5 Specific areas of enquiry

In the light of the above, it was decided to explore:

- the extent to which access to and awareness of the immediate, shared, environment is necessary to make sense of the two texts; how far this is explicitly signalled linguistically – by deictic means – and how far this differs between the two texts.

- the extent to which different role relationships (including the 'presence' of the computer in the Task extract) are reflected in the overall interactions represented by each text and how these changes and shifts are manifested.

5.5.1 Deixis

McTear (1985: 205–6) shows some approximate correspondences with the current study in his discussion of aspects of 'the later conversational development' of his young daughter and her friend (by then aged eight) in their interactions with an adult in different situations. He identifies differences between the children's use of deictic reference strategies (specifically 'anaphoric and exophoric reference') in different situations.

The relevant experiment contrasted the girls' telling of two stories (based on pictures placed between them) and the giving of instructions to the adult on how to play two games – the first game being placed immediately in front of them (the 'present' condition) and the second in a far corner of the room (the 'absent' condition). Each of these three situations was thus likely to involve some degree of reference to material in the immediate, non-linguistic, environment. McTear found, however, that when telling the stories (the 'language about' function) the children used mainly anaphoric devices – that is, interpretable from the shared linguistic environment – even though the relevant pictures were present. Further, when giving the instructions (the 'language to do' function) they made notably greater use of reference to the non-linguistic environment (via exophoric linguistic devices or gestures such as pointing) in the 'present' condition than in the 'absent' condition.

It is expected, therefore, that the Talk text discussion (Text 5.1), which mainly concerns descriptions of events and environments elsewhere, will be largely interpretable 'endophorically' (usually 'anaphorically') – that is, from material within the text. In contrast, the Task text (Text 5.2) is likely to be much more 'opaque' (Hasan 1994: 80) and will be expected to employ a higher proportion of exophoric devices than the Talk text precisely because of its close focus on the specific task in the shared environment and the 'presence' of the computer. The children do not need to describe or even explicitly identify what is clearly shared and/or can be seen, even though they are linguistically quite capable of doing so. (This consequent 'opacity' is, in fact, likely to have contributed to difficulties of transcription of the kind referred to in Section 5.3 – thus perhaps providing some degree of indirect support for the Talk v. Task approach.)

5.5.2 Participant role relationships

The Talk text involves A and R discussing and describing features of a particular swimming pool; the adult researcher H has no knowledge of the pool in question and the information is produced in response to questions by H in her role as informal interviewer. The Task text involves A and R, and to a lesser extent H, questioning each other about the current stage of the computer game, commenting on what they see on the computer screen and deciding what might be done next. A operates the computer keyboard, while R keeps a written record of potentially significant and useful information. Both boys have played the game before, but A is more familiar with the various stages, partly because he has a version of the same game on his home computer. H has no knowledge whatsoever of this specific game. (She does have some knowledge of an approximately comparable, though earlier and much less sophisticated, adventure game; see Hillier 1992.)

It will be apparent that the potential participant role relationships, and the consequent shifts and permutations in those relationships, are likely to differ between the two texts. The Talk text allows the specification of three participants, each having potentially equal access to Hymes's roles of Speaker, Addressee and Hearer (see Section 1.1.5). The Task text allows a similar initial specification of the human participants, with each having, at least potentially, the same equality of access to each of those roles. This equality may, however, be compromised by the less than equal role relationships brought about by the presence of the computer.

Hymes notes that different participant roles for speech acts within a speech situation will entail different 'specifications'. Goffman, in his *Forms of Talk* (1981), proposes a 'participation framework' (p. 3) with an identifiable participation status relative to every utterance. He also cites as evidence a stretch of language showing where 'significant shifts in alignment of speaker to hearers were occurring' (p. 127), and notes the 'structurally important distinction' (p. 132) between the participant who is selected as the addressee and one who is a 'ratified' hearer. Bell (1984: 158–61), in his important paper modelling sociolinguistic variation, 'Language style as audience design' (see also Bell (1997) for a much shorter paper bearing the same title), posits four audience roles which are hierarchically ordered in their degree of salience for a speaker's style design. His four roles are addressee, auditor, overhearer and eavesdropper, ordered according to whether or not they are addressed, ratified and known. Like Goffman, Bell accords greatest potential salience to the role of addressee, with the next greatest to 'auditor' (equivalent to Goffman's known and ratified hearer). 'Overhearer' is known but not ratified, and 'eavesdropper' is neither known nor ratified. (See further reference to Bell's hierarchy elsewhere in this book, for example Sections 6.2.1 and 8.6.2 to 8.6.3.)

Stubbs (1983a: 20–3) provides interesting support for some of these claims. His data shows his child subjects demonstrating great skill in marking the distinction between the conversational roles of addressee and hearer/auditor, by designing and redesigning their talk specifically to take account of the degrees of shared knowledge of different participants: ' . . . speakers must understand their audience: they must have some idea what the audience already knows and what they want to know, and therefore of how to select and present information' (1983a: 21).

It will be apparent that a significant feature of the data under consideration is likely to be that of the role of <u>addressee</u>. An analytical approach which draws on Hymes's and others' insights should, therefore, show how far the different purposes of the Talk and Task extracts, and the varying types and degrees of shared knowledge involved, will influence:

- the occupation of the role of addressee by particular participant/s;
- the extent of such occupation/s and differences between these;
- the ways such differences may be manifested, and what these might imply.

5.6   The frameworks for this study

The summarising frameworks offered here are highly condensed and simplified and can only offer signposts to full explication of the relevant areas. Readers are recommended to follow up specific points where necessary at each stage, both those raised here and in the commentaries on the respective analyses.

5.6.1   Deixis

Deixis is defined by both Quirk et al. (1985: 374) ('Q et al.') and Halliday and Hasan (1976: 58–9) ('H&H') as a kind of verbal 'pointing', with particular linguistic features being used to give information such as the time and place of an utterance and the persons or objects referred to in the utterance. These 'deictic' features thus rely for their interpretation on the specific context shared by speakers and hearers, that context being either the immediately surrounding <u>situation</u> or 'surrounding' <u>language</u>, or 'text'. Q et al. use the term 'situational reference' in the former case, while H&H (who are principally concerned with within-text cohesion) prefer 'exophoric reference', that is, 'outside' the text (pp. 32–3). For 'within text' reference H&H use the overall term 'endophoric reference', which they subdivide into 'anaphoric' reference (to an earlier part of the text) and 'cataphoric' reference (to a later part of the text) (compare the discussion of 'cataphoric ellipsis' in Section 2.9). Both 'anaphoric' and 'cataphoric' are used, and in similar ways, by Q et al. (for example pp. 861–2).

Both groups of writers, from their slightly different perspectives, are concerned to identify the kinds of deictic features involved. Q et al. (pp. 1025–6) do this by citing an example of reported speech and noting which features have to be changed in some way to accommodate differences between an utterance and the reporting of that same utterance. These include tense forms of verbs, other time references such as *yesterday* and *now*, place references such as *here* and *there*, personal pronouns such as *I, you, he, she*, and demonstratives such as *this* and *these*. All of these except the time references are included by H&H within their 'types of reference' (pp. 37–9 ff.).

The following are the deictic features to be investigated in this study. (Illustrative examples from the data refer to the relevant analysed text extract and the appropriate contribution number – see Appendix 1.4.)

- demonstratives *this, that, these, those* when acting as <u>determiners</u> within the noun phrase (see Section 2.6.3), for example <u>*that*</u> *shower* (Talk 11), <u>*this*</u> *computer* (Task 28)

- demonstratives *this, that, these, those* when acting as <u>pronouns</u>, standing in for a whole noun phrase (Crystal 1996: 146–50), for example <u>*that's*</u> *when you're coming out* (Talk 21), <u>*that's*</u> *the only way . . .* (Task 22)

- time references such as *yesterday, now* (Q et al.: 1025), for example <u>*now*</u> *we need to go west* (Task 31), <u>*last*</u> *Wednesday* (Talk 13), *we're there* <u>*at the moment*</u> (Task 15), typically realised by adverbs, noun phrases, prepositional phrases acting as Adverbials (see Section 2.6.2)

- place references such as *here, there* (Q et al.: 1026), for example *camping is* <u>*here*</u> (Task 1), *you get stuck* <u>*there*</u> (Talk 25), *go right up* <u>*there*</u> (Task 18), typically realised by adverbs (Crystal 1996: 166–7)

- forms of the third person personal pronouns such as *it, he, she, they* (see Section 6.6.1), for example *you do* <u>*it*</u> *in about ten seconds* (Talk 38), <u>*his*</u> *shorts* (Talk 15), *I've found a route by* <u>*em*</u> (Task 24)

First and second person pronouns have been used as evidence of identification, where possible, during the Addressee analysis stage (see Sections 5.6.2 and 5.7.2). They were, however, excluded from the Deixis analysis. A comparison of the use of the definite article (regarded by H&H: 70–4) as potentially significant in exophoric/endophoric terms) was also excluded, not least because the extent of its occurrence and the form of its realisation in the Erewash Valley region is itself an area of research (see, for example, Section 7.6).

5.6.2 Participant roles

Potential participant roles to be considered are those of Speaker/Addressor, Addressee and Hearer (see Hymes's components 5–8 in Section 1.1.5), the most significant for this study being that of <u>Addressee.</u>

Identification of Speaker/Addresssor for analytical purposes is straightforward. The voices of the three participants are in all cases clearly distinguishable in the two extracts and individual contributions can be reliably attributed to the relevant participants. Identification of Addressee, however, can be more problematic. Goffman notes that designation of the role of Addressee is 'often accomplished exclusively through visual cues, although vocatives are available for managing it through audible ones' (1981: 132–3). It will be apparent from this statement that it is not always easy to identify a specific 'Addressee' from a transcript of spontaneous conversation involving more than two participants. This is especially so when the data is audio-recorded and there is thus no recourse to observation of the 'visual cues' Goffman mentions (see discussion of data collection questions in Section 1.2.2).

The following general criteria for identifying 'Addressee' in these texts were therefore arrived at, using semantic and structural features and citing typical formal realisations where possible. The ordering of the criteria reflects the degree of certainty involved in arriving at the presumed Addressee.

1 Use of the name of a particular participant ('the Addressee'), realising a Vocative (Q et al.: 773–5).

2 An appropriate 'response' to a preceding utterance by a particular participant ('the Addressee'), the 'addressing' utterance being one which will usually, in chronological terms, precede the 'response' by no more than two utterances. 'Appropriacy' might well be indicated by the kinds of response identified by Stubbs (1983a: 104–27), for example:

   (i)   The answer to a question expressed by that preceding utterance, for example one that provides the variable required by a wh-question, or 'X-question' (1983a: 107–9) or some indication of polarity as required by a yes-no question, the latter typically realised by *yes, no* or their equivalent (1983a: 105–6) (see also Crystal 1996: 40–1).

   (ii) An indication of a relevant reaction to that preceding utterance, for example agreement or disagreement with a statement or comment or suggestion expressed by that utterance. Typical realisations involve elliptical elements or anaphoric pronoun reference requiring recourse to the preceding utterance for elucidation of meaning.

3 Use of a particular personal pronoun (principally, though not exclusively, *you*) having identifiable specific meaning.

4 A statement, question or suggestion which relates to the presumed knowledge, or lack of knowledge or responsibility of a particular participant ('the Addressee'). Typical realisations involve declarative, interrogative or imperative structures, with <u>no</u> evidence of ellipsis requiring

recourse to a preceding utterance for elucidation; there may be limited use of anaphoric pronoun reference. (Such utterances are specifically not responses of the kind identified in 2(i) and 2(ii) above. In discourse analysis terms they could in fact be regarded as 'initiating' utterances or moves (see Section 4.7).)

5.7 Method and presentation of analysis

Contributions (that is, chunks of text assigned to individual speakers) were numbered in each text extract for reference purposes.

5.7.1 Deixis

Each text was analysed for the features specified in the framework outlined in 5.6.1. Deictic items which were unproblematically represented in the texts (that is, which had not been placed in round brackets in the transcripts) were identified and highlighted according to whether their meaning was recoverable linguistically or extra-linguistically – that is, via 'endophoric' or 'exophoric' means.

Endophoric items are shown by underlining and exophoric items in bold. The presumed meaning of the item in each case is then indicated via underlined text placed in square brackets. Single square brackets are used for endophoric items and double square brackets for exophoric items, thus: it [the water] (Talk 17) and *there* [[in the direction indicated]] (Task 18).

The following broad analytical and presentational decisions have been made:

- Where a deictic item is repeated within the same utterance and the same interpretation has been made this is indicated by the use of [ditto], see for example Talk 21.

- Where items appear in tag-type questions, for example *that's . . . is it* (Talk 20), co-reference with the subject of a preceding statement is assumed (Q et al.: 810–11) and its status indicated via [tag].

Annotations (via superscripts [1, 2] and so on) have been added in support of choices and/or interpretations in individual cases as appropriate. The analyses are displayed as Texts 5.1A (Talk) and 5.2A (Task) (see Appendix 1.4).

5.7.2 Participant role relationships

Texts 5.1A and 5.2A were then re-analysed according to the framework outlined in Section 5.6.2 in order to identify the presumed Addressee of each 'addressing utterance' in each text. Each contribution by each Speaker/Addressor was examined in terms of criteria 1–4, and the identified Addressee in each case is shown in the right-hand column, followed by an indication of the relevant criterion or criteria used in each instance. Where the criteria suggest that different elements within the same contribution are being directed at <u>different</u> Addressees, those elements have been regarded as indicating separate 'addressing utterances' and the criteria are shown appropriately. (See Section 1.2.5 for the distinction between 'contribution' and 'utterance' as used in this book.) If the criteria do <u>not</u> so suggest, then the whole of that contribution has been regarded as a single 'addressing utterance' being directed at the same Addressee. Incomplete contributions/utterances and/or those contributions which are given wholly in round brackets (indicating uncertainty over transcription) have been drawn on during the analysis where there is sufficient useful material, but categorisations accompanied by a question mark have <u>not</u> been included in the totals presented in Section 5.9.

The framework presented in Section 5.6.2 is an attempted synthesis of a simplified version of Hymes (1994) together with the insights of Goffman (1981) and Bell (1984, 1997). In carrying out the analysis it has been assumed that:

- the data has three 'ratified' human participants;
- the roles of Speaker and Addressor can be conflated under 'Addressor' (see below);
- there is always an Addressor (realised by one participant) for each utterance;
- either one sole participant or two joint participants may occupy the role of Addressee;
- where the analysis identifies one specified participant as Addressee the third (unspecified) participant is to be regarded as the Hearer/Auditor;
- where the criteria cannot be used to identify <u>either</u> one or two specified participants as Addressee the default presumption will be that the two participants other than the Addressor are the Addressee (that is, rather than the Hearer/Auditor – see below). Those utterances which have been so regarded are coded D (for 'default').

It is acknowledged that both the conflation of Speaker with Addressor and the default presumption re Addressee (rather than Hearer/Auditor) could be regarded as rather large assumptions. 'Speech for self' and/or some kind of commentary accompanying an occurrence in the surrounding environment is always a possibility (see, for example, Hillier 1992: 70 and 185–6). However, in the interests of simplification it was decided to streamline participant roles as much as possible.

Annotations (via superscripts [a, b] and so on) give support for analytical decisions as appropriate.

5.8 Presentation of results: deixis

5.8.1 Deictic choices overall

Table 5.1 compares total deictic choices made in each extract, further distinguishing between endophoric and exophoric choices. It shows a notable dif-

Table 5.1 Total Deictic choices: Talk v. Task

	Total Deictic choices	Endophoric choices	%	Exophoric choices	%
Talk	25	21	84.0	4	16.0
Task	23	9	39.1	14	60.9
Total	**48**	**30**	**62.5**	**18**	**37.5**

ference between endophoric and exophoric choices overall – that is, in the two extracts combined, 62.5 per cent endophoric compared with 37.5 per cent exophoric. However, and significantly for the purposes of this study, the distribution of endophoric and exophoric choices across the two extracts is very different indeed, being in completely opposite directions. There are more than five times as many endophoric as exophoric choices in the Talk extract (84 per cent compared with 16 per cent) and more than one and a half times as many exophoric as endophoric in the Task extract (60.9 per cent compared with 39.1 per cent).

The following subsections examine how far such overall differences in particular deictic choices are reflected across the different participants, particularly child participants.

5.8.2   Deictic choices across participants: Talk

Table 5.2 shows the deictic choices made by each participant in Talk Text 5.1A. When the choices of individual participants are examined the numbers become rather small. Nevertheless, Table 5.2 shows consistency with the overall pattern in Table 5.1, with all participants in the Talk extract making substantially more endophoric than exophoric choices. (H's choices are in fact 100 per cent endophoric, but given their very small number this finding cannot be regarded as significant.) The figures for A and R are a little more substantial and also notable: R's endophoric usage is three times his exophoric (75.0 per cent compared with 25.0 per cent), while A's endophoric usage is more than six times his exophoric (86.7 per cent compared with 13.3 per cent).

The specific exophoric choices made – two by each boy – involve either a time reference (A's _last Wednesday_ in Talk 13) or accompany a signal of some

Table 5.2 Comparative analysis of Deictic choices made by each participant: Talk

	Total Deictic choices	Endophoric choices	%	Exophoric choices	%
Child A	15	13	86.7	2	13.3
Child R	8	6	75.0	2	25.0
H	2	2	100.0	0	0
Total	**25**	**21**	**84.0**	**4**	**16.0**

kind of descriptive demonstration: A's *it's only about that deep* (Talk 17) and R's *it goes like this* (Talk 8) and *about this ( )* (*(gesture demonstrates depth?)*) (Talk 22).

Table 5.2 shows that A in fact makes much greater use of deixis overall (both endophoric and exophoric) than either of the other two participants, even though he and R contribute equal amounts to the Talk text (47.0 per cent of the word count by A and 46.7 per cent by R, with just 6.3 per cent by H). A detailed breakdown of word counts and deictic choices is, however, beyond the scope of this study (see Section 5.12).

5.8.3 Deictic choices across participants: Task

Table 5.3 presents a similar comparison for Task Text 5.2A. Once again individual numbers are small, but the overall pattern shown in Table 5.1 is broadly maintained, at least so far as the children are concerned. (H uses the same number of each kind in the Task text.) Both A and R make more exophoric than endophoric choices but, as in the Talk text, the proportions are different for each. A's exophoric choices are one third again of his endophoric (57.1 per cent compared with 42.9 per cent) while R's exophoric choices are four times his endophoric (80 per cent compared with 20 per cent).

As expected, the majority of the exophoric choices are interpretable via reference to some kind of entity in the immediate environment. The 'entity' is most frequently some visible element of the 'scene' represented in the game as displayed on the map on the computer screen (for example Task 1, 15, 17, 26, 34). These items are in the form of a place reference (*here, there*) or a demonstrative (*that*). Sometimes a participant asks for clarification, as in the following:

32 H *where are you now* [[at this point in the game]]
33 A *just there* [[in the place indicated]]

Such references can remain somewhat obscure to the reader of Text 5.2A, even though they are, of course, quite evident and comprehensible to the three participants (see further discussion in Section 5.9.3). In addition, there are references to the game itself and to the computer (Task 6, 28) and there is one reference to a 'human entity', when A complains to H about R's behaviour (Task 35) (see Section 5.9.2). The remainder are time references (mainly

Table 5.3 Comparative analysis of Deictic choices made by each participant: Task

	Total Deictic choices	Endophoric choices	%	Exophoric choices	%
Child A	14	6	42.9	8	57.1
Child R	5	1	20.0	4	80.0
H	4	2	50.0	2	50.0
Total	**23**	**9**	**39.1**	**14**	**60.9**

now) in relation to the current stage of the game, used by all three participants.

In the Task text, as in the Talk text, the actual numbers of deictic choices (both exophoric and endophoric) by each participant differ, with A in particular making many more deictic choices overall than the other two participants. In the Task text, however, A contributes proportionately much more to the talk than either R or H. (A, R and H contribute 46.0, 26.4 and 27.6 per cent respectively.) The numbers and proportions of choices would seem to be connected in the Task extract with the practical roles involved. A is in charge of the computer keyboard and is more familiar with the game than either R or H; he uses more exophoric game-related items than they do and tends to make many of the decisions as to what should be done next. R is attempting to keep track of events by maintaining the written map, and he contributes suggestions based on this map and the one currently on the screen; he appears to have a slightly more peripheral role than A. H knows virtually nothing about this specific game and most of her exophoric items are used in the course of her trying to clarify what is going on. Her role appears to be even more peripheral than R's. Her relative 'presence' in the Task extract, therefore, as suggested by Table 5.3 (and her overall contribution to the talk) is more apparent than real.

The effects of the practical roles adopted by each participant are considered again in Section 5.9 when participant roles are examined.

5.8.4 Deictic choices by child participants: Talk v. Task

Table 5.4 explicitly compares choices made across the two extracts by child participants only. It shows that when both extracts are taken together child participants' choices (61.9 per cent compared with 38.1 per cent) pattern in roughly the same way as the total choices for all three participants set out in Table 5.1. However, the differences in distribution across the extracts vary a little from those in Table 5.1. Table 5.4 shows a slight reduction in the difference between endophoric and exophoric choices in the Talk text (now 82.6 per cent endophoric and 17.4 per cent exophoric compared with 84 and 16 per cent respectively). In the Task text, however, the difference has <u>increased</u> (being 36.8 per cent endophoric and 63.2 exophoric compared with 39.1 and 60.9 per cent respectively).

Table 5.4 Comparative analysis of Deictic choices – Talk v. Task – made by child participants only

	Total Deictic choices	Endophoric choices	%	Exophoric choices	%
Talk	23	19	82.6	4	17.4
Task	19	7	36.8	12	63.2
Total	**42**	**26**	**61.9**	**16**	**38.1**

To adopt a different, 'vertical', perspective, in the Talk extract the children make more than twice as many endophoric choices as in the Task extract (82.6 per cent compared with 36.8 per cent) and in the Task extract they make almost four times as many exophoric choices as in the Talk extract (63.2 per cent compared with 17.4 per cent).

It is clear, therefore, that the initial expectations in Section 5.5.1 have been fulfilled:

- the Talk text does draw to a much greater extent on the <u>linguistic</u> environment for its interpretation than the Task text, and

- the Task text does draw to a much greater extent on the immediate, shared, <u>extra-linguistic</u> environment for its interpretation than the Talk text.

These findings are considered and assessed in the light of the overall findings in Section 5.10 below.

5.9 Presentation of results: participant role relationships

The following subsections summarise the results for the Addressor/Addressee analyses of each identified 'Addressing utterance' in Talk Text 5.1A and Task Text 5.2A respectively. (All 'uncertain' items have been excluded from the summaries.)

5.9.1 Occupation of the roles of Addressor and Addressee

Table 5.5 shows the distribution of the role of Addressor across participants for each extract. It shows that in the Talk extract there is a marked difference between child and adult participants in the extent to which they act as Addressor. The boys R and A each contribute at least 40 per cent of total Addressing utterances, but H only just over 10 per cent. It would seem, therefore, that, from the perspective of Addressing utterances at least, the adult H does not dominate the interaction represented by the extract or appear to be 'in control' of the conversation. This serves to support the initial, intuitive, impression that the 'interview' was a very informal – even 'democratic' – one indeed.

In the Task extract the numbers of Addressing utterances are closer to being

Table 5.5 Comparative Analysis of Addressors: Talk v. Task

	Total Addressing utterances	Child R as Addressor		Child A as Addressor		Adult H as Addressor	
		No.	%	No.	%	No.	%
Talk	45	22	48.9	18	40.0	5	11.1
Task	34	10	29.4	13	38.2	11	32.4

Table 5.6 Occupation of role of Addressee – individual v. group – Talk v. Task

	Total Addressing utterances	Addressee – individual		Addressee – group (including Default)	
		No.	%	No.	%
Talk	45	40	88.9	5	11.1
Task	34	25	73.5	9	26.5

equal, though R does make fewer than A or even H (29.4 per cent compared with 38.2 and 32.4 per cent respectively of all Addressing utterances). This suggests, at least initially, that R assumes less dominance in this extract than A. This is considered in Section 5.10 below.

Table 5.6 compares the extent of occupation of the very significant role of Addressee, distinguishing between those utterances addressed to an individual Addressee and those to a 'group', that is, to a joint (including Default) Addressee.

As the table shows, the majority of the utterances in each text have been identified as being addressed to one individual participant within the triad rather than to the remaining two ('group') participants. The difference is greater, however, in the Talk text – with 88.9 per cent being individually addressed compared with 73.5 per cent in the Task text. In the Task text nine (26.5 per cent) of the utterances are to a group Addressee, four of these being 'Defaults'. (No Defaults at all were recorded in the Talk text.) Some possible reasons for this are considered in Section 5.9.3.

The following subsection examines these findings in a little more detail.

5.9.2 Individual v. group Addressee

Tables 5.7 and 5.8 present the results for each individual Addressee and then for each different group. Table 5.7 shows that in the Talk text 17.5 per cent of utterances are addressed to R and 25.0 per cent to A, with 57.5 per cent of all individually addressed utterances being directed at H. This is a notable finding. Some of the utterances are responses to her questions or to statements functioning as what Labov calls 'requests for confirmation' (1978: 253–4). They may thus be considered consistent with the original 'interview'

Table 5.7 Comparative Addressee Analysis – Individual Addressee Talk v. Task

	Utterances to Individual Addressees	Child R as Addressee		Child A as Addressee		Adult H as Addressee	
		No.	%	No.	%	No.	%
Talk	40	7	17.5	10	25.0	23	57.5
Task	25	8	32.0	10	40.0	7	28.0

format and not, therefore, particularly surprising. However, responses of this kind account for only five out of the 23 utterances.

The most interesting aspect here in fact centres on R and A's account of the slide and shower at Ilkeston baths. The specific topic of the slide is initiated by R's utterance at Talk 8, and the full account begins at Talk 22, extending through a remarkable and syntactically coordinated sequence through to Talk 31. This sequence shows the boys supporting, reinforcing, expanding and completing each other's utterances for H's benefit. It emerges in an almost seamless flow: the boys share in the construction of the talk 'as if they were a single speaker', which Coates (1996: 267) regards as 'a powerful way of doing friendship'. Stubbs too (1983a: 20–3) describes such joint production of talk by his 12-year-old boy subjects, as did Maybin (1994: 135–7), who commented on the 'duetting' appearing in the talk of her 10-year-old girls (see a comparable reference to Coates's findings in Section 4.7.1). Interestingly, both Stubbs's and Maybin's research involved pairs of children well known to each other in conversation with a friendly adult. (See further discussion in Section 5.9.3.)

In contrast, Table 5.7 shows that, in the Task text, A is the target of the majority of the individually addressed utterances (40 per cent in comparison with R's 32 per cent and H's 28.0 per cent) and this seems to be consistent with his practical role as keyboard operator. Questions and/or comments are addressed to him by both R and H in that capacity. Fewer utterances are addressed to R in his practical role as map-keeper. This role is a valuable one in that it helps to chart their progress and to record potentially useful information, but it seems to be a less salient practical role than that of keyboard operator. It can also be counter-productive at times, as will be seen.

The adult H is addressed with far lower frequency in the Task text than in the Talk text, and virtually all of those utterances individually addressed to her represent responses to her questions about where things are at a particular point in the game. Interestingly, the single initiating utterance addressed to H in the Task extract emerges as though to a teacher, being a complaint by A about a particular aspect of R's map-keeping behaviour: *he keeps marking where we are and I keep thinking they're traps* (Task 35). (This utterance might almost have been prefaced by the classic *Miss . . .*) There are no jointly constructed sets of utterances addressed to H of the kind produced in the Talk text. This reinforces the impression given by the Deixis analysis (see Section 5.8.3) that H's role is a very minor one in the Task text: to a great extent she is merely an observer and occasional – and largely superfluous – commentator on the significant action the others are engaged in.

Table 5.8 shows that A+R is Addressee of 60 per cent of the group-addressed utterances in the Talk text (the adult H being, of course, Addressor of both boys jointly), with R+H receiving the remainder. Numbers are, however, very small, with only five group-addressed out of a total of 45 Addressing utterances.

The Task text has proportionately more group-addressed utterances than the Talk text, and these are also a little more evenly distributed across the three potential groups. Four of the nine Addressing utterances (two by each

Table 5.8 Comparative Addressee analysis – group Addressee Talk v. Task

	Utterances to Group Addressees	A+H as Addressee		R+H as Addressee		A+R as Addressee	
		No.	%	No.	%	No.	%
Talk	5	0	0	2	40.0	3	60.0
Task	9	3	33.3	4	44.4	2	22.2

boy) have been analysed as Defaults: the Addressor is making some kind of comment or observation on some aspect of the current stage of the game, and there is no very convincing evidence as to the intended Addressee. (See Section 5.9.3 for further consideration of these findings.)

5.9.3 Participants' Addressor–Addressee relationships: who addresses whom

Tables 5.9 to 5.11 compare the different Addressor-Addressee combinations appearing in each text and for each participant in turn. Discussion here will focus principally on child participants, with minimal attention given to the addressing patterns of the adult H.

Tables 5.9 and 5.10 show that both R's and A's Addressee choices differ notably between the two extracts. In the Talk text either all or the vast

Table 5.9 A comparison of CHILD R's Addressor–Addressee relationships – Talk v. Task

	Total Addressing utterances	CHILD A as Addressee		ADULT H as Addressee		A+H as Addressee	
		Number	%	Number	%	Number	%
Talk	22	9	40.9	13	59.1	0	0
Task	10	5	50.0	2	20.0	3	30.0
Total	32	14	43.8	15	46.9	3	9.4

Table 5.10 A comparison of CHILD A's Addressor–Addressee relationships – Talk v. Task

	Total Addressing utterances	CHILD R as Addressee		ADULT H as Addressee		R+H as Addressee	
		Number	%	Number	%	Number	%
Talk	18	6	33.3	10	55.6	2	11.1
Task	13	4	30.8	5	38.5	4	30.8
Total	31	10	32.3	15	48.4	6	19.4

Table 5.11   A comparison of ADULT H's Addressor–Addressee relationships – Talk v. Task

	Total Addressing utterances	CHILD R as Addressee		CHILD A as Addressee		A+R as Addressee	
		Number	%	Number	%	Number	%
Talk	5	1	20.0	1	20.0	3	60.0
Task	11	4	36.4	5	45.5	2	18.2
Total	**16**	**5**	**31.3**	**6**	**37.5**	**5**	**31.3**

majority of <u>both</u> boys' utterances are to an individual rather than a group Addressee, and in each case the proportion is greater where the Addressee is the adult H. This latter is a reflection, at least to some extent, of the finding discussed in Section 5.9.2, where the two boys construct the series of interdependent utterances to H in describing the slide.

In the Task text, there is no comparably clear pattern. Both boys address predominantly an individual rather than a group Addressee, but the proportions of group-addressed utterances are much higher than in the Talk text – almost a third for both. These findings may be partially accounted for by some of the generalised comments made in the Task extract as part of the progress of the computer game, giving rise in some cases to the Default codings already referred to. R could almost be talking to himself in places as he reads from and/or comments on the computer screen or the map he is keeping (e.g. *camping is here* (Task 1) (see comparable utterances found by Fisher 1993: 100 and also Hillier 1992: 178). (The adult H also appears to read aloud from the computer screen. In fact this practice may well account for some of H's questionably decipherable (and frequently unanalysable) contributions – see, for example, Task 27, 30.)

So far as A is concerned, there are signs that he takes more or less independent decisions as to what should be done next, appearing to be announcing these rather than actually seeking to consult or gain approval, for example, *west – that's that way now we need to look (   )* (Task 26). (Again, Fisher (1993: 102) and Hillier (1992: 202 and 204) report comparable findings.) This tendency may be partly brought about by haste to find the last clue before the end of the school day (see Tasks 5–11).

All of the above factors may contribute to the overall impression of fragmentation given by the Task text in comparison with the Talk text. There is an intermittent sense of isolated and unconnected utterances going in separate and unspecific directions, which contrasts strongly with the coherent and integrated stages shown in the Talk text. This fragmentation in utterance terms in fact reinforces – as it is inevitably reinforced by – the amount of indecipherable and/or questionable material in transcription terms. The transcript itself, therefore, with all its shortcomings, could be regarded as providing some concrete evidence of the effects of an extralinguistic task-related focus (see Section 5.10).

Tables 5.9 and 5.10 show some interesting differences in the patterning of individually addressed utterances, particularly the inter-child Addressor–

Addressee relationships in the Talk text. (Addressing utterances to H have been discussed in Section 5.9.2.) In the Talk text R addresses nine utterances to A and receives only six in return (40.0 per cent compared with 33.3 per cent). Text 5.1A shows, however, that of A's six Addressing utterances to R half are initiations (Talk 11, 13, 15) whereas, in marked contrast, <u>none</u> of R's addressing utterances to A is an initiation. All of these respond directly to A (being second or third 'moves' – see Section 4.11.2) or to A following his initiations to H or R+H.

A's initiations to R occur in the sequence beginning at Talk 11. A begins to recount directly to R an incident which had happened to him on the slide at the Ilkeston pool the previous week, prefacing it with an explicit marker of shared knowledge: *R you know that shower at the end of it.* R's laugh acknowledges A's utterance and their shared knowledge (Talk 12a) and he then immediately gives H the explicit information about the location of the shower (detail of the specific 'scene') that she needs in order to follow and/or participate in the conversation (Talk 12b). A proceeds with his story, setting up the relevant time frame (Talk 13), suitably acknowledged by R, and then moves into the main body of the account, again including a marker of his and R's mutual knowledge (. . . *you know the man up at top who watches you go down* . . . Talk 15). Once again R acknowledges A's utterance (Talk 16a) and then brings H into the picture (*there's like a sprinkler what comes down* . . . Talk 16b). It is at this point that A seems to become aware of his wider conversational responsibilities, and he proceeds to provide H with a little more specific information – about the depth of water in the pool at the end of the slide (Talk 17). A's anecdote, in fact, combined with R's sensitive and skilful modulations, prepares the ground for the remarkable descriptive sequences beginning at Talk 22 as already discussed.

Patterns in the Task text are less striking, though once again R addresses a higher proportion of his utterances to A (50 per cent) than he receives in return (30.8 per cent), largely as a consequence of A's significant practical role as keyboard operator. Once again, too, A initiates more to R than the reverse, though less notably than in the Talk text. A uses three initiations (out of four utterances), two of which concern the next possible move in the game (Task 14, 17), the third being a mild complaint – *I can't see R* (Task 31). R's two initiations (of five) appear to comment directly (from the sidelines) on A's operator role (Task 3, 29).

5.10 Summary of findings

The principal motivation for this study seems to have been justified: the different purposes of the two extracts studied are reflected in <u>both</u> the kinds of deictic choices the children make <u>and</u> the participant roles they adopt *vis-à-vis* each other and the adult participant. The main findings may be summarised as follows:

• The children show great discrimination in the extent to which they make their different deictic choices: they make linguistically explicit what needs to be said and avoid giving what Stubbs (1983b: 50–54) would regard as 'redundant information': They leave detailed interpretation to be recovered from the immediate environment where this is self-evident, thus displaying linguistic economy (compare McTear 1985) (Section 5.8).

- They use a much higher proportion of endophoric items in the Talk extract than in the Task extract, and such use makes a significant contribution to the construction and overall coherence of the conversation represented by the Talk extract. The relatively few exophoric items are readily interpretable (and/or imaginable by the reader of the extract) in terms of the immediate situation (Section 5.8.2).

- The much higher proportion of exophoric items in the Task extract than the Talk extract is consistent with the concentration on the task in hand, the co-present computer and the associated depictions of aspects of the relevant game being played. Interpretation of the different exophoric items is readily apparent to all the participants, or can be easily clarified by visual and/or linguistic means, though this may present problems for the reader of the text (Section 5.8.3; and see below).

- The children show comparable adaptability and discrimination in their adoption and allocation of different participant roles. In the Talk extract they largely share their conversational responsibilities, alternating the roles of Addressor and Addressee to an approximately equal extent. More interestingly, they both address most of their utterances to the adult H, and in approximately equal proportions. In particular, they show striking skill, timing and coordination in constructing complex descriptive utterances for the benefit of H (Section 5.9.2). They also display discrimination and sensitivity to the degree of background knowledge she can be assumed to have (again, what needs to be made explicit), modifying their utterances to take account of this (compare Stubbs 1983a). The latter is particularly so for the child R, who appears to take the lead in this respect (Section 5.9.3).

- In the Task extract participant roles are less equally distributed, with the practical roles associated with the computer and the playing of the game influencing the adoption and allocation of the participant roles of both Addressor and Addressee. Thus A, the person in charge of the computer keyboard, is the dominant participant in both participant roles when compared with R, who is the comparatively unregarded keeper of the written map. The adult H, who has no practical role and whose evident ignorance of the game seems to be gently tolerated, is a mere observer (contrast the notable orientation towards H as Addressee in the Talk extract) (Section 5.9.3).

- The increased proportion of group-addressed, especially Default, utterances found in the Task extract (reinforcing the less-than-precise interpretation of some of the exophoric items used) may account for the disjointed effect created by the specific text. It should be remembered, however, that this 'fragmentation' is a construct of the investigative process itself. It arises from the act of (imperfect) *post facto* transcription of audio-recorded data, with all its uncertainties of attribution and interpretation. It is not, of course, a reflection of the progress of the discourse as it actually occurred. This proceeded perfectly comprehensibly so far as the participants were concerned, and it appears to have been largely successful in its achievement of its limited practical goals within the scope of the brief extract examined here.

5.11   Conclusion

This chapter has investigated the spontaneous talk of two children in conversation with an adult, comparing the language used in two contrasting situations, one Talk-centred and one Task-centred.

It has shown that the children successfully adapt specific aspects of their speech according to the needs of the particular context, both in their choice of appropriate deictic items and their adoption and assignment of particular participant roles. In doing so, they demonstrate sensitivity, discrimination and skill in assessing the requirements of the specific environment and the degree of shared knowledge of their co-participants, thus deciding just how much needs to be said and to whom.

5.12   Suggestions for further work

(a)   Other features which might be examined in detail include:

- different types of deictic item, including extent and type of deictic choice across individual participants, especially the children, in relation to overall amount of talk;

- different participant roles occupied and assigned, for example distinguishing between Speaker v. Addressor, Addressee v. Hearer/Auditor and so on.

(b)   The framework (modified as necessary) could be applied to comparable data but controlling, say, both Mode and Field but varying Tenor, for example, comparing different participants when engaged in the same task:

- (small) groups of children of contrasting age or sex or social/cultural background;

- children in comparison with adults.

Such studies might be especially productive if (suitably 'low-profile') video-recorded data were obtainable (see Section 1.2.2).

(c) Aspects of the framework (especially Deixis) could usefully be applied to different kinds of text, accompanied (or not) by visual material in support. Examples involving controlled Field but varying aspects of Mode might be:

- spoken v. written instructions for performing a particular task;

- sports commentaries of comparable events on television v. radio;

- advertisements for comparable products on television v. radio; an alternative approach here might be to prepare transcripts of <u>only</u> the spoken material of television advertisements, omitting <u>any</u> element of visual description of the kind included in texts presented in Chapter 8.

Comparisons of such texts should reveal which material (its extent and type) has to be made explicit in linguistic terms and which is assumed to be situationally recoverable, that is, from the extra-linguistic environment.

CHAPTER

Political Speeches
6

6.1   Introduction

This chapter will be concerned specifically with the language of speeches by two British politicians. In terms of the overall framework of the book as presented in Figure 1.1, political speeches will be regarded as coming under 'the speaking of what has been written to be spoken'.

The chapter will compare a short extract from a speech by Tony Blair, leader of the Labour party, to the Labour party conference and a comparable speech by John Major, leader of the Conservative party, to the Conservative party conference. It will explore how far the extracts differ in the linguistic choices made by each speaker.

6.2   Identifying the variables

6.2.1   The controlled variables

The variables to be controlled in this chapter are:

- **Mode**:   The language is 'spoken' in each case. It is produced via the oral channel and is intended to be processed by the ear; there is visual contact between the speaker and his immediate audience. Each speech, however, will have been thoroughly prepared in advance and will have its origins in some form of writing, being what Carter et al. (2001: 258) describe as 'scripted speech'. It may, indeed, have been constructed by more than one individual, including (perhaps) the actual deliverer of the speech.

  Even though there is visual contact between speaker and immediate audience the communication is almost entirely one-way. The audience has virtually no share in text creation, being limited mainly to non-verbal signals such as applause.

- **Field**:   The **purposeful activity** involved is the exposition of political discourse by the party leader at a party conference in a public space (the relevant designated conference hall in each case) in consecutive weeks of the same month (October) of the same year (1995). (The **Setting** – both spatial and temporal – is therefore congruent with aspects of Field; see

Section 1.1.6.4.) The chosen extract represents the closing stages of the speech in each case.

- **Tenor** (functional):   Each speaker is a new, relatively young, party leader trying to create a rapport with his audience – to establish himself as a leader who inspires confidence. His speech is intended to encourage the faithful (the delegates actually attending the conference), trying to balance need for change with a need to carry the old party along. Some degree of reassurance is therefore required.

   The target audience, however, also includes (via television and other media) the voters in the country. The party leader wants to address them and at the same time persuade them of a particular point of view. It is possible, indeed, that this wider audience (the electorate in general) is of at least equal significance in determining the content and style of the speech. In terms of 'audience design' as defined by Bell (1984, 1997), the electorate can be regarded as incorporating the roles of both 'auditor' and 'overhearer' – they are certainly 'known' members of the audience (see Sections 5.5.2 and 8.6.2).

6.2.2   The varying variables

Potentially varying variables arise under:

- **Tenor** (personal):   The immediate **participants** are the party leader (the speaker) and the relevant party delegates (the audience) in each case: Tony Blair and the Labour party members on the one hand and John Major and the Conservative party members on the other.

John Major had succeeded a charismatic leader, Margaret Thatcher, who was ousted by the party in 1990. He had won one election against the odds in 1992, and this had been considered something of a personal triumph. At the time of the speech Major is both party leader and incumbent prime minister; he is defending the government's record and seeking to justify more of approximately the same.

Tony Blair had succeeded a highly respected but short-term leader, the late John Smith, in 1994, at a time when the Labour party had suffered a series of election defeats. He was continuing the reforms of the party begun by Neil Kinnock, Smith's predecessor as leader. Blair is the challenger to Major, advocating change.

It is clear, therefore, that although the two party leaders are in what is essentially the same immediate situation, their current status, their different political philosophies and the expectations of their respective party audiences will influence the way those audiences are addressed. The two men may also be expected to differ in the way they try to appeal to the wider electorate.

Further, each party has broad areas of policy with which it has tended in the past to be traditionally associated – for example 'individual responsibility' and 'national pride' for the Conservatives, 'aspirations of equality' and 'social progressiveness' for Labour. However, given some of the fundamental changes in British society brought about under Margaret Thatcher, these traditional concerns cannot be so readily assumed. Topics chosen within the overall Field of political discourse – particularly the emphases accorded them by the two leaders in recognition of the perceived concerns of their audience – cannot, therefore, be predicted. They are likely to be a fruitful area of investigation.

From this point on, I will refer to the various politicians mentioned by their surname only. This is entirely for purposes of economy of reference: no ideological position is thereby implied!

6.3   Description of the data

The speeches were made on 3 and 13 October 1995, respectively, with the Labour party conference preceding the Conservative. Audiotapes of the speeches were obtained from the relevant political organisations, and these were transcribed in accordance with the conventions outlined in Section 1.2.5.

The extracts chosen for analysis represent the closing few minutes of each speech, since its climactic and persuasive purpose was felt likely to be most evident at this point. Each leader's speech might indeed have been the last opportunity for a conference speech (with its attendant media coverage) before the following election, though in the event the election was not called until May 1997 – almost at the end of the Conservative government's full five-year term.

The extracts differ slightly in length of recording time but they consist of approximately the same number of words. The Blair extract (**Text 6.1**) is just over four minutes long, but it is punctuated by applause. The applause has been noted in the transcript (though with no indication of its duration) since it seems to make an important contribution to the overall effect of the speech, especially in indicating how it was received in the conference hall (see reference to the role of applause in Section 6.4.1 below). It is 487 words long, and the start of the extract is immediately preceded by applause.

Text 6.1   Blair

and I say to you my party – be strong and of good courage –the Labour party that first won support from the British people – that was new Labour then – 1945 was new Labour – 1964 was new Labour – both new Labour because both had the courage to take the values of the Labour party and use them not for the world as it was but for the world as they wanted it to be – and new Labour now ready in 1995 to build new Britain — during those VJ day celebrations I was on the platform with Tory ministers and as we walked down the Mall there were thousands of people there holding their Union Jacks – and it became clear – to the horror of the Tories – that most of them were Labour ((*laughter*)) and they were waving and shouting and urging me to get the Tories out ((*laughter*)) ((*applause*)) these are our people – they love this country just as we do and it is because they love this country that they look for us to change it – so let us say with pride – we are patriots – this is the patriotic party because it is the party of the people – and as the Tories wave their Union Jacks next week I know what so many people will be thinking – I know what the people want to say to those Tories – it is no good waving the fabric of our flag when you've spent sixteen years tearing apart the fabric of the nation ((*applause*))

tearing apart the bonds that tie communities together and make us the United Kingdom – tearing apart the security of those people – clutching their Union Jacks swelling with pride at their victory over tyranny yelling at me to get the Tories out because they want security because they want to leave a better world for their children and their grandchildren than they created for themselves and they know the Tories can't do it – decent people — good people — patriotic people — and when I hear people urging us to fight for *our* people I tell you *these are our people* ((*applause*))

they *are* the majority – and we will serve them and build that new Britain – that young country for their children and their families and I make them this promise now – that I will do all that I can to get these Tories out and I will devote every breath that I breathe every sinew of my body to ensuring that your grandchildren do get to live in that new Britain in a new and better world – discipline – courage – determination – honesty – this victory can be won – the prize is immense – it is new Britain – one Britain – the people united by shared values shared aims – a government governing for *all* the people – and the party – this party – the Labour party – new Labour – founded by the people backed truly as the people's party – new Labour – new Britain – the party renewed – the country reborn – new Labour – new Britain ((*applause*))

The Major extract (**Text 6.2**) is also immediately preceded by applause. It is 471 words and just over three minutes long, with no intervening applause.

Text 6.2   Major

Mr Chairman — after four terms why a fifth – why should we be elected for a fifth time to serve our nation – because in a shifting world only we will build a safe future for our people and heal the scars of the past – because we're building a more secure economy as the enterprise centre of Europe – because we're reforming public service to make it more accountable to the public who pay for it – because we stand for choice and excellence in education and we are in the midst of the biggest revolution in education since Rab Butler — because we will retain the old rock-solid guarantee of the health service free at the point of delivery – and where improvement in the health service is necessary it won't be treated as a sacred cow we will seek to improve it – because defence and security of the realm in our streets and beyond our streets are of *paramount* concern to us and to our party and to your government — we Conservatives are for the individual not the state for choice not direction for ownership not dependence for liberty not for control – these are the enduring things – the cornerstones of our beliefs – the reasons that you and I joined the Conservative party and are meeting here today – we have worked for them – cared for them fought for them over the years – we are building in this country the greatest success for this nation that we have known in our lifetime – we will not surrender them to a lightweight alternative – we carry the scars of battle – that is true – but they are honourable scars – we know that no other party can win the battles for Britain that lie ahead – so when you go home – refreshed and uplifted I hope by this conference – remember these things and ask the people on the doorstep – would taxes be higher or lower under Labour – would inflation be higher or lower under Labour – would there be more or less choice under Labour – would our defence be more secure under Labour – would our constitution be safe under Labour – you and I have only to ask the question and the echo from our country will provide the answer – we stand – we Conservatives – we stand for a wise and kindly way of life that is rooted deep in our history – our hopes for our country aren't tired – our ambitions aren't dim – our message to our fellow countrymen is clear – millions of them have yet to make up their minds the choice is theirs – our nation's future is at stake and we Conservatives – who have served our country in office for longer and better than any other democratic political party in the world – we Conservatives are here and in the future we Conservatives stand ready to serve on behalf of the nation we love ((*applause*))

6.4   Expectations re the varying variables

6.4.1   Some general expectations

Work on persuasive speeches in general, and political speeches in particular, suggests that speakers adopt a range of rhetorical devices and strategies to appeal to their hearers.

Wooffitt (1996) notes the popularity of particular devices in the speeches of British politicians, both Conservative and Labour. He discusses the work of the sociologist Atkinson (1984) and others, in particular what Atkinson calls 'three-part lists' and 'contrasts', which appear to be successful in evoking applause from audiences at appropriate points. In a 'three-part list' a particular point is made by use of a series of three specific components, cited examples being: 'Soviet marxism is <u>ideologically politically</u> and <u>morally</u> bankrupt'; and 'I [have] a marvellous deputy who's wonderful <u>in all places</u> <u>at all times</u> <u>in all things</u> . . . ' (Atkinson 1984; cited in Wooffitt 1996: 125). In 'contrast', one argument is contrasted with another, a 'well constructed' example being: 'The fact is that <u>too much is spent on the munitions of war</u> and <u>too little is spent on the munitions of peace</u>' (Heritage and Greatbatch 1986; cited in Wooffitt 1996: 127).

Fairclough (2001, 2000) considers some of the linguistic features of political discourse, most specifically 'the discourse of Thatcherism' (2001: 140–62) and the language of New Labour, especially as the latter is embodied in the language style of Tony Blair (2000). He also (for example 2001: 153–5; 2000: 28) notes the fondness of Thatcher and Blair for 'lists' of various kinds, though Fairclough's lists appear to be rather different in both form and function from the 'three-part lists' discussed by Wooffitt. Fairclough takes a rather dim view of 'lists', claiming that they do ideological 'work' on audiences, leaving to them the task of 'inferring connections which are left implicit' (2001: 155). Further:

> The factors or elements in such lists are seen as connected only in the sense that <u>they appear together</u>. There is <u>no attempt at explanation</u> that tries to specify deeper relations among them (e.g. cause and effect) . . . This is <u>a logic of appearances</u> that manifests itself grammatically in a propensity towards lists, which is in contrast with a different logic in the left and social democratic tradition – a rational and explanatory logic. . . . (2000: 28; emphases added)

Fairclough focuses on a Conservative and a Labour leader, but his analyses do not involve systematic comparative approaches to his chosen text extracts, nor independent evaluation of the kind recommended in Section 1.2.6. It will be seen, however, that he makes many insightful and provocative points. Some of these can be related directly to the concerns of the current study and will be drawn on as appropriate in discussion of findings. He also makes some interesting claims about pronoun choices made by Thatcher and Blair respectively, and these are considered in a little more detail in Section 6.5 below.

Most significantly, however, Fairclough's analyses are placed against the context of what he sees as a politician's discourse aims, that is 'to either <u>maintain</u> or <u>create</u> commonality of ideology or allegiance among (<u>the sections of a population represented in</u>) an audience . . . ' (2001: 141; emphases added). The question of 'ideology' and its assumptions was, of course, one of the concerns addressed in Chapter 3 (see Section 3.4.1). The various strands identifiable in Fairclough's claim, therefore, appear to relate very precisely and succinctly to the significant aspects of Tenor relations outlined in Section 6.2, that is, the need for both men, from their different standpoints, to (appear to) assume a 'commonality of ideology' with <u>both</u> the committed constituency (the 'maintaining' function) <u>and</u> the electorate in general (the 'creating' function).

The ways in which each party leader appears to do this, including the linguistic choices he makes in addressing and/or referring to his 'audience', are the focus of this study. The areas each man chooses to emphasise (see the reference to the topic element of Field) are also likely to be significant in contributing to this overall aim. A close examination of each text should, therefore, give some indication of:

- the way each leader presents himself to his audience – both his party and the electorate in general;

- the kinds of assumptions each leader appears to be making about the concerns of his audience – again, both his party and the electorate in general.

6.4.2   Evaluative responses

While these speeches cannot – with any degree of certainty – be regarded as having played a significant role in either convincing or deterring the electorate, it is undeniable that the Labour party did win the May 1997 election. Whatever their actual persuasive force in 1995 and beyond, the Blair speech can in general terms – and with hindsight – be associated with success and the Major speech with failure.

More specifically, so far as these two particular extracts are concerned, it is pertinent to report on the results of a small informal enquiry. In order to explore in a little more detail what might be considered to constitute the 'persuasive' aspect of political speeches, I presented the two extracts to a group of ten adult students attending a course on persuasive language. The students listened as a group to each of the two taped extracts, while also reading the transcript, and they were then asked for their intuitive reactions. No specifically focused questions were asked of them, but a discussion followed in which they gave their evaluative responses. The discussion took place early in 1998 and the students therefore had the benefit of hindsight – both of the results of the 1997 election and their own opinions (from their individual political and personal positions) about the new government's record so far.

Their observations should therefore be regarded as a very small number of exploratory and qualitative responses to the data, not as a structured informant test (see Section 1.2.6 and also Section 3.4.2). The students did, however, make some interesting comments on the extracts, and they also identified some potentially significant linguistic features which were likely to repay further investigation. For example, during the discussion specific reference was made to:

- the contrasting use of pronouns by the two men (*I, me, my* by Blair compared with *we, our* by Major);

- the impression of wisdom and maturity conveyed by Major, compared with Blair's 'bossiness';

- Blair's apparent wooing of the middle ground;

- Major's rather 'preachy' style, his use of long sentences and of words like *battles* and *scars*.

6.5   Specific areas of enquiry

Informants had specified pronoun use as being notably different between the two men. It seemed, therefore, that a detailed examination of all personal pronoun choices was likely to be a fruitful area of enquiry, in assessing how personal reference (including to speaker and audience) is manifested and what that might imply about the way the relationship between speaker and audience is perceived.

Fairclough, in fact, identified use of personal pronouns as being significant in the political discourse of both Thatcher (2001: 148–50) and Blair (2000: 98–105). He comments (2001: 148–9) on the meanings expressed in Thatcher's uses of *we* and *you* in relation to 'the people', and how these may be presented as implying her own solidarity with 'the people'. He also discusses (2000: 98–105) Blair's use of *I* as a part of an overall strategy for constructing his personal identity – as a 'normal person' – in his public performances. Fairclough's claims will be considered as appropriate when the findings of the current study are discussed below.

It was also decided to focus on lexical and grammatical choices, specifically the extent of repetition involved in each case. Investigation of degrees of lexical repetition might indicate the relative importance assigned to specific themes or topics by each speaker and thus his assumptions about his particular audience's concerns. Grammatical repetition might suggest something about each speaker's personal style, both in the context of the 'rhetorical' strategies discussed by Wooffitt (1996) and the claims of Fairclough (2000). Both investigations might also go some way towards accounting for the informants' more general responses as presented in Section 6.4.2.

6.6   The frameworks for this study

6.6.1   Personal pronouns

The analysis, and therefore this framework, includes under the designation 'personal pronouns' all of the pronouns which Crystal (1996: 148) and Quirk et al. (1985: 346) categorise as the 'central pronouns', that is the personal, possessive and reflexive pronouns.

It was necessary to adopt a comprehensive and strictly formal approach to the descriptive framework (see Section 6.7.1 below). There would be no attempt to categorise in advance any specific use of a pronoun nor to decide on either its inclusion or exclusion on the grounds of its presumed meaning (contrast Wilson 1990: 45–76). Interpretation of possible meanings in each case would be considered at the analysis and results stage. The findings might then be more profitably related to the kinds of claims made by, for example, Fairclough (2001, 2000). The personal pronouns are set out in Table 6.1.

6.6.2   Lexical repetition

For the purposes of this study and this framework, 'repetition' will be defined as three or more uses of the 'same' lexical item.

In identifying items for potential repetition a distinction has been made between 'lexical items' and 'grammatical items' (Halliday 1989b: 63–4) (see too 'open class' and 'closed class' items as designated by Quirk et al. 1985: 67). Those items considered for lexical repetition fall within the 'lexical'/'open' category – that is, nouns, adjectives, full (lexical) verbs and

Table 6.1 Personal pronouns

Person	Personal		Possessive		Reflexive	
	Singular	**Plural**	**Singular**	**Plural**	**Singular**	**Plural**
First	I, me	we, us	my, mine	our, ours	myself	ourselves
Second	you*	you*	your, yours	your, yours	yourself	yourselves
Third	he, him, she, her, it	they, them**	his, her, hers, its	their, theirs	him-/her-/itself**	themselves

* The same forms of *you* are, of course, used for both singular and plural in Standard English (for example, there is no equivalent of the dialect form *thou* still found in some non-standard dialects; Trudgill 1999: 90-4). The most likely meaning in any individual case has to be decided by reference to context.

** The use of the so-called 'singular they' with its associated forms – including *themself* – is still controversial, and it is not fully addressed by Crystal even in his discussion of 'sexual bias' (1996: 156–7) (*they* does not in fact appear to be used with singular meaning in either of these extracts, but it should be noted that its adoption is increasing, even in relatively formal contexts). (See 'A note on style' in the Preface.)

adverbs. Auxiliary verbs will <u>not</u> be candidates for repetition, <u>nor</u> will the verbs *be, have* and *do*, whether acting as auxiliary verbs (*She has seen it*) <u>or</u> as main verbs (*They are happy*) (Crystal 1996: 69).

When calculating the number of times a particular lexical item is used I have followed Halliday in regarding different morphological forms of a word as tokens of the 'same' lexical item (1989b: 65; 1994a: 330–1) – thus *Tory/ies, people/'s, Conservative/s, serve/service.* (Hoey too (1991: 107–9) brings comparably variant forms within his different categories of 'lexical repetition'.) Amalgamation within other words has also been admitted, for example *children* within *(grand)children, country* within *country(men).*

6.6.3   Grammatical repetition

Those items <u>not</u> classed as lexical items under the criteria in Section 6.6.2 have been considered to be potential candidates for grammatical repetition, more specifically where these items have initiated more extensive grammatical structures (phrase, clause and so on) which <u>themselves</u> involve some form of repetition. The framework for analysing these extended grammatical structures has drawn (where appropriate) on that outlined in Section 2.6. Other clarifying references will be indicated as necessary and/or appropriate.

As with lexical repetition, three or more uses of the same grammatical item and structure have been regarded as constituting 'repetition'.

6.7   Method and presentation of analysis

Each text was analysed in three distinctly separate ways, applying the different frameworks set out in Section 6.6. Line numbers were added to each text and, for economy of space, all three analyses are displayed on the <u>same</u> text as described below (see Section 1.2.9 for generally recommended procedure).

Analyses are presented as Texts 6.1A (Blair) and 6.2A (Major) respectively (see Appendix 1.5), with exemplifying references being made to appropriate line numbers in the following form: B16, M15 and so on.

6.7.1 Pronoun choice

Each text was analysed according to the framework set out in Section 6.6.1. Each pronoun, whether personal, possessive or reflexive, and whether singular or plural, is

- highlighted in the text in bold
- assigned a superscript [1, 2, 3] according to whether it is first, second or third person
- placed within square brackets, also in bold

6.7.2 Lexical repetition

Three or more occurrences of the same lexical item within each extract were regarded as constituting 'repetition' for that particular speaker, and the initial identification stage was carried out using a rather complex system of colour coding, cross-matched (where possible) between the two texts. Colour coding was not a practicable method of displaying the analysis for this book (see Section 1.2.9) so the following alternative method was adopted:

- each 'lexical repetition' by a particular speaker was highlighted in bold in the relevant text;
- a list of 'lexical repetitions' was assembled for each text and these were placed in alphabetical order;
- the two separate lists were then amalgamated and each lexical item on the combined list was assigned a number according to its overall alphabetical place, that is, from *Britain* (1) to *world* (23);
- the appropriate number has been added as a superscript to the relevant lexical item in each text;
- superscript numbers assigned to 'lexical repetitions' for a particular speaker are also shown in bold: thus **country[5]**, **nation[9]**.

6.7.3 Grammatical repetition

Analysis of grammatical repetition had to be rather more selective and sensitive to surrounding text than the procedure described in Section 6.7.2. (Its display also proved to be slightly less complex in 'coding' terms.)

Those grammatical items which occur three or more times in what are considered to be notable ('marked') structural environments (see Section 6.6.3) have been underlined, together with their significant 'structural environment'.

Instances of such grammatical repetition in fact appear only in the Major text – see Section 6.10 below.

6.8   Presentation of results: pronoun choices

Table 6.2 presents the different pronoun choices made by each party leader. Results have been calculated according to choice of person in each case and as a proportion of total pronouns used overall.

This table shows that Blair and Major use approximately the same actual number of pronouns in the extracts (63 and 60 respectively). These are, in fact, in virtually identical proportion to the total number of words each speaks (487 and 471) – that is, 12.9 per cent and 12.7 per cent respectively. Overall pronoun use alone is not, therefore, particularly remarkable. Interesting differences do, however, arise in terms of individual choices for first and third person pronouns. The choices for all persons are therefore examined in some detail in the following subsections.

Table 6.2   Personal pronouns (including possessive and reflexive): in proportion to total pronouns used

	Total	First person		Second person		Third person	
		Number	%	Number	%	Number	%
Blair	63	27	42.9	4	6.3	32	50.8
Major	60	44	73.3	4	6.7	12	20.0

6.8.1   First person pronouns

Table 6.3 presents the number of first person pronouns used by each party leader, further differentiating between singular and plural pronouns.

It shows that Major uses a far higher proportion of first person pronouns overall than Blair – 73.3 per cent of total pronouns used by Major compared with 42.9 per cent by Blair. The majority of these are in fact first person plural pronouns – variants of *we* – a striking 68.3 per cent of his total pronoun use compared with only 19.0 per cent for Blair. The second notable contrast lies in their use of the first person singular pronoun – with Blair using *I* and its variants more than four times as often as Major: 23.8 per cent of all pronouns

Table 6.3   First person pronouns, singular v. plural: numbers and proportions of total pronouns used

	Total pronouns	Total first person pronouns		First person singular		First person plural	
		Number	%	Number	%	Number	%
Blair	63	27	42.9	15	23.8	12	19.0
Major	60	44	73.3	3	5.0	41	68.3

used by Blair compared with only 5.0 per cent by Major. The different choices and their meanings are examined below.

(a)   The meaning of we: The first person plural pronoun *we* (with variants) is, of course, already ambiguous in terms of potential meaning, since it can mean <u>either</u> inclusive <u>or</u> exclusive of addressee/s. The fluidity of meaning of *we* in actual use – with its persuasive potential – has also been identified by others (for example Fairclough 2001: 148–9; 2000: 35–7; Wilson 1990: 50–3; Hillier 1992: 391–3) and it is therefore ripe for exploitation.

For Major it would seem that there are three potential referents for *we*: '*we* the Conservative party', '*we* the (Conservative) government' and '*we* the people'. In the first instance the *we* is clearly <u>in</u>clusive of addressee (the relevant addressee being the immediate audience, fellow members of the Conservative party); in the second instance the *we* (the government) is essentially <u>ex</u>clusive of addressee; in the third the *we* is again <u>in</u>clusive of addressee (but this time the relevant addressee is being extended to include the population of Britain in general, the people). How far, then, might these different referents be distinguished? How far might they tend to slide into an imprecise meaning embracing all three together?

Of Major's 41 uses of variants of *we*, approximately half can be fairly reliably assigned to the first meaning – the most explicit form being *we (Conservatives)* . . . (**M1, M2, M13, M29** and so on – see also Section 6.10.5 below). Elsewhere it is often uncertain where the Conservative party ends and the incumbent Conservative government begins (for example *we're building, we're reforming* – **M4, M5**). Similarly, there is a blurring of the distinction between Conservatives and Britons: presumably *our streets* (**M11, M12**) and *our country* (**M28, M30**) mean 'the (British) people's' *streets, country* and so on, but what about *our people* (**M3**)? Whose people are being referred to here? (see Fairclough's discussion of Thatcher's use of *we* in conjunction with *(the) people* ; 2001: 148–9).

The extract seems to begin and end with clear indications that Major is speaking as the voice of the Conservative party, but in the intervening section the precise referent can be much more difficult to pin down. This may perhaps be intentional – encouraging the listener to infer (even take for granted) an identity of purpose, even actual identity between 'Conservatives', 'the government' and 'the people'.

For Blair, comparable blurring is not an option to quite the same extent: he cannot incorporate the implied power and authority of government into his use of *we*. Instead he can only seek to align 'the (British) people' with 'the Labour party'. Most of his uses of *we* and *our* appear to refer unambiguously to the Labour party (for example **B13–15**) but these lines are followed almost immediately by uses of *our* and *us* which in fact refer to 'the people' – presented as a quotation by Blair of what 'the people' are supposed to want to say to *those Tories* (**B17–22**). Thus Blair, like Major, makes ambiguous use of 'our people' to suggest an identity of interest between his own political party and a particular group of people.

(b) *The use of* I: Major in fact uses *I* only three times: two of these occur in the collocation *you and I* (**M16, M27**) (compare the discussion of *we* above) and the third is the one openly personal reference (*I hope*) addressing *you* (the delegates) in the immediate situation of the conference hall (**M23**).

Blair's uses of *I* and its variants are striking. He is making a clear presentation of himself to <u>his</u> party (**B1**) (and the wider audience) as a single individual pledging himself (**B32**) to change the government of the country (**B11, B24, B32** and so on – see also Section 6.10.7) and bring about the desired 'new Britain'. His stance is personal, unique, and apparently unchallengeable: *I know what so many people will be thinking – I know what the people want to say to those Tories* . . . (**B17–18**). This claim to unique insight and capacity is particularly interesting in view of the later (that is, post-1997 election) accusations in the press and elsewhere of excessive attempts to exert personal authority and control. (Fairclough, 2000: 97–108, discusses the 'tough' and 'authoritative' dimension to Blair's presentation of himself, alongside the 'normal person'.)

6.8.2   Second person pronouns

Table 6.4 compares the number of second person pronouns used by each party leader in proportion to his total pronoun usage.

Second person pronouns represent only a very small proportion of total pronoun use by both men – just four uses each by Blair and Major (6.3 per cent and 6.7 per cent respectively). Neither man, therefore, makes frequent explicit reference to a potential addressee or group of addressees who are – at least notionally – distinct and separate from the speaker. However, some of their individual uses may be noteworthy since the use of *you* can in certain circumstances allow a degree of ambiguity which has exploitative potential. (Fairclough, 2001: 149, for example, interprets Thatcher's use of *you* as an indefinite pronoun, referring to people in general, as a claim of solidarity with 'the people'.)

Three of Major's uses of *you* appear to be unproblematic. Two (**M16, M27**) are in the collocation *you and I* (see discussion of *we* and *I* above) and therefore clearly mean 'members of the Conservative party', while one addresses the delegates in the hall: *so when you go home* . . . (**M22**). The remaining use is, however, rather less clear, since it refers to *your government* (**M13**) and it comes at the end of a series of long subordinate clauses (the last beginning at **M11**) which are full of first person plural pronouns culminating in . . . *to our party and to your government* (**M13**). *Your government* at this point can at one level be interpreted as meaning 'the government which you

Table 6.4   Second person pronouns: numbers and proportions of total pronouns used

	Total pronouns	Total second person	%
Blair	63	4	6.3
Major	60	4	6.7

as Conservatives support', but the abrupt change to a second person (speaker-exclusive) form is marked and presumably deliberate – perhaps intended to reach beyond the immediate audience and introduce the kind of ambiguity of identification between Conservatives and 'the people' discussed above.

Blair's four uses of *you* appear to have different meanings in each case. The first (**B1**) is in apposition (see Section 2.9) to the noun phrase *my party;* the second (**B19**) refers to 'the Tories', being presented as part of a quotation of what *the people* want to say to *those Tories*. The third (**B29**) is rather unclear – perhaps 'you the (Labour) party' or 'you the people'. The fourth (**B34**) compares interestingly with the Major strategy discussed above: it represents a switch to second person reference following a long sequence of, in his case, third person plural pronouns referring to 'the people', including . . . *their children . . . their grandchildren . . . their children . . . their families . . .* (**B25** . . . **B31** . . .) *your grandchildren* (**B34**). He thus moves from designating 'the people' as outside the immediate interactive situation (*their*) to directly addressing them (*your*) – again appearing to blur the distinction between party and people.

6.8.3   Third person pronouns

Table 6.5 compares the use of third person pronouns by each party leader, again differentiating between singular and plural pronouns. It shows that over half of Blair's pronouns are in the third person (50.8 percent) compared with only one-fifth for Major (20.0 per cent). Both men prefer the plural form to the singular, though this preference is greater for Blair.

For Blair, the vast majority of the referents for *they* and its variants (20 out of 23) are 'the people', the remainder being a portmanteau reference to the 1945 and 1964 Labour parties (**B6**), Labour values (**B5**), and the Tories (**B16**). The confluence of 'the people' and *they* when acting as subject of the verb 'want' (**B18** and two instances in **B24–5**) gives a (retrospective, and perhaps over-fanciful?) resonance to the comparable form *they wanted* at **B6**, where *they* means the 1945 and 1964 Labour parties – an elision in *they* of Labour and the people? (compare Section 6.8.1).

Major too uses variants of *they* to refer to '(our) fellow countrymen' (three uses), and there is one reference to 'scars' (**M21**). There are, however, four notable uses of *them*, beginning at **M17**. These follow a statement of 'the enduring things' set out in **M13–15**, which are the most likely referent of

Table 6.5   Third person pronouns – singular v. plural – numbers and proportions of total pronouns used

	Total pronouns	Total third person pronouns		Third person singular		Third person plural	
		Number	%	Number	%	Number	%
Blair	63	32	50.8	9	14.3	23	36.5
Major	60	12	20.0	4	6.7	8	13.3

them. It is notable, however, that a potential alternative referent does intervene at **M15**, that is, 'the cornerstones of our (Conservative) beliefs'. Again we have a blurring of meaning boundaries – here leaving open the distinction between Conservative beliefs and enduring things (eternal truths?) – leading to their possible interpretation as the same thing.

The use of the singular form of the third person pronoun seems not to be particularly remarkable. It is always *it* for both men, sometimes empty or 'prop' *it* (Crystal 1996: 153) for Blair (**B9, B13**). Major's *it*s (all non-'prop') refer to public service (**M5, M6**) and the health service (**M10, M11**). Blair's have a range of referents: the world, this country, this party, the prize and the concept of giving the people what (according to Labour) they want.

6.8.4   Singular v. plural pronouns

Table 6.6 compares use of singular and plural pronouns (all persons) by each party leader in proportion to his total pronoun use. (All second person pronouns have been considered to have plural meanings (see Section 6.8.2).) The table shows that both men prefer to use plural pronouns of all types. Major's preference, however, is noticeably greater – 88.3 per cent of his pronouns are in plural form compared with 61.9 per cent for Blair. Blair's use of singular pronouns is, correspondingly, much higher – more than three times that of Major. These findings are considered in conjunction with other findings in Section 6.11.

6.9   Presentation of results: lexical repetition

All lexical repetitions identified in Texts 6.1A (Blair) and 6.2A (Major) were totalled for each item and each speaker respectively. Each total was then calculated in proportion to the total number of words in each extract. (The hyphenated *rock-solid* (**M8**) has been counted as <u>two</u> words – see Section 1.2.10 for identification of 'running words'.)

The individual items chosen by each speaker for repetition (together with their frequency of occurrence in each case and proportion to the total number of words in the extract) were tabulated and listed. This was done first in order of frequency for each man (Table 6.7) and then in alphabetical order of all lexical items chosen for repetition by either man (Table 6.8). The designated superscript, indicating place in overall <u>alphabetical</u> order (see Section 6.7.2), has been included in each case for reference purposes.

Table 6.6   Singular v. plural pronouns: numbers and proportions of total pronouns used

	Total pronouns	Total singular pronouns (all persons)		Total plural pronouns (all persons)	
		Number	%	Number	%
Blair	63	24	38.1	39	61.9
Major	60	7	11.7	53	88.3

6.9.1 Orders of frequency

Table 6.7 lists lexical repetitions in order of frequency. It shows much greater lexical repetition by Blair over all – 21.6 per cent of the words in the extract are lexical items which are used three or more times by him compared with 9.3 per cent by Major. There is thus more than twice as much lexical repetition by Blair. If we consider average use, we find an average of 6.6 uses of the 16 lexical items appearing in the Blair table, compared with 4.4 uses (of ten items) for Major. The most striking figures, however, are those for Blair's top four lexical items (*people, new, Labour* and *party*) which together account for 55 occurrences – an average of 13.8 uses each. These four lexical items alone account for more repetitions than all of Major's put together.

The actual items each man prefers for repetition are also interesting. Perhaps predictably, both leaders choose to give frequent repetition to the item *party* and the name of their own party. Blair uses *Labour* 12 times and *party* ten times; Major uses *Conservative* six times (equal first in the extract) and *party* four times (his choices being appropriately scaled down in accor-

Table 6.7 Lexical items in order of frequency (three or more occurrences) and in proportion to total words in each extract

Blair			Major		
Total words = 487	Number of times used	Percentage of total words	Total words = 471	Number of times used	Percentage of total words
people[13]	17	3.5	Conservative[4]	6	1.3
new[10]	16	3.3	serve[16]	6	1.3
Labour[8]	12	2.5	country[5]	5	1.1
party[11]	10	2.1	Labour[8]	5	1.1
Tory[19]	8	1.6	party[11]	4	0.8
Britain[1]	8	1.6	nation[9]	4	0.8
country[5]	4	0.8	choice[3]	4	0.8
children[2]	4	0.8	stand[17]	4	0.8
world[23]	4	0.8	secure[15]	3	0.6
want[21]	4	0.8	scars[14]	3	0.6
courage[6]	3	0.6			
get[7] *	3*	0.6			
patriot[12]	3	0.6			
Union Jack[20] **	3	0.6			
waving[22]	3	0.6			
tearing apart[18] **	3	0.6			
Total repetitions 105		**21.6**		**44**	**9.3**

* *get (to)* in **B34** has <u>not</u> been included as a lexical repetition, given its 'intermediate' status between auxiliary and full (lexical) verb (Quirk et al. 1985: 136–48).
** *Union Jack* and *tearing apart* respectively have been treated as <u>a single lexical item</u> for the purposes of repetition analysis, but counted as <u>two</u> words when calculating the total of running words.

dance with his generally lower repetitive tendency). Blair reserves his main repetitions, however, for the items *people* (17) and *new* (16). (Fairclough 2000: 17–19) found these two items heavily represented in a computer corpus of New Labour texts.)

New collocates most frequently with *Labour* (eight instances) and *Britain* (six instances), with just one occurrence of *new and better world* (**B35**) and one of *the party renewed* (**B40**). The repeated association of *Labour* and *the party* with *new* (notwithstanding the assertions in **B2–4**), underlines the progression away from 'old Labour' – see Section 6.2.2 and consideration of *new* in advertising in Section 8.10.2. Even more striking, however, is the actual orchestration of the use of *new* and its main collocates. At the very beginning of the extract there are five occurrences of *new Labour* in six lines of transcript, followed by one *new Britain* (**B6**). At the very end of the speech *new* reappears, and the two noun phrases *new Labour* and *new Britain* are woven together to summarise the thrust of the whole extract – *(new) Labour* is synthesised with *(new) Britain* (**B40–1**) (see further discussion in Section 6.10.7).

6.9.2   Comparison of individual lexical preferences

Table 6.8 lists in alphabetical order all the lexical items chosen for repetition by either speaker in the two extracts and allows a direct comparison between the preferences of each. It shows that some lexical items are used by both party leaders with more or less comparable frequency (compare discussion of Table 6.7). There are, however, some items within the extracts which are preferred by one leader but may be virtually or completely ignored by the other. For example *Conservative* (Major's equal favourite lexical item) is not used at all by Blair in his extract: *Tory* is chosen – and repeated – instead. (It may be significant that, according to the *Hutchinson Encyclopedia* (1992: 828), *Tory* is a colloquial term which has some negative historical associations.) Major's *serve* appears only once in the Blair extract (**B30**), and, rather surprisingly, its variant *service* (as in Major's collocations *public service* (**M5**) and *health service* (**M8–9, M9–10**)) does not occur at all.

It is not, perhaps, surprising that Blair's *new* is not used by Major, given the latter's inevitable position as defender of the status quo. Major's four uses of *stand* underline this, especially the three occurring towards the end of his speech (**M29, M36**). What is more surprising is the heavy (and non-ironic) use by Blair (with little or no use by Major) of such explicit items as *Britain, patriot, Union Jack*. (Major's use of *nation* (four occurrences to Blair's one) is his principal claim in this area.) Blair's choices suggest that he may be colonising – via lexical repetition – what has always been considered to be traditional Conservative territory. Even his emphasis on *children*, with no use at all by Major, appears to be an appropriation of the ground of 'the party of the family'.

6.10   Presentation of results: grammatical repetition

Grammatical repetition, as defined in Section 6.7.3, appears only in the Major text. It is notable, in fact, that his relative lack of lexical repetition, as shown in

Table 6.8 Comparison of frequency of repetition of individual lexical items: presented in alphabetical order (times used and proportions of total words in extract)

Lexical item	Blair		Major	
	Times used	**Percentage of total words (487)**	**Times used**	**Percentage of total words (471)**
Britain[1]	8	1.6	1	0.2
children[2]	4	0.8	0	—
choice[3]	0	—	4	0.8
Conservative[4]	0	—	6	1.3
country[5]	4	0.8	5	1.1
courage[6]	3	0.6	0	—
get[7]	3	0.6	0	—
Labour[8]	12	2.5	5	1.1
nation[9]	1	0.2	4	0.8
new[10]	16	3.3	0	—
party[11]	10	2.1	4	0.8
patriot[12]	3	0.6	0	—
people[13]	17	3.5	2	0.4
scars[14]	0	—	3	0.6
secure[15]	2	0.4	3	0.6
serve[16]	1	0.2	6	1.3
stand[17]	0	—	4	0.8
tearing apart[18]	3	0.6	0	—
Tory[19]	8	1.6	0	—
Union Jack[20]	3	0.6	0	—
want[21]	4	0.8	0	—
waving[22]	3	0.6	0	—
world[23]	4	0.8	2	0.4

Section 6.9, is counterbalanced by a relative frequency of grammatical repetition. Certain grammatical items are repeated, and in marked circumstances which use the repeated items to initiate certain structures (for example clauses) which then incorporate <u>both</u> a further element of grammatical repetition <u>and</u> some form of lexical variation or contrast – thus creating sets of parallel structures. As Hoey points out, repetitions and parallel grammatical constructions in themselves make significant contributions to interpretation: 'it is what is <u>changed</u> that receives attention . . . while the repeated material acts as a framework for the interpretation of the <u>new material</u>' (1991: 25; emphases added). (Compare Wooffitt's 'well-constructed contrast' in Section 6.4.1.)

Quantitative results were felt to be less appropriate here, and the discussion which follows is therefore in a more discursive style, organised under headings for the different kinds of grammatical repetition found. The findings are grouped under five main headings.

6.10.1 Clauses initiated by *because*

The Major extract has six occurrences of the subordinating conjunction *because* (see Section 2.6.1) (equal in fact to the totals for his preferred lexical items *Conservative* and *serve*; see Table 6.7). The extract begins with the use of a wh-question (see Section 5.6.2) *why should we be elected . . .* (**M1–2**), and this is followed by a sequence of six subordinate clauses initiated by *because*, each answering his own question and offering a justification for the Conservatives' being given a fifth term. It will be seen that five of the clauses have the basic structure *because . . . we . . .* , and the sixth introduces a final variant *because . . . x . . . to us . . . .* The series of clauses thus has consistency, repetition and rhythm in both meaning and structural patterning. The whole sequence extends from **M2** to **M13**, one third of the entire extract. The momentum thus created builds towards the introduced structural variant *to us* in the sixth clause. This, in turn, allows the *us* to be expanded to embrace both *our party* and *your government*, suggesting an identity of purpose between these two concepts and appearing to blur the boundaries between Conservative party, Conservative government and even the British people (see discussion in Section 6.8.1).

The Blair extract does, in fact, have five occurrences of *because*. They are, however, distributed at widely spaced and unequal intervals – one each in **B4**, **B14**, **B16** and two in **B24–5**. Further, the grammatical patterning of the first three occurrences varies, in that each selects a different pronoun subject: *because both . . . ; because they . . . ; because it . . . .* They also offer reasons or justifications for different claims: why the 1945 and 1964 Labour parties were 'new Labour'; why 'our people' want us to change 'this country'; why 'this is the patriotic party'. The fourth and fifth occurrences (**B24–5**) do have some similarities in structural and semantic patterns – the form *because they want . . .* offering reasons 'to get the Tories out' – but they constitute only two occurrences which have no obvious link with the preceding *because they . . .* (**B14**). No overall cumulative effect is created which compares to that in the Major extract.

6.10.2 Complement realised by prepositional phrases initiated by *for* and followed by *not*

Lines **M13–14** of the Major extract feature four prepositional phrases, together acting as Complement to *we Conservatives are. . . .* Each has the structure *for x not y*. The preposition *for* is consistently used to express 'support' (Crystal 1996: 185) and the prepositional complements, *x* and *y*, are noun phrases (see Section 2.6.3) having similar structures – either determiner+headword or headword alone. Each is presented as an individual instance of the group of 'enduring things' which are 'the cornerstones' of Conservative beliefs (**M15**) (see also Section 6.8.3). The strict formal patterning and rhythm is slightly disrupted in the fourth instance when the ellipted second preposition *for* resurfaces to give *for liberty not for control*. This may or may not be interpreted as intentional artistic variation – as an anti-control declaration?

No comparable structural patterning is discernible in the Blair extract.

6.10.3   Preposition *for* plus *them*

Line **M17** of the Major extract has three occurrences of preposition *for* followed immediately by the pronoun *them* within a series of three clauses in which there is what Quirk et al. call 'coordination of predications' (1985: 949–50), with the second and third clauses ellipting the subject and operator *we have* . . . . The structure is *(we have) x'd for them y'd for them z'd for them* . . ., where the repetition of *for them* serves to highlight the 'new material' represented by the series of three verbs *worked, cared* and *fought*. The *them* itself refers to 'the enduring things' identified in the immediately preceding series of structural patterns, as discussed in Section 6.10.2.

In clause terms *for them* could be analysed as a prepositional phrase acting as Adverbial following each of the lexical verbs *worked, cared, fought*. Alternatively, *for* could be regarded as a particle within a multi-word verb (Crystal 1996: 82–3) in each case (*worked for* . . . and so on) – that is, as part of the Verb element – with *them* acting as Object. Whichever way they are analysed, however, the stress patterning links *for+them* more closely and naturally than verb+*for* in creating its rhythmic effects, and it is the rhythmic effects which give the repeated structures their rhetorical power.

There is no comparable grammatical patterning in the Blair extract.

6.10.4   Interrogative structures initiated by *would . . . be . . .*

M24–7 of the Major extract has a sequence of five interrogative (VS) structures realising yes–no questions (see Section 5.6.2) initiated by *would . . . be . . .*, each one featuring an Adverbial element realised by the identical prepositional phrase *under Labour*, thus: *would x be y under Labour* . . . . Again, the repeated material serves to frame the *x* and *y* variables, and the whole sequence is presented as a series of questions which delegates are exhorted to 'ask the people on the doorstep' (**M23–4**).

There is no similar pattern in the Blair extract.

6.10.5   Subject realised by pronoun *we* plus *Conservatives*

The final instance of grammatical repetition in fact brings together two aspects of frequency of choice by Major which have already been separately discussed – his preference for the pronoun *we* (see Section 6.8.1) and his notable repetition of the proper noun *Conservatives* (see Section 6.9.1). There are five occurrences of *we Conservatives*, (**M13, M29, M33, M35–6** (two). In each case they are acting either as the <u>entire</u> Subject of the relevant clause or as a <u>part</u> of the Subject, either in apposition (see Section 2.9) to a preceding (and following) *we* (**M29**) or by repetition to reinstate after an interpolated non-restrictive relative clause (see note **5** to Text 3.1A) (**M35–6**). (The construction itself would seem to be a complex noun phrase consisting of a head (pronoun *we*) postmodified by a reduced restrictive relative clause ((*who are*) *Conservatives.*)

Four of the repeated structures come in the closing stages of the extract (**M29–36**), with three occurring in the last four lines. It may indeed be significant that the final occurrence in the extract (and the speech) has *we Conservatives* acting as Subject of the defiant verb *stand* (see consideration of *stand* in Section 6.9.2).

6.10.6 Summary of discussion of grammatical repetition in the Major text

The Major extract makes notable use of repetitive patterning of a grammatical, rather than a lexical, nature and, as the display in Text 6.2A shows, these patterns occur in five broadly distinct phases across the extract. An additional phase appears to be about to begin at **M30** (the two instances of *our x aren't y* would presumably be an example of a 'contrast' – see Section 6.4.1) but it is brought to an end just before the final *we Conservatives* phase begins. (The decision had perhaps been taken to accentuate the positive.)

The overall phasing gives a clear structural underpinning to the Major extract as well as an impression of carefully constructed 'balance'. This reinforces the measured effects created by each individual pattern within the total structure.

6.10.7 A coda: the Blair strategies

The Blair extract shows no directly comparable use of structural patterning signalled by grammatical repetition. It is important to note, however, that it does nevertheless make very significant use of a different <u>kind</u> of structural repetition, both clausal and phrasal. This is, however, signalled almost entirely lexically.

The Blair extract shows two instances of clausal repetition, each initiated by non-finite Verb forms (Crystal 1996: 74–5). The first instance involves three repetitions of virtually the same items (both lexical and grammatical) though, in contrast to the Major text, at irregularly spaced intervals. In each case the initial verb *to get* is in its base, or infinitive, form and *to get the Tories out* (**B11–12** and **B24**) is presented as being what the people 'want'). He thus creates his repeated clause by bringing together two of his separate lexical repetitions *get* and *Tory* (see Section 6.9). He then follows this with the variant *to get these Tories out* at **B32–3**. The replacement of *the* by the demonstrative determiner *these* (see Section 5.6.1) seems designed to emphasise and reinforce the personal 'promise' being given (see discussion in Section 6.8.1). This, together with the choice of the lexical item *get* (and the subsequent *out*), creates an informal, colloquial effect consistent with the way such a sentiment might be presumed to be expressed by 'the people' (and, by implication, by

Blair himself). It provides some support for Fairclough's claims (2000: 100–1) about the 'normal person' dimension of Blair's rhetorical style.

The second instance of repeated non-finite clauses begins at **B19–20** with his use of the *–ing* form of a multi-word verb (Crystal 1996: 82–3), *tearing apart*. This is closely followed at **B21–2** by use of the same (rather dramatic) lexical verb but with varying Objects: producing the pattern *tearing apart the x . . . the y . . . the z . . . .* The repeated element thus serves to focus attention on the new material, including the punning use of *fabric (of the nation)* (**B20**) and the unity and security of the people of the United Kingdom which is apparently threatened (**B21–2**). The repetition also serves as a bridge over the hiatus created by the audience's demonstration (by its applause) of their appreciation of the pun.

Blair's most significant grammatical strategy, however, is the frequent use of serial noun phrases, especially when initiated by repeated premodifiers. The most notable of these is the repetition of *new* with its varying headwords (see Section 6.9.1). This particular construction is used as the climax of the extract – and therefore the speech. It crowns the sequence which begins at **B35** with a series of unmodified abstract nouns – *discipline, courage, determination, honesty* – progresses through definite noun phrases centring on *party – the party, this party, the Labour party* – and ends *new Labour, new Britain . . . new Labour, new Britain.* This form of <u>structural</u> repetition seems designed to suggest an identification of the (new) Labour party with the preceding virtues and aspirations – the kind of 'ideological work' referred to in Section 6.4.1 – building towards the ultimate implied identity (via insistent <u>lexical</u> repetition) between Labour and Britain.

6.11 Summary and overall comparison of findings

Section 6.8 has shown that both men exploit the persuasive opportunities provided by the use of plural pronouns, and in comparable ways: to suggest an identity between their audience and their own party. They thus try to encompass both the immediate audience in the conference hall and the wider electorate beyond. They differ, however, in the extent to which they do this and the preferred choice of person for the purpose. Major adopts a first person (*we* and variants) strategy (see Section 6.8.1) whereas Blair, to a lesser extent, prefers the third person (*they* and variants) (Section 6.8.3). Alongside this, Blair is notable for his use of the first person singular pronoun (variants of *I*), appearing to claim an individual and unique power to bring about political change (Section 6.8.1). There would seem, in fact, to have been an unexpected exchange made between the two party leaders, given the traditional – even stereotypical – associations made with their respective parties. Thus, an apparent marker of group solidarity (*we*) is used on behalf of the Conservatives, while a clear marker of individuality (*I*) is used by a Labour leader.

So far as the different kinds of repetition are concerned, on the evidence of these brief extracts both men use specific lexical choices combined with selective forms of repetition to convey their own party concerns and philosophies.

They also imply an identity between those philosophies and the assumed aspirations of both their immediate audience and the electorate in general. The means adopted, however, differ in interesting ways, with Blair choosing the heavily and directly repetitious lexical route and Major the more modulated and indirect, though still repetitious, grammatical route.

This difference is also evident in terms of the personal style of each man, especially when combined with the pronoun choices mentioned. Blair's choice of grammatical style, with its easily remembered and frequently repeated 'sound-bite' noun phrases, combines with his ready use of the pronoun *I* to give an informal, emotive, apparently spontaneous impression. It is clearly very carefully crafted, however. Lexical choices and the insistent repetition together create an impression of an irresistible force, hammering home a message that claims to be modern, egalitarian, populist (centring on *people* . . . and what *they* are declared to *want*), that is urging change (*new* . . .) but is at the same time safe and reliable (*Britain, country, children* . . .). It would seem, therefore, explicitly to reflect the concerns outlined in Section 6.2 in attempting to appeal to both a committed constituency <u>and</u> the electorate in general.

Major adopts a more formal grammatical style, with traditional 'complete sentences' throughout the extract, which could have been transcribed using all the conventions of written punctuation. It presents a modest defence of traditionally Conservative values, via moderate use of *country, nation, choice* . . . , though in fact Major gives much less emphasis than Blair to the openly patriotic approach. The style is therefore reassuring (*stand, secure* . . .) but seems – presumably intentionally – somewhat old-fashioned, maintaining the 'known' constituency. This effect is emphasised by the repetitive structures within that formal style which work to create carefully balanced rhetorical – indeed incantatory – patterns, having almost religious overtones. (His *remember these things* (**M23**) especially coming after *uplifted*, has echoes, for this hearer/reader, of the Authorised Version (of course) of *Saint Luke's Gospel*, chapter 2, verse19: '(Mary) kept all these things, and pondered them in her heart'.)

6.12 Evaluative responses revisited

The evidence of both the pronoun and lexical choices in these extracts suggests that there has been some attempt by each man to colonise territory traditionally associated with the other side, especially perhaps in terms of making the more direct appeal for the patriotic vote. Blair would seem to do the latter more clearly than Major in these extracts – see the students' comments in Section 6.4.2 re his apparent wooing of the middle ground. Indeed it may not be coincidental that Blair's directly populist appeal has some parallels with that of Margaret Thatcher. Fairclough (2001: 147–50) notes Thatcher's predilection for *the people* and makes direct comparisons between Blair and Thatcher in this respect (2000: 106–7, 114–15).

The findings do also provide support for other of the student evaluations. The 'wisdom and maturity' accorded to Major, as well as his 'preachy' style, may be partly accounted for by his choice of formal grammatical structures, and the carefully orchestrated repetition and staging of those structures. The impression of 'bossiness' accorded to Blair may be partly a result of his repetitive noun phrases. Cockcroft and Cockcroft (1992: 153) describe such unlinked 'staccato' phrases as having a 'sharper and more aggressive' rhetorical effect than explicitly linked ones.

6.13 Conclusion

This chapter has examined some aspects of the language of political speeches, using two brief extracts from the addresses of Tony Blair and John Major to their party conferences, Labour and Conservative respectively.

It has considered the choice and deployment of personal pronouns and the extent and type of lexical and grammatical repetition, and has shown that close examination of the patterning of particular linguistic choices can provide evidence of notable emphases within the political programmes and philosophies themselves. It can also provide insights into the way these philosophies are expounded via each speaker's persuasive personal appeal both to his immediate audience and the electorate in general. On the evidence of these extracts <u>both</u> men, in their very different ways, adopt a style which is a vital element in the delivery of their message.

6.14 Suggestions for further work

(a) Other features which might be investigated and/or approaches adopted for this specific data include:

- demonstratives (both determiners and pronouns – see Section 5.6.1) and how they may augment the findings for personal pronouns;

- contractions (see Section 8.9) and the extent of their use in these examples of 'scripted speech';

- rhetorical figures (which would require careful definition and description) such as the 'three-part lists' and 'contrasts' referred to in Section 6.4.1. (The discussion of the findings in Section 6.10 might provide a basis for such an approach, but it has merely touched on such phenomena.)

(b) A version of this framework could be applied to addresses by other persuasive speakers, whether politicians or religious leaders. Such speakers might represent alternative ideological perspectives or come from different cultural backgrounds. (Wooffitt, for example, discusses speech styles of some Indian politicians and black Pentecostal evangelists; 1996: 131 ff.) (If video-recorded data were available, non-verbal strategies such as gestures, body language and so on might be related to rhetorical style – see Wooffitt 1996; Fairclough 2000.)

(c)   Variation within Mode could be explicitly built in, for example a comparison of possible shifts in a given speaker's style in different contexts: a 'formal' address (written to be spoken, one-way) and participation in an interview or a discussion (spoken, two-way, some degree of spontaneity). This could involve a systematic investigation of the extent to which features identified in this study are found in the different contexts. It might also include some pronunciation features (see Fairclough's (2000: 99–101) comments on Blair in this respect) (see also Section 7.17).

(d)   The framework used in this chapter could be applied to other types of 'persuasive' text, for example advertisements of all kinds, whether written or spoken (compare those in Chapter 8). Areas of enquiry might be:

   ● the kinds of pronouns used (if any) to address/refer to potential consumer and advertiser and the apparent meanings of such uses;

   ● the extent and effects of <u>both</u> kinds of repetition, for example lexical items and their associations for a given product, and 'grammatical parallelism' as referred to in Section 8.4.

Evaluations by informants could be obtained as appropriate (see Section 1.2.6).

Fictional Narrative in a Regional Dialect

7.1   Introduction

This chapter has some areas of correspondence with Chapter 2. Each examines a 'literary' text, whose form of expression is an essential part of both its content and its creative impact. The chosen text in this chapter, however, comes from a rather different literary background from that examined in Chapter 2.

Bleak House is part of a substantial body of work by Charles Dickens, a classic English author; it is an extensive fictional narrative written in standard English, by a third-person omniscient author. *Our Mam un t'Others* is a short fictional narrative written in the first person and in the dialect of Kirkby-in-Ashfield, a small town in Nottinghamshire, in the English East Midlands. It was originally intended for oral presentation to the members of an adult education class, the Teversal Living Memory Group, and was subsequently published under the Group's own auspices in 1998. It was the first serious attempt at writing by its author, Fred Wetherill.

The narrative represents the voice and persona of a young member of a mining family of the Kirkby area and it draws on many of the author's own memories and experiences. These are, however, processed through and transformed by a creative sensibility which shows characters and events as seen through the eyes of its young protagonist, who remains unnamed throughout. It appears to fall somewhere between 'oral narrative' (see Gregory and Carroll's 'reciting' in Figure 1.1) and what may perhaps be called 'literature proper' – perhaps as 'oral literature'. In terms of the broad overall framework in Fig.1.1 it has been regarded as 'writing intended to be read, but <u>as if</u> heard' (see, however, Sections 7.2 and 7.3 below).

Although the kinds of text extract chosen for this chapter are in some respects notably different from those in Chapter 2, the approach adopted has some parallels with the earlier one. Comparisons are being made between different versions of essentially the same text – original and rewritten – thereby throwing into relief some of the special linguistic characteristics of the original. In this chapter, therefore, the rewritten version translates the dialect into standard English grammar. In this chapter, however, I have also been able to make use of a reading of the original published version which the author had tape-recorded for a blind friend. This enables a dual perspective to be adopted in terms of variables, which is different from that of Chapter 2 and, in fact, different from any other chapter in the book. The oral rendering allows <u>both</u> an examination of pronunciation features of the dialect <u>and</u> how these are represented.

7.2 Identifying the variables: perspective one

7.2.1 The controlled variables

The variables to be controlled are:

- **Mode**: The original and standardised versions are in written form in each case. The graphic channel is used and they are intended to be processed by the eye. From perspective one, therefore, both versions will be regarded as falling under 'writing (intended) to be read'. (It will be apparent, however, that different assumptions are being made about <u>how</u> these written forms might be processed; see Section 7.2.2.)

- **Field**: The overall **purpose** is to constitute (a part of) a literary narrative, a fictional story created to divert, entertain and delight its audience. The basic **content** of the extract is the same, since each text is a version of three paragraphs taken from the early part of the same novella. The reader is introduced to the persona's sister Ada, and is then told a short anecdote involving her.

- **Tenor (functional)**: Tenor relations here would seem to be consistent with the purposes set out under Field above.

7.2.2 The varying variables

The Preface to the published text of *Our Mam un t'Others* includes the following:

> Fred Wetherill was born seventy-eight years ago in Mansfield, moving to Kirkby at an early age. He has spent the major part of his life living and working in the Ashfields, apart from the War years when he served with the RAF.
>
> The incidents and characters depicted, though fictional, are loosely based on people and events in Fred's own life.
>
> Originally written in pure local dialect, some slight changes have been introduced into the script for ease of reading.
>
> Fred belongs to the Teversal Living Memory Group where fellow members have supported and encouraged him in this, his first piece of serious writing.

The story was originally produced for a specific audience, one which would be familiar with both the topography and the language used to describe it. The 'slight changes' made when the book was prepared for publication (by fellow group member Jack Townsend) were intended to render the text more easily understandable to the eye, but the final published version, promoted and sold locally, was clearly still intended for a specifically local readership. In this it proved to be very successful, attracting attention from newspapers and television and radio stations across the county. Indeed Fred Wetherill became something of a local celebrity, as will be seen from the article by Ian Drury in the Nottingham *Evening Post* of 31 July 1998 (Figure 7.1).

The rewritten and standardised extract to be used for comparison in this chapter was prepared by me. I am very familiar with the dialect, since my mother was born in Kirkby, I lived there for a time as a child and I still have close family connections there. The rewritten version is intended to be readily comprehensible and accessible to a non-local audience. Deliberately varying variables will therefore arise under:

- **Tenor (personal)**: The significant **participant** relationships here are between the author and the potential readership in each case. The principal varying factors are the regional and social origins of the target audience, since the original version was written for residents (present and past) of the Kirkby/Sutton/Mansfield area, and the rewritten version has no specific target audience, requiring no knowledge of the local dialect and little or no knowledge of topography. As with the rewritten version of *Bleak House* in Chapter 2, the personal characteristics of the participant who has done the rewriting are not considered likely to have any substantial bearing on the aims and outcome of this study: the primary factor here is the <u>addressee</u> relationship.

7.3 Identifying the variables: perspective two

7.3.1 The controlled variables

- **Field**: Both overall **purpose** and basic **content** are the same; see Section 7.2.1. (The small changes of content between the two versions – see Section 7.4 below – are not regarded as being significant for current purposes.)

- **Tenor**: The participants are Fred Wetherill (as both writer and reader-aloud) and a 'readership' in each case having the same regional and social origin as himself.

7.3.2 The varying variables

- **Mode**: There is deliberately varying variation between the written and spoken use of language; consequently, from this perspective each version would be placed under <u>different</u> nodes of Figure 1.1. The written version is to be processed by the <u>eye</u> (the graphic channel is used), but will be regarded as being 'intended to be read <u>as if</u> it were 'real' speech'. In the spoken version the author is reading aloud from the 'same' written text (for

Figure 7.1 An article from the Nottingham *Evening Post*, 31 July 1998

the benefit of a non-sighted friend), which is consequently intended to be processed by the <u>ear</u> (the phonic channel is used). Since the reading is into a tape recorder this is entirely a one-way process, and there is no visual contact between participants (see Section 1.1.6.3). It will be regarded as being placed under 'the speaking of what has been written not necessarily to be spoken'.

It should be emphasised that the transcribed version of the reading – represented by Text 7.3 – is solely a means to an end. For the purposes of this study the 'actual' texts being compared are the written version and the spoken version.

7.4   Description of the data

Several kinds of data were made available to me by Fred Wetherill. In addition to the published text, I had access to a copy of the original manuscript and I also have tape recordings of readings from both the published and manuscript versions. All of these versions could be drawn on as and when appropriate. Interestingly, all four versions of the narrative differ slightly in matters of detail, having small variations and embellishments as might be expected in the retelling of a familiar tale. The published version also shows some internal inconsistencies in terms of spelling. These factors would seem to have some links with the 'reciting' mentioned by Gregory and Carroll (1978: 42) as being part of an oral tradition.

The study has chosen to focus on three specific texts for analysis:

Text 7.1 consists of three paragraphs (473 words) reproduced from pages 4–6 of *Our Mam un t'Others* by Fred Wetherill, published by the Teversal Living Memory Group in 1998, from the section headed *Now I'll tell yer about our Ada*. These paragraphs were chosen on the rather arbitrary basis that they constituted a manageable amount of text, and told a complete and amusing anecdote which was expressed via the use of a range of dialect features. This has been regarded as the primary text for the study.

Text 7.1   Published version

Now I'll tell yer about our Ada.

Our Ada loved ter go ter school, specially went Teacher took class inter fields unt woods. She soon lont alt names at flowers, leaves ont trees, un grasses. I thort grass wer just grass un orlt same. Ont dark nights when we couldn't go ert to play she'd be doin drawins on um, real clever wer our Ada.

Ada wer four year older than me, un five year older than Dollie, the youngest, Bill wer somewhere in between. Int summer when we wer little, unt sun wer shining, she'd tek us a walk on Sunday afternoons. Our Mam ud say to her 'Tek our Bill with yer', but we dint want him we us cos we wer orlus up to summat. Anyroad, he said he dint want to go with lasses, he'd sooner go ter farm. We'de go ter Newstead Abbey, yer could go round by Newstead pit, but favourite walk wer ovva Misk-Hills ter Beauvale. It wer a long way un we'de getta bit tired, un Ada would let us rest for a bit. She'd be tellin us abert wild flowers un things, un if we wer good she'd show us some Bee-orchids, but we wer'nt to touch um, not to tell anybody, it wer a secret.

One Sunday, we had little Audrey with us from next door, her Mum ud asked Ada if she'd tek her with us. Her husband liked her out ut road on Sunday afternoon. I don't know why cos she wer such a quiet kid, un well mannered anorl. We wer cummin back through Annesley park, we wer orl tired, our Ada said ter hurry up or we'd be late for us tea, un she'd got ter get ready for Chapel. We'd just got by 'Badger' goin towards Mutton hill when our Dollie said "What's that in that front garden?'. It wer a hearse. Ada told us it wer a funeral car, what yer go in when yer dead. We all went nearer ter have a proper look, little Audrey let ert a yell, then we could see a man layin in it, we soon run off. We'd gone up road a bit when we saw Bobby Brown on his bike cummin towards us. Our Ada shouted to him, 'Please sir, there's a man layin in a hearse inna front garden'. 'Yer what me lass?' he said, un she told him again, 'Un he's not in a coffin, is he dead?' Bobby laughed un said, 'He's only asleep', un not to be frightened, 'Its only old man Jones, he often as a sleep innit on Sunday afternoons'. We could still hear him laughing as he peddled away, I said to our Ada what a nerve she'd got talkin to a bobby, but then that wer her, nowt bothered our Ada.

Text **7.2** is a standardised version of Text 7.1 (496 words), which draws where necessary and/or possible on the kinds of features identified by Hughes and Trudgill (1996) and others, both to translate non-standard grammatical features into their standard forms and to remove indications of specific regional pronunciation by substituting standard orthography. Changes (including lexical changes) have been kept to a minimum, and an attempt has been made to retain the informal, colloquial style of the original. (I have followed Hughes and Trudgill (1996: 11–12) in regarding informal features as instances of stylistic rather than specifically dialectal variation.)

Text 7.2   Standardised version of Text 7.1

Now I'll tell you about our Ada

Our Ada loved to go to school, especially when the Teacher took the class into the fields and the woods. She soon learnt all the names of the flowers, leaves on the trees, and grasses. I thought grass was just grass and all the same. On the dark nights when we couldn't go out to play she'd be doing drawings of them – really clever was our Ada.

Ada was four years older than me, and five years older than Dollie, the youngest. Bill was somewhere in between. In the summer when we were little, and the sun was shining, she'd take us for a walk on Sunday afternoons. Our Mam'd say to her 'Take our Bill with you', but we didn't want him with us cos we[1] were always up to something. Anyway, he said he didn't want to go with lasses, he'd sooner go to the farm. We'd go to Newstead Abbey, you could go round by Newstead pit, but the favourite walk was over the Misk-Hills to Beauvale. It was a long way and we'd get a bit tired, and Ada would let us rest for a bit. She'd be telling us about wild flowers and things, and if we were good she'd show us some Bee-orchids, but we weren't to touch them, and not to tell anybody, it was a secret.

One Sunday, we had little Audrey with us from next door, her Mum'd asked Ada if she'd take her with us. Her husband liked her out of the way on Sunday after-noon. I don't know why cos she was such a quiet kid, and well mannered as well. We were coming back through Annesley park, we were all tired, our Ada said to hurry up or we'd be late for our tea, and she'd got to get ready for Chapel. We'd just got by the 'Badger' going towards Mutton Hill when our Dollie said "What's that in that front garden?' It was a hearse. Ada told us it was a funeral car, that you go in when you're dead. We all went nearer to have a proper look, little Audrey let out a yell, then we could see a man lying in it, we soon ran off. We'd gone up the road a bit when we saw Bobby Brown on his bike coming towards us. Our Ada shouted to him, 'Please sir, there's a man lying in a hearse in a front garden'. 'What d'you say my lass?'[2] he said, and she told him again, 'And he's not in a coffin, is he dead?' The bobby laughed and said, 'He's only asleep', and not to be frightened, 'It's only old man Jones, he often has a sleep in it on Sunday after-noons'. We could still hear him laughing as he pedalled[3] away, I said to our Ada what a nerve she'd got talking to a bobby, but then that was her, nothing bothered our Ada.

Notes

1   The manuscript (pre-editorial process) has 'e', not 'we', and 'he' seems in fact to be more likely (see also Text 7.3).
2   Literal translation presumably: 'you what my lass?'
3   The published version (see Text 7.1) has 'peddled'.

Text **7.3** is a transcript (475 words) of a reading-aloud of the published version by Fred Wetherill. The transcript has been modelled on the orthography of the original (as in Text 7.1), and Text 7.3 plus the actual reading have been used as the basis for an analysis of specific pronunciation features. There are several minor diversions from Text 7.1 in terms of content, and these have been signalled via annotations on the text.

Text 7.3   Transcript of reading of published version

Now I'll tell yer about our Ada.

Our Ada loved goin[1] ter school, specially went Teacher took class inter fields unt woods. She soon lont alt names at flowers, leaves ont trees,[2] grasses. I thort grass wer just grass un orlt same. Ont dark nights when we couldn't go ert to play she'd be doin drawins on um, real clever wer our Ada.

Ada wer four year older than me, un five year older than Dollie, the youngest, Bill[3] were somewhere in between. Int summer when we wer little, unt sun wer shining, she'd tek us on[4] a walk on Sunday afternoons. Our Mam ud say[5] 'Tek our Bill with yer', but we dint want him cos he wer orlus gettin up to summat[6]. Anyroad, he said he dint want to go with lasses, he'd sooner go ter farm. We'de go ter Newstead Abbey, yer could get[7] round by Newstead pit then,[8] but favourite walk wer ovva Misk-Hills ter Beauvale. It wer a long way un we'de getta bit tired, un Ada would let us rest for a bit. She'd be tellin us abert wild flowers un things, un if we wer good she'd show us some Bee-orchids, but we not to touch um, un not tell anybody else, it wer our secret.[9]

One Sunday, we had little Audrey with us from next door, her Mum ud asked Ada if she'd tek us[10] with us. Her husband liked her out ut road on Sunday afternoon. I can't think why cos she wer a right quiet kid,[11] un well mannered anorl. We wer cummin back through Annesley park, un[12] we wer orl tired, our Ada said ter hurry up or we'll be late for us tea, I've got to get ready for Chapel anorl.[13] We'd just got by 'Badger Box'[14] goin towards Mutton hill when our Dollie said 'What's that in that front garden?' It wer a hearse. Ada says[15] it wer a funeral car, what yer go in when yer dead. We all went nearer ter have a proper look, little Audrey let ert a yell, then we could see a man layin in it, we soon run off. We'd gone up road a bit when we saw Bobby Brown on his bike cummin towards us. Our Ada shouted to him, 'Please sir, there's a man layin in a horse[16] int front garden of that house'.[17] 'Yer what me lass?' he said, un she told him again, 'Un he's not in a coffin, is he dead?' Bobby laughed un said, 'He's only asleep', un not to be frightened, 'Its only old man Jones, he often as a sleep innit on Sunday afternoons'. We could still hear him laughing as he peddled away, I said to our Ada what a nerve you've[18] got talkin to a bobby, but then that wer our Ada, nowt bothered her.[19]

Notes to Text 7.3: reading of published version
Text 7.1 differs from the reading in the following ways:

1 *ter go.*
2 *un* precedes *grasses.*
3 There is no comma after *Bill,* which the intonation and pause in the reading would seem to require. This has been regarded as a reading performance error, probably brought about by the editorial choice of a comma rather than a full-stop after *youngest.* (Clearly Dollie, not Bill, is the youngest.)
4 *on* does not appear.
5 *to her* follows *say.*
6 *we dint want him we us cos we wer orlus up to summat.*
7 *go.*

8   *then* does not appear.

9   *we wer'nt to touch um, not to tell anybody, it wer a secret.*

10   *her* (a reading performance error, probably a result of distraction caused by the barking of the author's dog; there is a pause in the recording at this point).

11   *I don't know why cos she wer such a quiet kid.*

12   *un* does not appear.

13   *said ter hurry up or we'd be late for us tea, un she'd got ter get ready for Chapel.*

14   *'Badger'.*

15   *told us.*

16   *hearse.* (The author confirms that his use of the word *horse* is an error, perhaps influenced at this point by the fact that the hearse itself would have been horse-drawn. He is <u>not</u> using /ɔːs/ as a variant pronunciation of *hearse!*).

17   *inna front garden.*

18   *she'd.*

19   *that wer her, nowt bothered our Ada.*

7.5   General aims and expectations

The general aim of this study is to investigate some of the linguistic choices made by a writer using a very specific regional dialect of English and to explore the contribution these choices appear to make to the impact created by the particular narrative.

An immediate question arises over the possible 'authenticity' of the dialect in linguistic terms: how far does authenticity in a literary text matter? Is it in fact possible? Is it feasible to regard a given literary text as a potentially accurate and informative <u>linguistic</u> text? These questions have been addressed by a number of writers interested in the use of dialect in literature, notably Page (1988) on the work of, for example, Emily Bronte, Dickens, Gaskell, Hardy and Lawrence, and Shepherd (1990) on Hardy, Tennyson and Barnes. Both Page and Shepherd note that compromise is likely to be inevitable between strict representational 'accuracy' and authorial creativity and sensitivity to the needs (and tolerance) of the reader. Both, however, emphasise the significance of a writer's deep <u>knowledge</u> of a dialect in enabling them to use it to give full creative expression to their own personal vision.

The newspaper article reproduced as Figure 7.1 suggests both success with the local readership <u>and</u> a warm acceptance of the authenticity of the dialect used. This study will, therefore, treat the small piece of data represented by Text 7.1 as, at least potentially, an accurate representation of the Kirkby dialect, one that can give, in conjunction with standardised Text 7.2 and the taped reading as represented in Text 7.3, significant information about both the grammar and accent of that dialect. Thus the study will:

• regard Text 7.1 as an authentic <u>linguistic</u> text, which can provide the basis for the formulating and testing of tentative hypotheses about the patterning of this particular dialect in terms of some of its grammar and pronunciation features;

● regard Text 7.1 as a <u>literary</u> text and examine how particular pronunciation features are represented in written form, considering these in the light of claims about the conventions adopted for dialect speech in literature.

The implications of all of the above can then be explored for the creation of a 'successful' example of literary narrative written in a particular regional dialect.

This general approach has proved to be a fruitful strategy in the past, for example in examining use of dialect in the work of D. H. Lawrence (Hillier 1993a, 1993b, 1993c; 1994; 1996). Lawrence is an author who has demonstrated his 'masterly' command of the dialect of Eastwood, Nottinghamshire, by using 'one of his actual voices' (Worthen 1991: 63). The dialect used by Lawrence has, in fact, many features in common with that of the Kirkby area, partly as a result of their geographical link via the River Erewash. Exploration of the overall geolinguistic area for this particular study will be found in Section 7.6.

7.6   The geographical and linguistic area of enquiry

Kirkby lies in roughly the north-west region of Nottinghamshire, in a part of the Erewash Valley, the Erewash being a narrow river which forms the county boundary between Nottinghamshire and Derbyshire for much of its length. This may indeed be a significant factor in helping to account for what seem to be a number of similar features in the speech of those who live close to the river – whether on the Nottinghamshire or Derbyshire side. (Anderson, 1987: 4, in his discussion of dialect boundaries distinguishes between non-navigable and navigable rivers. The former create 'good' boundaries and therefore maintain difference, but the latter (the Erewash type) tend to encourage the spread of <u>similar</u> features.)

Trudgill's (1999) descriptions of the Traditional and Modern dialect areas of England provide some geographical and linguistic clues as to the likely linguistic features of the particular region. In terms of Trudgill's Traditional dialect regions, parts of the Erewash Valley show some affinities with both Western and Eastern Central dialects (1999: 41–3, 87–101). (Some older dialect features might be expected to occur in Text 7.1, given the age of the author and also the nostalgic perspective of the book.) So far as Modern dialects are concerned, the Kirkby area, like Trudgill's own example of Sheffield, would fall within the broad Central North (1999: 67). Within that region, however, it has affinities with both Central Midlands (its Nottinghamshire connections) and Northwest Midlands (its Derbyshire influences).

Hughes and Trudgill's (1996) invaluable introduction to accents and dialects in the British Isles does not, unfortunately, discuss the Erewash Valley area – the closest region both geographically and linguistically seems to be Bradford in Yorkshire. They do, however, record many broad regional features which are directly relevant, and their work has strongly influenced the approach adopted for this small study. Another valuable reference work has been Edwards et al.'s (1984) survey of dialect grammar research in Britain. More specific, though very small, studies have been carried out by Hillier of the accent and dialect of a retired miner in Mansfield and of schoolchildren in Eastwood, Nottinghamshire (Hillier 1993a, 1994, 1995, 1998; and see Section 5.3). (Eastwood lies approximately seven miles south-west of Kirkby, still within the Erewash Valley, and it shares at least some of Kirkby's dialect features.) There are, too, a small number of non-specialist books, intended for a general audience, which contain much useful information. The most significant of these are Scollins and Titford (1976a, 1976b) on the dialect of Ilkeston. Ilkeston lies approximately three miles south of Eastwood, on the Derbyshire side of the Erewash, and it seems to share some of the features of both Eastwood and Kirkby.

All of these resources, both general and specific, have been drawn upon for this study.

7.7 The descriptive frameworks: the overall approach

The overall approach adopted will be to identify within Text 7.1 a range of dialect and accent features, relating these where possible to those outlined by Hughes and Trudgill (1996) (from this point referred to as 'H&T'), and Edwards et al. (1984) ('E et al.'). Supplementary reference will be made to Trudgill (1999), Hillier (1994) and Scollins and Titford (1976a, 1976b) where additional features and/or comments prove necessary and/or useful. In considering specific accent features I have made use of H&T's framework for identifying and describing vowels and consonants, and have adopted their chosen system of notation. The account of the frameworks has been limited to a summary of the most significant features for the purposes of this study. Readers should seek out the original sources for fuller explication where necessary.

The term 'dialect' has in fact been used in slightly different ways in this chapter so far – as an overall term for language variation in general and also to indicate a particular type of variation. From this point on H&T's practice will be followed of making an important theoretical distinction between '**dialect**', meaning features of grammar and vocabulary, and '**accent**', meaning features of pronunciation (H&T: 3). The former will be described in Section 7.8 and the latter in Section 7.9.

7.8 The descriptive frameworks: selected dialect features

In investigating dialect the principal focus for this study will be the identification of grammatical features within Text 7.1 which show systematic variation from standard English. Occasional reference is made to vocabulary features as appropriate. Several of the features of non-standard grammar identified by H&T and others were found to be significant in arriving at the standardised version of the extract (Text 7.2). (Reference will also be made, where appropriate, to instances found in the Chapter 5 data.) The principal features are:

(a) **Past tense of irregular verbs:** This is a complex area, as E et al.: 19 acknowledge (see also Crystal 1996: 70–3). Non-standard forms may involve the use of the past participle for the past tense; thus standard English *I see, I saw* and *I have seen* may be *I see, I seen, I have seen* (H&T: 24). E et al.: 20 note alternative possible 'generalisations' for some verbs, for example of the past tense (*I go, I went, I have went*) and of the present tense (*I come, I come, I have come*). Scollins and Titford (1976b: 11) note the apparent regularisation of some irregular verbs, for example *knowed, telled, catched*.

For the verb *to be,* E et al.: 20 identify a range of possible variations: generalisation of *was* or *were* with all persons, or of *were* with singular persons and *was* with plural. The geographical regions mentioned by them which are closest to the Kirkby area seem to be Yorkshire (generalisation of *were*) and North Staffordshire (*were* in the singular and *was* in the plural).

Instances of all of these various processes and forms have been observed by Hillier (1994).

It should be noted that E et al.: 19–20 discuss 'irregular forms' and *to be* under separate headings. For this small study they have been placed within one category, though they are considered separately at a later stage.

(b) **Relative pronouns:** Use of *what* to refer to all antecedent nouns, human and non-human, thus *that was the man what done it* (H&T: 27; Hillier 1994). (See also Talk Text 5.1A: 8, 16.)

(c) **Possessive pronouns:** Use of first personal plural pronoun *us* as a possessive form (standard English *our*) (E et al.: 27). Trudgill (1999: 88) also notes the comparable use of *me* (for standard English *my*).

(d) **Adverbs without –ly:** No addition of -*ly* to adjectives to form adverbs of manner, thus *slow, real* rather than standard English *slowly, really* (E et al.: 24; H&T: 29; Hillier 1994).

(e) **Unmarked plurality after a numeral:** No explicit indication ('marking') of plural meaning of nouns of measurement and quantity after a numeral, thus *twenty year* (H&T: 30; E et al.: 25; Hillier 1994). (The terms 'unmarked/marked' here have a more restricted meaning than as used so far in this book, for example in Chapter 2: see Glossary in Appendix 2, and also Section 7.14.1.)

(f) **Preposition on for of:** Use of *on* where standard English would have *of* (E et al.: 24)

(g) **The definite article:** Either omission of definite article (E et al.: 28) or realisation by /t/, thus *t'fire* (H&T: 92; Hillier 1994) (and see Section 7.9). (See also Talk Text 5.1A: 15, 35.)

7.9   The descriptive frameworks: selected accent features

7.9.1   RP as a background framework

As with standard/non-standard English for dialect description, the approach adopted for accent description will be to identify features represented in Text 7.1 which show systematic variation from those of a perceived 'norm', in this case 'received pronunciation' (RP). As H&T state (p. 3), RP is by far the most well known, widely understood and fully described of British accents, even though only a very small percentage of the English population speak it. It is the prestige accent of British English, associated with high social status in terms of education, income and profession. Crucially, it gives no indication of any particular regional origin: 'It is quite impossible to tell from pronunciation alone where an RP speaker comes from' (H&T: 3).

H&T describe RP in some detail (pp. 33–53). The basic descriptive method they adopt is to present a broad, phonemic, description (shown between slants) of the typical consonant and vowel features of RP supported by a list of 52 key words (H&T: ix). They also identify variations within RP, including different possible realisations of particular phonemes, showing these narrower, phonetic, descriptions between square brackets. They use the framework thus established as a background against which specific features of a particular regional accent can be compared and identified. (A version of this procedure will be followed for this study, though necessarily in a highly selective and simplified form.)

The following, therefore, presents a broad transcription of those vowels and consonants of RP which appear to be most significant for the current study. Each is accompanied by one or more exemplifying key words, given in both standard orthography and broad transcription. (H&T's own Word List numbers are added, as appropriate, for cross-reference purposes.)

Vowels – Monophthongs (single sounds)
/iː/ as in *bee* /biː/ (WL7)
/ɪ/ as in *pit* /pɪt/ (WL1)
/ɛ/ as in *pet* /pɛt/ (WL2)
/æ/ as in *pat* /pæt/ (WL3) and also *hat* /hæt/ (WL21)
/ʌ/ as in *putt* /pʌt/ (WL5)
/ɑː/ as in *bard* /bɑːd/ (WL17) and also *dance* /dɑns/ (WL22)
/ɒ/ as in *pot* /pɒt/ (WL6)
/ɔː/ as in *board* /bɔːd/ (WL18)
/ʊ/ as in *put* /pʊt/ (WL4)
/uː/ as in *boot* /buːt/ (WL11)
/ɜː/ as in *bird* /bɜːd/ (WL16)
/ə/ as in *father* /fɑːðə/ (WL25) (final vowel – always unstressed – referred to as a 'schwa')

Vowels – Diphthongs (two vowels in one syllable)
/ɛə/ as in *bear* /bɛə/ (WL15)
/ɑu/ as in *bout* /bɑut/ (WL13)

Consonants (in addition to those illustrated as part of the above description of Vowels)

/ŋ/ as in singing /sɪŋɪŋ/

7.9.2 Kirkby accent features

After having described RP, H&T go on to identify broad kinds of regional accent variation currently found across the British Isles (pp. 54–67). This is followed by more detailed descriptions of the speech of thirteen specific areas (pp. 68–119), though <u>not</u> the area which includes the Erewash Valley. They do, however, identify a number of broad regional accent features which are also characteristic of the Erewash Valley area (having been noted by Hillier 1993c, 1994) and might therefore be expected to be represented in various ways in Text 7.1.

Kirkby's geographical position in the Northern and/or Central regions (see Section 7.6) would in fact lead us to expect certain consistencies, as follows:

(a) **use of the vowel /ʊ/** (as in RP *put* WL4) in words such as *putt* (WL5) and *but* (H&T: 54–5);

(b) **use of the vowel /æ/** (as in RP *pat* WL3) in *path* and *dance* as well as in *pat* (H&T: 56);

(c) **use of the consonant /n/** in the suffix *-ing* (where RP would have /ŋ/) (H&T: 63);

(d) **absence of the consonant /h/** (H&T: 62).

Other potentially significant features which have been noted by Hillier (1994) are:

(e) **realisation of the consonant /t/ as a glottal stop [ʔ]** when the /t/ is itself realising the definite article (see Section 7.8). (H&T comment on the use of the glottal stop to realise /t/, but limit their discussion to word-medial or morpheme-final or word-final position (see for example H&T: 39, 62, 90).)

(f) **frequent use of what appears to be a lengthened monophthong [æː]** in words like *bout* (WL13) where RP would have the diphthong /aʊ/;

(g) **use of [ɛː], but occasionally [ɒ]**, in some words, for example *bird* (WL16) where RP would have /ɜː/.

The three vowel pronunciations under (f) and (g) are referred to in Scollins and Titford (1976a), who make the following interesting comments:

> The vowel sound in words like 'now', 'town' etc is usually pronounced nowadays with an open 'aah' sound: 'nah', 'tahn' . . . 'out' becomes 'aht'; 'cow' becomes 'caa' . . . older people, especially, may still be heard using a more closed sound,

approximating to 'air'. Thus, 'town' becomes 'tairn'; 'about' becomes 'abairt' etc. (1976a: 15)

Traditionally, words like 'bird' and 'shirt', which contain an 'er' sound, were usually pronounced 'bod' and 'shot'. Increasingly, however, an intermediate vowel is used – an 'air' sound.'   (1976a: 15)

Trudgill (1999: 94) does in fact illustrate the [ɒ] pronunciation of RP /ɜː/ (though without comment) when he quotes a folk-song in a version from western Derbyshire (collected by Scollins and Titford) which contains the words *choch* and *tonnip* (for 'church' and 'turnip').

7.10   Method and presentation of analysis

7.10.1   Grammatical features

Each of the non-standard features in Text 7.1, identified according to the framework outlined in Section 7.8 (and standardised in arriving at Text 7.2), was highlighted in upper-case lettering. In addition, those features were similarly highlighted where, again according to the framework, a non-standard form might <u>potentially</u> have been chosen but was not. Features were grouped into relevant categories and assigned a code, shown in bold superscribed lower-case letters, as follows:

a   Past tense of certain irregular verbs (*see, tell, run* and also *be*)
b   Relative pronouns
c   Possessive pronouns (first person)
d   Adverbs without –*ly*
e   Unmarked plurality following a numeral
f   Preposition *on* for *of*
g   Definite article

Line numbers were added to the text, together with a glossary of lexical items. The complete analysis is displayed as Text 7.1A (see Appendix 1.6).

7.10.2   Accent features

The analysis was carried out in two stages.

Stage one: The transcript of the reading of the published version (Text 7.3) was scrutinised, and notes were made on the text of the precise points at which each of the accent features described in Section 7.9.2 might <u>potentially</u> occur. Neither Texts 7.1 nor 7.2 could give anything more than possible clues as to either regional or RP pronunciation, but both texts were drawn on in arriving at initial identifications. The relevant points were indicated by the use of annotations of superscribed lower-case letters, again in bold, to show the relevant category of feature in each case, and, where possible, of upper-case lettering to show the approximate orthographic environment of the particular sound. The annotations were coded in accordance with the categories in Section 7.9.2, summarised as follows:

a   /ʊ/ for RP /ʌ/
b   /æ/ for RP /ɑː/
c   /n/ for RP /ŋ/ in suffix –*ing*
d   zero (0) for RP /h/
e   [ʔ] for /t/ as definite article
f   [æː] for RP /ɑu/
g   [ɛː] (or [ɒ]) for RP /ɜː/

Stage two: The tape recording of Fred Wetherill's reading of the extract was then replayed. The <u>actual</u> pronunciation of each of the identified potential occurrences of each of the selected features was noted, with each category of feature being taken separately and each feature within that category being given individual attention. The description of each actual pronunciation is shown in bold and in square brackets placed immediately after the relevant superscript, for example [n], [0], the descriptive system being in accordance with that summarised in Sections 7.9.1 and 7.9.2. Line numbers were added, and the complete analysis is displayed as Text 7.3A (see Appendix 1.6).

7.11   Presentation of results: grammatical features

Table 7.1 summarises the findings of the analysis presented in Text 7.1A. On the evidence of these selected features, it will be seen from the table that a high proportion of grammatical features in the text extract (at 65.5 per cent,

Table 7.1   Summary of selected dialect features in Text 7.1A

Code	Non-standard feature	Potential occurrences	Actual non-standard occurrences	Percentage actual of potential occurrences
a	past tense of irregular verbs	22	13	59.1
	see, tell, run	4	1 = *run*	25.0
	be	18	12 = *were*	66.7
b	relative pronouns	1	1 = *what*	100.0
c	possessive pronouns	12	1 = *us*; 1 = *me*	16.7
d	adverbs without –*ly*	1	1 = *real*	100.0
e	unmarked plurality after numeral	2	2 = *year*	100.0
f	preposition *on* for *of*	1	1	100.0
g	realisation of definite article by zero or by /t/	19	18	94.7
			10 by zero	52.6
			8 by /t/	42.1
	Total	**58**	**38**	**65.5**

almost two-thirds) are non-standard. Given its ostensible status as a dialect text, however, the corresponding proportion of <u>standard</u> features seems surprisingly high. This could be at least partly a consequence of the editing process (see Section 7.2.2), though reference to the relevant section of the manuscript would suggest that this mainly affected representation of <u>pronunciation</u> features via the spelling.

It will be apparent that not all of the seven individual categories have an equal effect on the figures. The different categories are therefore treated in slightly different ways in the following discussion. (Line references are to Text 7.1A unless otherwise stated.)

7.11.1   Relative pronouns; adverbs without –ly; preposition *on* for *of*

Each of the above categories is consistently in a non-standard form. Each is, however, represented by only <u>one</u> token.

7.11.2   Past tense forms of irregular verbs

Of the four occurrences of the verbs *tell, see, run* only the one instance of *run* is in a non-standard form. The others are in standard form, so on this evidence there is little or no support for the claims of Scollins and Titford (1976b) and Hillier (1994). (The standard forms *told* and *saw* also appear in the manuscript.)

Forms of *be* seem to show a generalisation of *were* for all persons. Two-thirds (12) of the forms have a singular subject, and the remaining six a plural subject (*we*). (It should be noted that in Fred Wetherill's reading of the text – see Text 7.3A – he substitutes *he* for *we* in line **12** and this too is followed by *were*.)

7.11.3   Possessive pronouns

Only two (16.7 per cent) of the first person pronouns are non-standard. The remainder involve the standard form *our*, and all of these are followed by a proper noun (Crystal 1996: 110–11) – either *Mam, Ada, Bill* or *Dollie*. The use of *our* in conjunction with a proper noun referring to a specific person is a traditional regional signal of kinship (note *our Dollie* compared with *little Audrey*). The two non-standard instances, *us* and *me* (pronounced [mɪ]), are followed by common nouns *tea* and *lass*. It will, however, be noted from line **20** of Text 7.3A that the author reads *our secret* (that is, *our* in conjunction with a common noun) and it is possible that stress is the significant factor here. On this small evidence there may be some correlation between stress patterns and choice of form in some environments, with low stress influencing choice of non-standard form and high stress standard form. (The effect of stress on accent and its representation is considered in Sections 7.12.2 and 7.14.8 below.)

7.11.4   Unmarked plurality after a numeral

There are just two instances of unmarked plurals following a numeral (*four* and *five* respectively), both involving *year* (line 7). There are many instances elsewhere in the text where plural meaning <u>is</u> explicitly indicated (by –*s*) (for example in lines **3, 4, 5** and so on). In these instances, however, there is <u>no</u> preceding numeral and thus formal marking of the relevant noun is a <u>require-ment</u>. Standard English chooses to mark the plural <u>twice</u> in such constructions as *four years*, which might – from a non-standard speaker's perspective – be viewed as excessive (see also Section 7.14.1 below).

7.11.5   The definite article

Table 7.1 shows that occurrences here are almost entirely non-standard (94.7 per cent), with the definite article being realised in Text 7.1A either by zero or by an indication of /t/. (Section 7.14.1 considers how these realisations are – or are not – actually represented in the written text.) There is just one occurrence of *the* in the extract (line 7), and the manuscript in fact reads 'Dollie youngest, we Bill somewer in between'. It is possible that the insertion of *the* in the published text was another contributing factor to the author's misreading on the tape – see note 3 to Text 7.3. (See also Section 7.12.2.)

7.12   Presentation of results: accent features

Table 7.2 summarises the findings of the analysis for accent features presented in Text 7.3A. It shows that although the text extract is quite short there are nevertheless substantial numbers of instances of the seven accent features selected for analysis. There are therefore rather more tokens to work with than for some of the grammatical features examined in Section 7.11. Of the 142 potential occurrences of the regional accent features outlined in Section 7.9.2,

Table 7.2   Summary of selected accent features in Text 7.3A

Code	Regional accent feature	Potential occurrences	Actual occurrences	Percentage actual of potential occurrences
a	/ʊ/ for RP /ʌ/	38	31	81.6
b	/æ/ for RP /ɑː/	10	10	100.0
c	/n/ for RP /ŋ/	13	13	100.0
d	zero for RP /h/	30	30	100.0
e	[ʔ] for the definite article	20	22 *	110.0*
f	[æː] for RP /ɑʊ/	23	20	87.0
g	[ɛː] or [ɒ] for RP /ɜː/	8	5	62.5
	Total	**142**	**131**	**92.3**

* See Section 7.12.2 for discussion of this apparently anomalous result.

the author's reading of Text 7.1 (as transcribed and analysed in Text 7.3A) shows an almost complete choice (92.3 per cent) of the expected features. There is complete consistency for categories **b, c** and **d**, in that /æ/ is always used for the *path* and *dance* vowels, /n/ occurs in the suffix –*ing*, and there is zero for RP /h/. The remaining categories are considered separately below. (Line references are to Text 7.3A unless otherwise indicated.)

7.12.1 /ʊ/ for RP /ʌ/

[ʊ] almost consistently realises RP /ʌ/, with 81.6 per cent of a possible 38 occurrences. Other pronunciations may occur when the relevant word is unstressed, the tendency then being in the direction of [ə] – a schwa (H&T: 46, and see Section 7.9.1) (see for example the instances of *us* in lines **17–18**).

7.12.2 [ʔ] for the definite article

Several complicating factors arise under this category. First, the figure for potential occurrences in Table 7.2 (20) differs from that in Table 7.1 (19) since the author's slightly divergent reading (line **35** of Text 7.3A) introduces an extra definite article – *int front garden of that house* instead of *inna front garden* (see note **17** to Text 7.3). Second, the number of actual occurrences of [ʔ] is the apparently anomalous 22 (110 per cent). This comes about as a consequence of three interpolated instances of [ʔ] in the reading (two of them particularly surprising) in that no 'potential occurrence' has been provided for in the annotation and analysis of Text 7.3 – see Text 7.3A. The first of these interpolations is in line **13**, where [ʔ] is inserted before *lasses,* thus seeming to convert *lasses* from lasses in general to these lasses in particular. The second and third are in line **15** (before *Newstead pit*) and line **27** (before *Chapel*). In neither of these two cases (especially the latter) had a definite article been expected in standard English (see Text 7.2) or, indeed, in the Kirkby dialect. E et al. (pp. 28–9) make the following comment, which may or may not be relevant in this particular case:

> [Sometimes the definite article] is used where standard English requires a possessive adjective, an indefinite article or no determiner at all (Ireland, Scotland, N. England, S. Wales, S. W. England). The environments where it can occur seem to vary from dialect to dialect. Most commonly mentioned were: before ailments . . . before trades, sciences and languages . . . before institutions such as *church* and *school* (Scotland, N. England) and before parts of the body. . . .

The effect of these 'extra' occurrences is to produce the surprising result in the percentage column. This skewing is compounded by the fact that the *the* in line **8** is fully realised in the reading as [ðə] (see Table 7.1 and discussion in Section 7.11.5). What is clear, however, is that whether or not the definite article is represented in the written text it is overwhelmingly realised in speech by the glottal stop.

7.12.3 [æː] for RP /aʊ/

This category is (at 87 per cent) almost consistently [æː]. There are two occurrences of something approaching [æu], both in the word *flowers* (see lines **4** and **18**), and these may have been influenced by the following syllabic [wəz]. (Hillier found a comparable pronunciation of *shower* in her Eastwood data – see Talk Text 5.1.) The third slightly questionable occurrence is in line **41**, where *our* seems to fall somewhere between [æː] and [æu], approximately [æʊ].

7.12.4 [ɛː] or [ɒ] for RP /ɜː/

Of the eight potential occurrences four are realised as [ɛː] and one as [ɒ]. Of the remainder, one receives very low stress and is a schwa (see the *her* following *liked* in line **23**) (compare the discussion of /ʊ/ above) and two (*sir* in line **34** and *her* in line **42**) receive fairly prominent stress and seem to be close to a diphthong [ɛə].

The single occurrence of [ɒ] is noteworthy. The manuscript in fact has *lernt* rather than the *lont* in **line 3**, so it would seem that the editorial process actually made it potentially <u>less</u> accessible to the general reader. Given the fact that this is an older pronunciation (see Section 7.9.2) it is possible that it was a deliberately 'literary' addition of what was felt to be local colour.

7.13 Summary of findings for both dialect and accent features

On the evidence of the findings for this text extract as described and discussed in the preceding sections, there is strong support for regarding it as an 'authentic' linguistic text. It appears to represent many of the dialect and accent features of Kirkby and the Erewash Valley (the notable exception being the past tense forms of irregular verbs other than *be*) and it deploys these in a largely consistent and thus 'reliable' manner.

Some of its specific effects are considered in Section 7.15 below, but first I want to consider the related – and important – question of how the different regional features appear to be represented in the written text.

7.14 Some observations on the representation of accent and dialect in Text 7.1

It is accepted that there is no <u>consistent</u> matching of letters to sounds in the English spelling system (see for example Stubbs 1983c: 281–3). Furthermore, there are no agreed conventions available to writers who wish to use traditional orthography to represent the authentic sounds of speech, though Upton and Widdowson (1996) and Trudgill (1999), for example, try possible strategies. The problem is particularly acute for writers of novels, stories and plays. They must to some degree construct their own approximations of the sounds they wish to convey (always keeping in mind reader tolerance; see Section 7.5) and they may do this with varying degrees of consistency.

Several writers, for example Traugott and Pratt (1980: 338–9), Leech and Short (1983: 167–70), Freeborn et al. (1993: 212–15), Short (1996: 87), have discussed the forms of representation of non-standard varieties in literature in English, using such terms as 'normal' v. 'deviant' spellings, and 'eye-dialect'. Traugott and Pratt make the interesting observation that when a writer uses 'normal' English spellings in dialogue:

> we infer that the pronunciation intended is the <u>standard</u> of the audience for which the work is written, while special deviant spellings indicate the pronunciation of a dialect that is <u>not</u> the audience's standard. This can lead to some rather unusual variations. For example, a writer representing an Irishman to a predominantly English audience might be inclined to use spelling to indicate Irish pronunciation, while the same writer might not do so when presenting an Irishman to a predominantly Irish audience. (1980: 339; emphases added)

What then might be inferred from some of the orthographic choices made by Fred Wetherill and his editor and the approximate patterns (if any) suggested by those choices? In the observations which follow, line references will be to the published text as presented in its analysed version (Text 7.1A) unless otherwise indicated. (Confirmation of actual pronunciation will be via explicit reference to Text 7.3A.) The terms 'standard' and 'non-standard' spellings will be used instead of Traugott and Pratt's 'normal' and 'deviant'.

7.14.1   The definite article

Section 7.12.2 states that virtually all realisations of the definite article in the reading aloud are via the glottal stop, and that this is so whether or not the presence of the article is formally indicated in the written text. Where there are in fact traces of the definite article in the written text these are shown by the attachment of the letter *t* to the end of the preceding word. This word is always a grammatical (rather than a lexical) item (see Sections 6.6.2 to 6.6.3) – see, for example, *went* (when the) (line **2**) and *unt* (and the) (line **3**), *alt* (all the), *at* (of the) and *ont* (on the) (line **3**). This practice contrasts, therefore, with the conventional attachment of *t'* to the beginning of the <u>following</u> word (its relevant noun), see for example *t'fire* (H&T: 92), and indeed the formally designated title of the book under discussion.

What might be called the 'suffix *t*' seems to be much more convincing in its representation of the relevant sound than the 'prefix *t*', though it may be less immediately comprehensible in <u>visual</u> terms to a non-local audience (hence perhaps the title accorded to the book). The finding does, however, suggest two potentially interesting general points. It confirms that the conventional use of 'prefix *t*' is designed to give purely <u>visual</u> information to a largely 'standard'-speaking readership about the approximate regional and/or social origin of a particular speaker, and does not (as 'suffix *t*' does) attempt to represent with any degree of accuracy the actual <u>sound</u> of the particular speech. It also makes a rather neat connection with H&T's claim about the glottal stop and its occurrence in word-final position (see Section 7.9.2). In this particular written text 'suffix *t*' <u>does</u> appear in word-final position. (This is not the whole story, of course, since the glottal stop in fact also realises the definite article at the <u>beginning</u> of a sentence – see Text 7.3A, line **37**, where the glottal stop is inserted before *Bobby* ((the) policeman) even though there is no formal indication of this in the text.)

This whole discussion raises wider – intriguing – issues around the question of degrees of explicitness required in a non-standard dialect – issues which are highlighted when that dialect has to be written down (arguably an unnatural act in itself). It may be that there is a working presumption of definite meaning, with already-shared knowledge being assumed between speaker and hearer (see the discussion of shared knowledge, and the ways it is manifested, in Chapter 5). The hearer is assumed to 'know' the specific entity being referred to. On this reading, 'definiteness' would in fact be the most expected ('<u>unmarked</u>') interpretation, hence its variable and inconsistent realisation in the written form: it is not really 'necessary'. (This could also suggest a reason for the uncertainties and interpolations referred to in Sections 7.11.5 and 7.12.2.)

The less usual/expected meaning would therefore require to be explicitly indicated ('<u>marked</u>') in a text – in this case the signal of <u>in</u>definiteness – and the small evidence of the current study gives a degree of support to this theory. There are, in fact, many uses of the indefinite article *a* throughout Text 7.1/A and in every case either its omission would be impossible (** it wer long way*) or it would have to be replaced by a 'spoken' glottal stop. In the latter event this would create a new and different – definite – meaning. This is in fact illustrated by one of the changes brought about in the reading-aloud. The general and unspecific *inna front garden* in line **28** of Text 7.1A becomes, in line **35** of Text 7.3A, *int front garden of that house*. A specific garden (the front) (and of a now-specified and mutually visible house) is being referred to. A further example is *a bobby* in line **32** of Text 7.1A. The child narrator is commenting admiringly on Ada's nerve in general – not just at talking to this particular bobby, Bobby Brown (whom they clearly all know, though note the respectful *sir* in line **27**), but to <u>any</u> bobby at all.

The economy thus being claimed for this dialect can perhaps be related to the comments in Section 7.11.4 on the marking (or not) of plurals, and also to Hillier's findings for non-standard forms of the verb phrase in particular environments (Hillier 1995). (It might even suggest a tenuous link with the discussion of assumptions of 'shared knowledge' and 'linguistic economy' in Section 5.10.) Such considerations are, however, beyond the scope of the current study.

7.14.2   Zero /h/

Table 7.2 shows 30 potential occurrences of the phoneme /h/, but in no case was /h/ sounded – that is, there was 100 per cent 'realisation' by zero. Reference to Texts 7.1A and 7.3A shows that, even though the letter *h* appears in almost every instance, Fred Wetherill makes no attempt <u>at all</u> to pronounce /h/. There is only one instance of 'no *h*' in the spelling – *he often as a sleep innit on Sunday afternoons* (Text 7.1A, line **30–1**) – and it may or may not be significant that this occurs in quoted dialogue (by Bobby Brown) rather than in the narrative voice of the persona.

The conventional literary device of signalling zero /h/ is via the attachment of an apostrophe to the beginning of the relevant word (see *'it*, though <u>not</u> *'issen*, in the headline of Figure 7.1), which in this text would be *'er, 'ill, 'earse* and so on. This device can, however, be irritating to the eye when it is carried out consistently and authentically. (D. H. Lawrence appears to opt for a judicious mix of *h* and use of apostrophe, perhaps for this reason.) Consistent omission of <u>both</u> letter *h* <u>and</u> apostrophe might have been felt to impede overall comprehension when processed by the eye of a standard speaker, though as Stubbs notes (1980: 37–8) genuine ambiguities over pairs such as *ill, (h)ill* and *as, (h)as* would be unlikely to arise, given that such pairs usually come from different grammatical categories. (The manuscript does in fact adopt this last strategy (that is, no *h* <u>and</u> no apostrophe) and it is possible that the *as* in line **30** just slipped through the editing process – other quoted dialogue by Bobby Brown in lines **29–30** does include *h*.)

The findings for this text confirm some of Stubbs's observations (1980: 36–40) about what he calls 'this peculiar consonant', particularly that a sharp distinction should be made between the phoneme /h/ and the letter *h*. Aitch (the phoneme) is <u>not</u> part of the Kirkby accent, and aitch (the letter) seems to be a purely <u>visual</u> symbol required by convention.

7.14.3 Suffix /ɪn/

Text 7.1A represents the suffix almost entirely as *–in*, and the reading pronounces it consistently as [ɪn], even when it is written as *–ing* (for example in line **31**). (The manuscript has *laffin* at this point.)

7.14.4 /æ/

Words written as *class, afternoon* are consistently pronounced [æ], as are *laughed, laughing*. Standard spelling is used throughout for this vowel. (The manuscript, however, has *laffed, laffin*.)

7.14.5 /ʊ/

Words written variously as *loved, just, youngest, somewhere, front* (that is, in standard spellings) are all pronounced [ʊ], as is the only non-standard spelling *cummin* (for example lines **20, 27**). (The manuscript has one additional non-standard spelling *luvved*.) A few words (five tokens of *us* and two of *but*) (see Section 7.12.1) are accorded low or no stress in the reading and these may move towards a schwa rather than the expected [ʊ]. They are all, however, written with standard spelling. (See Section 7.14.8 for a consideration of strategies for indicating low stress which are shown elsewhere in Text 7.1/A.)

7.14.6 [æː]

Words having this pronunciation are virtually all written with standard spellings, for example *now, about, our, Brown*. The only instances of non-standard spelling are *ert* and *abert* (for example lines **5, 15**), though these do not appear consistently (see *about* and *out* – lines **1, 18**) in either Text 7.1A or the manuscript. (The manuscript has *ar* for *our*.)

7.14.7 [ɛː] or [ɒ]

Words having the pronunciation [ɛː] in the reading are all fully stressed items, and they are written with standard spellings, for example *her, hearse, nerve*, as are those (also fully stressed) which are realised by a diphthong (see Section 7.12.4), for example *sir*. (The questionable case of *wer* is discussed below.)

The single non-standard spelling *lont* (line **3**) is used specifically to indicate a different, alternative, pronunciation.

7.14.8 Strategies for indicating low (or no) stress

Reference has been made at several points in preceding sections to the effects of stress patterning, and it may be fruitful to explore the degree to which assumptions about natural rhythm and stress appear to be manifested in the written text. The following represent just a few preliminary indications of such assumptions in Text 7.1/A.

- The letters *u* and *er* (and to a lesser extent *a*) are used to indicate that a word should be 'heard' as having low or no stress – that is, to represent an approximation of schwa. The environments and meanings differ, however, with *u–* (and *a–*) occurring in word-initial position and *–er* in word-final position;

- *un* is used for 'and' (for example *wild flowers un things* (line **15**); (*an* may also be used for 'and', for example the cover of the book displays *Our Mam an t'Others* while the title page inside has *Our Mam un t'Others*);

- *ud* is used for syllabic "d' (being a contracted form of either standard English 'would' (*Our Mam ud say to her* – lines **9–10**) or 'had' (*her Mum ud asked Ada* – line **17**));

- *ut* (and also *at*) is used for 'of'-plus-definite-article (*Her husband liked her out ut road* – line **18**; *alt names at flowers* – line **3**);

- *–er* is used in *yer* (meaning 'you', and possibly standard English 'you're' – *what yer go in when yer dead* – line **24**), *ter* ('to'), and *inter* ('into').

A note on *wer*: The use of *wer* is in some ways comparable to *–er* in that it indicates a pronunciation which is similar to the preceding *–er* examples, but it also differs in some interesting ways. The spelling *wer* is less non-standard than the *–er* examples, being merely a reduced version of the standard *were*.

Thus the spelling of the word nicely parallels its stress allocation. The fully stressed form of the vowel (RP /ɜː/) would in fact bring it potentially under category **g** in Section 7.10.2 and thus liable to be pronounced [ɛː] or [ɒ]. Such pronunciations of *were* have in the past been informally observed by Hillier, but these have tended to be in restricted linguistic environments and/or notable in some way, such as having a strong contrastive stress. The many instances of *wer* in Text 7.1/A were not, therefore, highlighted as potentials under category **g** or included in the analysis displayed in Text 7.3A. (All were in fact pronounced with a schwa [wə].)

There is only one environment in the extract where a fully stressed *wer* might possibly have been encountered, and that is in line **16**, where the child narrator is reporting Ada's prohibition on touching the Bee-orchids: *we wer'nt to touch um*. Unfortunately, the author's reading converts this into *we not to touch um* (see Text 7.3/A) and we are thus denied the opportunity to check the pronunciation of the *wer'nt* which was published. (The form of the conversion does raise interesting questions in itself, but these are beyond the scope of this book; see Hillier 1998, for some possibly comparable constructions using *not*.)

7.14.9 Summary of observations

While not wishing to make too strong a claim on the evidence of such a small piece of data, the preceding observations do appear to give some support for Traugott and Pratt's theories regarding inferences made from the spelling in which a literary text is presented.

Text 7.1/A, together with the analysis of the reading in Text 7.3A, suggests that local readers of the final published version would take it for granted that the various 'sounds' of the written language are their own, whether the spelling is (relatively) standard or not:

- the phoneme /h/ does not occur whether or not the letter *h* appears;
- the suffix /ɪn/ is used whether or not it is represented as *–ing*;
- vowels are pronounced as expected whether or not their spelling is non-standard;
- signals of 'definiteness' are made whether or not these are formally indicated in the text.

Thus grammatical features and vocabulary choices are consistent with accent features for local readers: the text is all of a piece.

What, then, might a non-local reader infer from Text 7.1 – a reader for whom Text 7.2 has been prepared? It will be apparent from the above discussion, and from reference to Text 7.2, that in fact minimal spelling changes were required for lexical items – in strictly lexical terms there are few signs of regional pronunciation in Text 7.1. The few there are, however, would be expected to give clear signals to readers. In Traugott and Pratt's terms, readers would make conflicting inferences: standard spelling would suggest 'standard' pronunciation, but non-standard spelling (for example *cummin* and *lont*) would declare 'difference', especially when this was reinforced by non-standard grammatical features of the kind discussed in Section 7.11 (whether or not those features were represented in non-standard spelling). They would therefore have to retrospectively 're-hear' the narrative voice in regional terms.

It should be remembered that, unlike much traditional published work involving dialect, the text is written in a consistent voice throughout: non-standard spelling is not being used to differentiate one character from another or characters from omniscient author/narrator. The story is written entirely from 'inside' the experience, with limited concessions being made to the non-local reader. This might, in fact, demand too great an effort from all but the most committed reader. (The question of 'acceptability' to a non-local readership is considered briefly in Section 7.15 below.)

What arises from these findings, however, is the clear evidence that the natural rhythms and stress patterns of speech are actually built in to the written text, and that this effect is created almost entirely via the non-standard representation of accent features. Many (though obviously not all) of the manifestations of stress patterning discussed could in fact be equally appropriate to speakers of a different regional variety or of RP-accented standard English in informal situations. Comparable tendencies in the production of unstressed words have been noted by others, for example the 'dropping' of aitches (Stubbs 1980: 37; H&T: 40) and, especially, the weakening of vowels towards schwa (H&T: 5; Quirk et al. 1985: 1595–7; Gimson 1989: 125–7). Quirk et al. claim that 'we do not find variation in writing corresponding to the range of reduced forms in speech' (1985: 1596), drawing a contrast with the 'institutionalized' written forms for contractions such as *I'm, that'll, won't* and so on. The findings of this study show that a written narrative <u>is</u> able to represent <u>both</u> of these kinds of variation – and with a high degree of consistency. On these grounds alone, therefore, it would appear to make a strong claim to be regarded as '<u>oral</u> literature'.

7.15   Overall discussion of findings

The findings overall suggest that this text should be regarded as a 'successful' text both from a linguistic point of view and, for a local audience, from a literary point of view. It represents the authentic sounds and structures of a particular dialect by adopting the form of a fictional narrative. In the course of the specific anecdote which is the focus of Text 7.1 the author shows skill and economy in his scene-setting, his retailing of humorous incident and his characterisation, especially in his creation of 'our Ada'. He shows a clear awareness of the distinction between author and 'I-narrator' (Leech and Short, 1983: 262–6, identify potentially different levels of 'I-narration'), presenting an 'I' who is also a character in the story. The anecdote – and the book – is processed entirely through the consciousness of his young narrator, with the author clearly signalling to us (and in a nicely understood way) the child's naïvety, for example in the account of how little

Audrey comes to be included in the Sunday outing (see lines **17–19** of Text 7.1A).

His character/narrator indeed progresses from a naïve child of unspecified gender to become an observant adult, reporting on various family happenings, including Ada's subsequent marriage to her 'Yanky' boyfriend and emigration to America. Eventually – with great simplicity and poignancy – s/he gives us the death of our Mam. The final paragraph of the book reads:

> Int morning, I took her up a cuppa tea, as I orlus did before I went ter work. 'Here yer are Mam, yer tea.' There were no response. I touched her shoulder, un said 'Come on sleepyhead, here's yer tea'. I looked down at her un suddenly realised she wern't asleep, she'd gone, an I wer on me own.

As will be apparent from Section 7.14, it is not certain how far the content of the narrative and, especially, the language of its expression, would be successful with a non-local audience. A small informant test with a group of students at an adult education class in Nottingham produced very mixed results. Some found it appealing – especially those with some familiarity with the dialect (two students were from the Erewash Valley) – but others were not at all ready to give it a positive evaluation. It is pleasing to record, therefore, that Fred Wetherill has received some wider recognition for his little book. He received an Individual Award for Adult Learners (under the auspices of the National Institute of Adult Continuing Education – NIACE) and, together with other regional winners from the UK and Europe, attended a Tenth Anniversary Ceremony in London in May 2002.

What remains unquestionable, however, is the book's evaluation by its local audience. Its form of expression is integral to its particular content, and both have been essential to its success with the audience for which it is intended (see Section 7.2.2). That audience is able to identify both with the events of the narrative and with the language in which they are expressed: this is their story and in their language.

7.16   Conclusion

This study has examined some of the linguistic features of a fictional narrative written in a regional dialect. It has related selected non-standard grammatical and accent features to their particular geolinguistic background – the Erewash Valley area in the English East Midlands. It has also examined the ways in which the different features are represented in the written text and the implications of such representations.

It is hoped that this study, like that presented in Chapter 2, has demonstrated that unity of linguistic form and related creative content can together constitute a 'successful' literary text. More specifically, it is hoped that the analyses presented and the detailed discussion of findings have provided support for the claim that *Our Mam un t'Others* should be regarded as a valuable instance of 'oral literature'.

7.17   Suggestions for further work

(a)   Additional features of Text 7.1/A might well be examined (for example the pronunciation – and its representation – of *tek* (line 10) and *ovva* (line 13) (for RP diphthongs /ei/ and /ou/ respectively) and added to those investigated here to form hypotheses to be tested against other extracts from the same book.

(b)   The same kinds of features, and the extent of their occurrence, could be investigated in extracts from other literary texts coming from the same region. A particularly fruitful source would be some of the plays of D. H. Lawrence, for example *A Collier's Friday Night* and *The Widowing of Mrs Holroyd* (see also references in Section 7.5) and short stories such as *Odour of Chrysanthemums*. These could also be compared with suitable spoken data (such as that presented in Chapter 5), thus introducing broad Mode variation.

A modification of this framework could be applied to other literature written in an apparently 'authentic' dialect. This might be from a neighbouring region (for example some of the early work set in Nottingham by Alan Sillitoe) or from elsewhere in Britain (for example the writers discussed by Page (1988) and Shepherd (1990) and referred to in Section 7.5). Gervase Phinn's accounts of his experiences as a schools inspector in North Yorkshire would seem to be highly suitable for such an approach, particularly since accompanying audiobook versions are readily available.

Of particular interest too might be an examination of literature written in 'non-British' varieties of English, for example Mark Twain's classic *The Adventures of Huckleberry Finn* (presented, like *Our Mam*, through a non-standard and youthful narrative voice) or the work of the Caribbean poet Jean 'Binta' Breeze. In the latter case, as with Gervase Phinn, recordings have been made by the author which allow close examination of actual pronunciation features alongside their representations.

(c)   An adapted version of the framework could be applied to <u>spoken</u> data involving speakers from <u>any</u> geolinguistic and/or social background. One potentially fruitful approach would be a development of a study suggested in Section 6.14(c), comparing the speech in different situations of one or more speakers having 'known' origins. The approach could pursue Bell's account of 'audience design' (see Section 5.5.2), especially his theory of 'referee design' (1984: 186–96; 1997: 247–8), where linguistic features associated with a particular (non-present) group can be used to express identification with that group. Bell (1997: 248) cites as examples the adoption of <u>non</u>-New Zealand accents in the New Zealand media and features of American English by British pop singers (see Trudgill 1997).

(d)   A version of the framework, and the findings of this chapter as presented in Section 7.14, might be applied to other kinds of texts which represent 'spoken' forms in writing, whether or not they suggest particular regional origins. Examples might be found in product names, packaging and related advertising material. (A type of toilet tissue sold in Britain uses the brand name *Sofcell*, representing the way it would be pronounced in very informal speech – that is, with elision of the intervening consonant /t/ (H&T: 5–6). This also, of course, creates a 'softening' of the sound of the name.)

Television Advertisements

8.1   Introduction

This chapter uses a small sample of data as a basis for the comparison of British television advertisements broadcast in the 1950s ('the Past') and the 1990s–2000 ('the Present'). Its principal place within the overall structure of the book (see Figure 1.1) falls under Gregory and Carroll's 'writing which is intended to be spoken as if not written'. That is, it is presumed to be intended to be heard by viewers in the main as though it is 'real' speech. How far, and in what ways, might the use and manifestation of that speech differ in the light of a time lapse of almost fifty years? Each advertisement also makes some small use of written language; that is, it is intended to be <u>read</u> by the viewer. The degree to which such language is used is also considered.

8.2   Identifying the variables

8.2.1   The controlled variables

The variables to be controlled are:

- **Mode**:   All of the advertisements within each set of texts are based on <u>written</u> language. The most significant Mode dimension, however, is 'the <u>speaking</u> of what has been written to be spoken as though <u>not</u> written'; communication is via the phonic channel and is intended to be processed via the ear. A small proportion of the language used in each advertisement is presented in written form, via the graphic channel, and is intended to be processed by the eye. The purposes and possible effects of the latter will be examined in the context of the overall analyses. It is important to note, however, that:
  – the 'interaction' between the primary participants in each set of texts (whether the language is to be heard <u>or</u> read) is entirely one-way: there is no visual contact between participants, and the desired consumer is merely the 'recipient' of the language produced by or on behalf of the advertiser and cannot share in the process of text creation (see Section 1.1.6.3);
  – the kinds of 'speaking' which are represented within and across the texts can be further categorised according to Gregory and Carroll's 'speaking' dimension (see the incorporation of 'monologuing' and 'conversing' under the appropriate node); this is in fact one of the main concerns of this study.

- **Field**:   The overriding **purpose** of the language used in each case is to persuade the viewer to buy a particular product – to present that product in as attractive and desirable a way as possible.
  The ads chosen for this study focus on two basic products, Persil washing powder and/or tablets and Kellogg's Corn Flakes (see Section 8.3). The products themselves may be regarded as 'being' the **broad content;** they have many similarities in terms of both function (each is inexpensive and 'consumable'/'usable' in the same domestic environment) and presumed 'beneficial consumer' (we all need to wear clean clothes and are all likely to eat some kind of breakfast). For present purposes they will therefore be

regarded as coming within a single controlled Field variable. (Lexical choices in relation to the particular product – washing powder as distinct from cereal – are discussed as appropriate; these are not, however, the object of study.) The **detailed content** for the two products across the Past and Present sets is approximately comparable, each being concerned with the social and/or practical benefits of use of the relevant product and the possible role of the women involved.

● **Tenor**:   The purposes as set out under Field are consistent with Gregory and Carroll's functional tenor (see Sections 1.1.6.1 to 1.1.6.2). Thus the principal participants in each set of ads are presumed to be the persuader, the advertiser (the would-be seller of the product), and the consumer (the potential buyer of that product).

● **Setting**:   The two sets of texts can, in broad terms, be regarded as having similar **spatial** parameters, to the extent that each set of texts has been produced by or on behalf of the would-be seller of the product in a given commercial/industrial setting and was or is expected to be viewed by the potential buyer in a given domestic setting.

8.2.2   The varying variables

The varying variables are considered to be:

● **Mode** – specifically **temporal Setting**:   The two sets of texts differ in their temporal settings, since each was produced, and expected to be received, in different chronological periods, the former (the Past set) in the middle of the twentieth century and the latter (the Present set) at the end of that century. The Past set were shown in black and white and the Present set in colour.

● **Tenor**:   Changes in **personal** tenor are likely to be brought about by the shift in temporal setting. Social changes which have taken place in Britain in the intervening forty to fifty years, especially changes in the role of women, will be reflected in the way the advertisements present their message to the consumer.

8.3   Description of the data

The data consists of transcripts and visual descriptions of a total of six television advertisements. Two represent the Past (one each for Persil washing powder and Kellogg's Corn Flakes respectively) and four represent the Present (three for Persil Tablets (presumed to be essentially the same powder but in tablet form) and one for Kellogg's Corn Flakes).

The collection of the data has a rather complicated history. The two Past ads were extracted from a BBC2 programme called *Washes Whiter*, an extensive survey of British television advertising broadcast in 1990. (The names attached to them, 'Woman Alone' and 'Executive', are as given in the television programme.) They were chosen for this study partly on the practical grounds that they were shown in their entirety rather than in the truncated, illustrative, form adopted for some of the advertisements cited, and partly because Persil and Kellogg's are consumer products with a wide popular appeal which are still regularly advertised. Two of the four Present ads were chosen from extensive videotape recordings made during October and November 1998 on a relatively haphazard basis. This was a time-consuming, and rather tedious, procedure, though I was grateful to receive some valuable guidance at one stage from the Sales Administration Director at Carlton Television, Nottingham, on the approximate dates and times on which suitably 'matching' products were likely to be advertised. The remaining two Present ads were obtained during a supplementary recording session in September 2000. (The names given to the four Present texts are fairly transparent labels chosen by me.)

Each text presents a description of the visual and musical elements of the particular ad in the left-hand column, numbered in sequence of occurrence. Written contributions are included with the visual elements and are shown in square brackets, thus: [Persil]. (No attempt has been made to reproduce the size or appearance of the written text.) The transcribed spoken contributions which are relevant to a particular shot or 'scene' (which may perhaps be very loosely linked to Hymes's 'scene' – see Section 1.1.6.4) are placed alongside in the right-hand column, numbered according to their own sequence. Transcription conventions are as set out in Section 1.2.5. The approach adopted is an attempt to give as accurate a word-picture as possible of the overall action of the advertisement, and to overcome at least some of the difficulties discussed by Cook (2001: 42–4) in the presentation of multi-media advertising. (It appears that Leech, whose work features significantly in this chapter, had access to at least some advertisement production scripts (1966: 39) in arriving at his own mode of presentation.) The six texts are:

Past Text 8.1   Persil, 1959, 'Woman Alone' (45 seconds)

1. Dreamy, romantic music which continues throughout

2. Woman in kitchen/dining room arranging dishes etc., smiling – picks up toy – close-up – looking thoughtful

   1. ((male voice)): this woman is alone – yet *not* alone

3. Daughter at school, husband at office – each wearing brilliant white blouse/shirt, in contrast to those around them

   ((same voice))
   even though her family may be apart *from* her they are still a part *of* her –

4. Close-up of woman's face – thoughtful

5. Husband's face at office – thoughtful – colleague silently compares whiteness of respective shirts

being judged by the care she takes of them – being judged by how clean and white she keeps their clothes – just as she is being judged by that same whiteness

6. Woman puts Persil packet back on shelf – close-up of packet: [New Persil washes even whiter]

7. Woman takes husband's arm – they go to child sitting at table arranging lettered bricks – parents bend over her on either side – join in

so Persil is part of *her* strength and *their* happiness – as a wife she uses Persil – as a mother she uses Persil

8. Close-up of packet: [New Persil washes even whiter]

Persil washes whiter

Past Text 8.2 Kellogg's Corn Flakes, 1956, 'Executive' (55 seconds)

1. Woman sees man off from home – he waves his newspaper to her

1. ((male voice)): this is how his wife sent him off to work this morning

good job she didn't see him two hours later

2. In the office – man at his desk listening to voice on telephone – secretary (female) stands watching (a little anxiously?)

2. Telephone voice (male): really Jones I can't wait any longer – you promised me that quote today

3. Jones: just a moment Mr Watkins ((covers mouthpiece)) ((to secretary)) where is that schedule

4. Secretary: you didn't complete Mr Jones

5. Telephone voice: I told you Jones I can't wait

3. Jones replaces receiver – close-up of telephone

6. ((male voice)): his wife's fault really – he's had almost nothing since supper twelve hours ago

4. He rubs his head, looking harassed

no proper breakfast – he said he hadn't time – what nonsense

5. Dissolve to close-up of toast in toast-rack, then cup of tea, then bowl of corn flakes

before his toast and tea give him a good big plate of corn flakes – delicious

6. Jones leaving for office again – smiling, waving

after a breakfast like that his wife needn't worry

7. Back in the office – Jones, wearing flower in buttonhole, holding two telephones, speaking into and then covering each mouthpiece – secretary sits at desk making notes as necessary

7. Jones ((into first telephone)): I'll fix you up Mr Watkins – yes just hold on ((into second)): I'll take that five hundred – yes today – goodbye ((replaces receiver)) ((returning to first)): that's ok Mr Watkins – not at all – goodbye ((replaces receiver))

8. Jones sits down and turns to secretary

well that's quite a good day's work – remind me to take some flowers home to my wife

8. Secretary: yes sir ((makes note))

9. Packet of [Kellogg's Corn Flakes] [Start <u>your</u> day the Kellogg's way]

9. ((male voice)): start *your* day the Kellogg's way ((word-by-word in synchronisation with Written))

Present Text 8.3   Persil Tablets, November 1998, 'Sports Kit Mother' (20 seconds)

1. Woman – seated – with two boys – all looking at camera – rather serious expressions ((photographed in muted colour))

1. ((male voice)): how well do these new Persil tablets clean then

2. Woman: they get the boys' sports things lovely and clean

2. Close-up of net bag containing tablets dropping amongst clothes in washing machine ((brilliant colour))

3. ((male voice)): but all washing powders do that don't they

3. Back to woman and boys ((again muted colour))

4. Woman: oh yeah – and how many dirty sports kits have you washed recently

4. (('upbeat' music)) – sports shirt blowing on line – blue sky ((brilliant colour))

5. Back to woman and boys – slightly different angle and closer up – woman has arm round younger boy, who scowls slightly at camera. ((muted colour)) [Persil tablets] ((red lettering))

5. ((female voice)): Persil's new tablets – a great wash – a great deal easier

6. Close-up of packet: [Persil Performance tablets] and net containing tablets ((brilliant colour)) – written text: [a great wash, a great deal easier]

Present Text 8.4   Persil Tablets, November 1998, 'Pregnant Woman' (20 seconds)

1. Heavily pregnant woman (seated) looking serious – female child standing next to her – both looking at camera – woman holding net of tablets in right hand ((muted colour))

1. ((male voice)): so they clean brilliantly

2. Woman: yeah

3. ((male voice)): they're dermatologically tested

4. Woman: mhmm

2. Close-up of net of tablets and right hand

5. ((male voice)): and the tablets give your clothes a (sort of) Persil soft-ness – what more could you ask for

6. Woman: some help with the ironing?

3. (('upbeat' music)) baby clothes blowing on line – blue sky – ((bright colours))

4. Close-up of woman and child half-smiling ((muted colour)) [Persil tablets] ((red lettering))

7. ((female voice)): Persil's new non-bio tablets – a great wash – a great deal easier

5. Close-up of packet: [Persil the original non-biological tablets] and net containing tablets ((brilliant colour)) – written text: [a great wash, a great deal easier]

Present Text 8.5   Persil Tablets, September 2000, 'Kidding Woman' (20 seconds)

1. Very attractive young woman looking at camera, frowning a little in concentration as she listens to his question ((muted colours))

   1. ((male voice)): why do you think Persil's Performance Tablets are such a great way to wash

   2. Woman: well – they don't just clean brilliantly

   3. ((male voice)): right

2. Close-up of net of tablets and right hand

   4. Woman: they leave clothes soft

   5. ((male voice)): uhuh

   6. Woman: they freshen

   7. ((male voice)): yeah

3. Back to woman

   8. Woman: and they do wonders for your love life

   9. ((male voice)): really

4. Woman shakes head and laughs

   10. Woman: no-o-o – only kidding

5. ((upbeat music))
   Line of washing blowing in the breeze photographed in brilliant colours

   11. ((female voice)): Persil Performance Tablets clean soft and fresh

6. Close-up of packet: [Persil], plus tablets and net bag. [clean, soft and fresh] then added beneath

Present Text 8.6   Kellogg's Corn Flakes, September 2000, 'Early Man' (30 seconds)

1. Dark primeval forest

2. Music – opening bars of soundtrack of *2001: A Space Odyssey* – music continues throughout

3. [645 BC]

4. [(Before Corn Flakes)] added beneath – [6] moves to left to leave space

5. A red [:] appears in the space and begins to flash, accompanied by loud beeps

6. Close-up of man's face: ape-like, unshaven, wild hair, blinking, vacant expression

1. Man: uggghh

2. ((female voice)): early man

3. Man: uggghh

4. ((female voice)): and it's not a pretty sight

7. He rolls out of bed, half-stands half-crouches by the bed – thumps the alarm clock to stop the beeps

– even the simplest of tasks seem beyond his primitive brain

8. He staggers to next room (bathroom?) – his Y-fronts on back to front

9. In the kitchen: he looks in cupboards, fridge etc. now with his shirt on but still with his Y-fronts back to front

the hunter-gatherer's first instinct is to find food

10. Upper cupboard door opens revealing [Kellogg's Corn Flakes] packet

11. Close-up of his face looking in cupboard, the light directed on his face (enlightenment demonstrated)

5. Man: uggghh

12. Close-up of bowl of corn flakes with milk splashing on to them [© Kellogg Co. 2000] ((very faint))

6. ((female voice)): particularly if it helps him to *wake up*

13. Close-up of him, still unkempt, eating (wolfing) corn flakes ((crunching sound))

14. Series of five images of him, moving from crouching (and scratching) figure in just underpants to ones with gradually-added clothes, ending with him standing erect, fully-

amazing — Neolithic to modern man in the time it takes to eat a bowl of Kellogg's Corn Flakes

dressed, smart, and ready for work (holding a
briefcase) ((compare anthropological charts
tracing stages in development of Man))

15. Man now sitting at table calmly eating more
    corn flakes – packet of [Kellogg's Corn Flakes]
    close to camera – now looking relaxed and
    confident, smartly dressed, with well-groomed
    hair, wearing a tie

16. Momentarily dark screen lights up to show
    packet of [Kellogg's Corn Flakes] ((packet
    photographed from below, so that it appears
    to be towering above viewer))

17. [Have you woken up to:] appears above   have you woken up to Kellogg's
    packet.   Corn Flakes
    Music builds to final triumphant conclusion

8.4   General expectations re the varying variables

A number of writers (for example, Goffman 1976; Williamson 1978; Geis
1982; Vestergaard and Schrøder 1985; Cook 2001) have examined the relationship between advertising and the perceived role of women. Vestergaard
and Schrøder (1985: 79–81 – 'V&S'), for example, discuss some of the ways
images of domesticity have been represented in advertising. Women have been
targeted in terms of 'their duties', and their shortcomings and inadequacies
exposed in terms of fulfilling the functions of a 'good wife and mother':

> The problems of the family, frequently socially determined, are thus individual-
> ized, and incipient despair is converted into a consumption-directed effort, which
> is allegedly capable of reinstating the agreement between the ideal image and
> experienced life.   (1985: 79)

V&S contrast the mid-1950s focus on women's role as exclusively serving
husband and family's needs with the broader perspective adopted in later
advertising, where a woman's multiple roles are acknowledged – including the
possibility that she might do paid work outside the home. They note,
however, that in spite of this a woman will remain responsible for household
chores – thus providing a further market opportunity.

Cook too (2001: 140–1) focuses on a woman's domestic role when he
analyses in detail a magazine advertisement for Sunny Delight fruit juice. He
shows the way grammatical parallelism (compare Section 6.10) can be used to
give a dual perspective: woman as 'a Good Mother' and woman as 'a Great
Mom'. He draws the conclusion that in the first perspective 'being a mother is

a position in society; in the second, it is a relationship with one's child(ren)' (2001: 141).

These claims suggest that Past Text 8.1 (with its woman protagonist happily fulfilled in her sole role as a supportive wife and mother – with the aid of Persil) and Past Text 8.2 (with its wife learning the error of her ways thanks to Kellogg's Corn Flakes) will constitute a promising basis for this study. The two texts are excellent instances of the 'idyllic' (V&S: 80) view of domesticity apparently expected to be held by – and of course created by – women, through which they will be rewarded with 'some sort of emotional satisfaction' (Packard 1960: 131). The Present Texts (8.3 to 8.6) offer potentially useful contrasts in showing different facets of women's lives now and enabling an exploration of how far things might have changed. If (as both intuition and others' claims suggest) there have been changes in the way that women are regarded in specific domestic circumstances – that is, in the washing of clothes and the providing of an adequate breakfast – how might these changes be manifested, and how do the relevant messages appear to be being created and conveyed?

8.5 Specific areas of enquiry

In the circumstances it was decided to approach the data with the following questions:

- How does the particular message appear to be presented in each ad?
- Are there any discernible patterns across (sets of) texts?
- How are gender roles assigned in each ad?
- Are there any discernible patterns in such assignment?
- What do the overall findings suggest about the potential consumer being addressed?
- What appear to be the differences (if any) between Past and Present texts?

In order to try to answer these questions it is necessary to examine in some detail the potentially multi-layered character of the discourse represented by each individual advertisement (Cook 2001: 18). A framework for such an analysis is presented in the following section.

8.6 The framework for the study

8.6.1 Leech and the advertising situation

As long ago as 1966, Leech presented a framework for a linguistic description of 'the advertising situation' which has proved to be a powerful tool for identifying and accounting for a range of types of advertisements, particularly television advertisements. His framework, with some modifications, has been used with my students over many years, and it forms the basis for the approach adopted in this chapter. (Cook agrees that 'Some of the earliest academic analyses of advertising are still well worth reading' (2001: 24), and he particularly recommends Leech 1966.)

The foundation of Leech's approach is his concept of primary and secondary situations, with their corresponding primary and secondary participants. The primary situation of an ad involves an advertiser and a consumer (as primary participants), the purpose of the ad being the sale of a given product by the former to the latter. In very simplistic terms, a message with that aim is directed by the advertiser (the initiator of the message) to the consumer (the recipient of the message). The advertiser may appear to be appealing to the consumer directly, typically by the use of a disembodied and anonymous 'voice-over' (see below) which gives explicit signals that it is addressing the consumer directly (for example, *start your day the Kellogg's way*). This is characterised by Leech as 'Direct Address' advertising (1966: 34–5).

Very often, however, the message to the consumer is much less starkly delivered, being mediated in some way. Such an advertisement will introduce Leech's 'secondary participants', and it is <u>they</u> who convey the desired message to the consumer. A 'secondary situation' is thus created within the primary situation, one of 'Indirect Address'. In this situation the consumer may be addressed via a monologue produced by a range of secondary participants such as 'real' celebrities, so-called 'ordinary housewives' or wholly fictional characters – all of whom speak in support of the product. Alternatively, the same kinds of secondary participants may appear in a form of dramatised dialogue with one another, with the product's merits being more indirectly extolled for the consumer's benefit (the consumer having the status of 'spectator' – 1966: 50). Leech makes the following interesting observation about the status of a visible participant in the context of Indirect versus Direct Address:

> Whenever a speaker appears on the television screen in a commercial, we may take it that he [*sic*] is identifiable as an individual personality, and speaks in his own right as a secondary participant. There are consequently only two ways in which direct address copy may be transmitted in commercials: by SUPERS (printed messages superimposed on the screen), and by COMMENTARIES spoken off the screen. In the script, the speaker of commentaries is variously designated 'commentator', 'announcer' and 'voice over'. Nothing could better symbolise the idea of the 'hidden persuader' than this anonymous, cajoling voice which invades the privacy of countless homes. (1966: 37)

Many advertisements in fact use a mixture of Indirect and Direct Address, as Leech shows in his transcript of a commercial for Polo Mints (1966: 35–6). Following an extended dialogue between secondary participants ('Interviewer' and 'Girl') about the special delights of Polos, there is a return to the 'primary situation'. A commentator's voice produces typical 'advertisingese' (1966: 46), in this instance stating the price and quoting the product slogan: *Polo's only 2d. Polo the mint with the hole* (1966: 36).

Leech's book is in fact devoted principally to the linguistic characteristics of

Direct Address advertising, as he makes clear (1966: 38). However, he makes many insightful observations on the ways that <u>both</u> types of Address are manifested. All of these appear to be still highly relevant and topical, and they are drawn on, as appropriate, at the analysis stage – see Sections 8.8 to 8.11 below. Indeed, one valuable aspect of the current study is that it presents an opportunity to explore how far Leech's 1966 framework continues to account for today's advertising texts.

8.6.2 Participant roles in the advertising situation

The status and roles of different participants in any discourse situation have been considered in each chapter of this book via specification of controlled and varying variables. In Chapter 5 a primary focus of attention was the effect of context in bringing about shifts and permutations of particular participant roles at discourse level – Speaker/Addressor, Addressee and Hearer/Auditor (see Sections 5.5.2 and 5.6.2). This subsection uses some of the concepts introduced in Chapter 5 (which in turn drew on Hymes 1994, as summarised in Section 1.1.5) to identify and define the participant roles which are most useful for present purposes and in the specific context of the advertising situation. It will then bring these together with the Leech concepts introduced in Section 8.6.1 in order to present a revised overall framework to be used in this study (see Section 8.6.3).

Both Leech (1966: 33–4) and Cook (2001: 180–2) acknowledge the shadowy and multifarious nature of the individuals and/or institutions likely to feature as 'primary participants' in a television advertising situation, whether as senders or receivers of a given message. 'Advertiser' in particular must subsume manufacturer, advertising agency and copywriters, actors and producers, and so on. No single identifiable 'voice', therefore, can be presumed to be speaking as 'the advertiser' in a television ad. Nevertheless, it will be convenient for present purposes to go along with Leech (1966: 34) in regarding the Speaker in Direct Address situations as 'being' the ultimate initiator of the message – that is, as being the 'advertiser'. Similarly, no precisely identifiable consumer can be pinpointed with certainty as the intended recipient (or Addressee) of a specific advertising message. An exploration of this very area is, indeed, one of the aims of this study – see Section 8.14.

With an Indirect Address situation the position is rather less complicated, at least so far as secondary participants and their discourse roles are concerned. The 'secondary situation' monologues and dialogues which Leech describes are entirely artificial constructions, and this is, presumably, accepted (at least tacitly) by the viewer/consumer. Secondary participants (whether 'real' celebrities or entirely fictional creations) perform their different discourse roles in accordance with a required script, acting as Speaker (in monologues) or alternating Speaker and Addressee roles (in dialogues). The consumer, on the other hand, remains unspecifiable: s/he is assigned the role of Addressee (of a monologue) or Hearer/Auditor (of a dialogue).

The choice of monologue or dialogue within Indirect Address situations is, however, likely to influence the form in which the particular message is expressed:

> The dialogue situation, in which secondary participants address one another, is still further removed from the primary situation than is monologue, and its language has accordingly a still more distant affinity to the language of direct address. (1966: 50)

Leech thus appears to be claiming that there will be some kind of progression from 'direct address' language, through indirect-monologue, to indirect-dialogue, in terms of the degree to which 'unrealistic sales talk' (1966: 51–2) is tolerable.

More immediately, however, his claim has interesting implications for the specification of participant roles in the final overall descriptive framework, particularly in the light of Bell's (1984, 1997) theories about 'audience design' (see Section 5.5.2). In a 1991 account, in fact, Bell considers the different roles immanent in the mass media audience, particularly for advertising. Bell himself draws on Leech (1966: 63) in seeing commercials as being implicitly or explicitly addressed to a specific section of the population (Bell 1991: 93). This 'specific section' will be the 'envisaged addressee' (compare Fairclough's 'ideal reader'; see Section 3.2.2), and the form and style of the message will be designed to target it/them. In Leech's terms, such an addressee would be viewed as a primary participant, almost certainly in a primary (Direct Address) situation, though Bell does not actually use or discuss such terms. He does, however, refer a little later to the potential for 'audience embedding' and the need for 'a dual set of roles' (1991: 95) in mass communication.

A development of that insight would seem, therefore, to be consonant with Leech's characterisation of the different 'audience' roles within an Indirect Address situation – that is, the consumer as addressee in a monologue situation (1966: 45) and as spectator in a dialogue situation (1966: 50). The latter role appears to coincide to some extent with Bell's definitions of 'auditor' – 'present but not directly addressed . . . known and ratified but not addressed' (1991: 91) and 'expected but not targeted' (1991: 92), and its effect on language style at the 'local' discourse level would be likely to support this view. The presence of a secondary participant <u>addressee</u> within a dialogue, however, may well be indicated explicitly, for example by the use of a question or the pronoun *you* (see Section 5.6.2), and something similar might in fact be found within a monologue addressing the (primary participant) consumer (Leech 1966: 46). In contrast, it would be unusual to find within a dialogue any comparably explicit linguistic signalling of the presence of the consumer in the role of <u>auditor</u> (though the exercising of what Leech refers to as 'theatrical licence' (1966: 55) is always a possibility).

It should always be remembered, however, that the consumer is the individual ultimately being 'targeted', and the advertisement overall (and the dialogue/s within it) will be designed to reach, appeal to, impress, activate that consumer, even though not explicitly. On this reading, it would seem to be both desirable and possible to redefine very slightly Bell's valuable role of

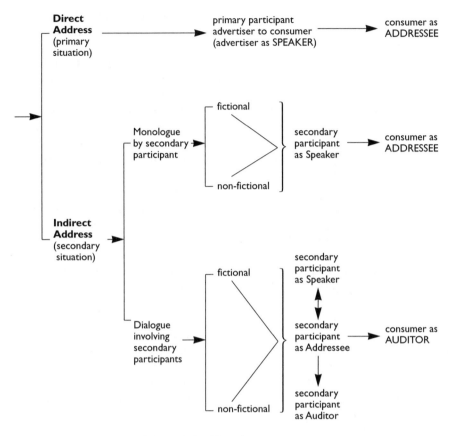

Figure 8.1 The advertising situation
(Categories based on and developed from Leech (1966: 34–8) and drawing on insights and
roles outlined in Bell (1984: 158–61; 1997: 246–7; 1991: 90–7).)

'auditor' when assigned to a primary participant in an advertising situation
(that is, to the consumer). The proposed redefinition of 'auditor' would be:
an audience who is <u>envisaged</u> but not <u>explicitly</u> targeted. The role as redefined
has, therefore, been incorporated into the revised descriptive framework set
out in Section 8.6.3.

8.6.3 Modified and rationalised framework for this study

Figure 8.1 represents an attempt to bring together, in a formalised way, the
concepts introduced and modified in the preceding subsections to create a
framework for describing the ads used in this study. Each contribution (or,
where appropriate, each utterance <u>within</u> a contribution) in each text can be
examined against this framework and the following can be identified:

- its address situation;
- the relevant participant role/s which are being assigned.

('Utterance' will, of course, include the use of written language. See also Section 1.2.5 for definitions of 'utterance' and 'contribution' as used throughout this book.)

As will be apparent, the framework in Figure 8.1 is founded on Leech (1966), particularly his concepts of Direct and Indirect Address and primary and secondary situations and their respective participants. However, it tries to arrive at a more systematic categorisation of the different participant roles which are operating within the different situations by incorporating specifically defined discourse roles as identified by Hymes (1994) and Bell (1984, 1997, 1991). The hierarchical ordering denoted by the terms primary and secondary situation is indicated by the use of upper-case lettering for roles within the primary situation (SPEAKER, ADDRESSEE, AUDITOR) and upper- and lower-case for those within the secondary situation (Speaker, Addressee, Auditor).

The different terms used within Figure 8.1 are in the main transparent or have already been introduced and defined. These will not, therefore, be repeated here. Confirmation and clarification of the way some of the terms are being used may, however, be helpful:

- 'advertiser' incorporates all the various elements mentioned in Section 8.6.2 above, including manufacturer, advertising agency and so on.

- 'consumer' is the presumed viewer, the ultimate purchaser (or instigator of the purchase) of the product. It is acknowledged that the person who earns, provides and/or actually hands over the money (for example a spouse or parent of either sex) may <u>not</u> be the person who is required to be <u>persuaded</u> by any advertisement.

- 'SPEAKER' will subsume Hymes's Addressor and will include the producer of written text, including that displayed on the packet containing the product.

8.7   Method and presentation of analysis

The analysis was carried out in two broad stages. Each utterance (spoken and written) in each text was analysed according to the situational framework presented in Section 8.6.3 and designated in terms of:

- situation, shown in bold (**Direct** or **Indirect Address**);
- type of situation within **Indirect Address** (Monologue or Dialogue);
- different participants and roles (for example, primary participant (advertiser) as SPEAKER, or secondary participant (Woman) alternating as Addressee and Speaker).

Both spoken and written contributions have been presented under their relevant **Address** situation, with sequences of **Indirect Address** being indented to indicate their secondary, or 'embedded', status. Where different parts of a contribution are considered to be being directed at identifiably different

Addressee/s these have been analysed as separate utterances occurring within the same contribution (compare Section 5.7.2). The analysed texts, Past Texts 8.1A and 8.2A and Present Texts 8.3A to 8.6A respectively, will be found in Appendix 1.7.

A commentary was prepared for each text, identifying what seem to be the most significant linguistic features in the presentation of the particular message (including aspects of Mode choice) and relating these to the claims and insights of others where appropriate, principally those of Leech (1966) and Cook (2001). The situational analysis (which is based only on the <u>linguistic</u> contributions in each text) was examined in conjunction with the text's visual and musical elements, in order to arrive at an overall grasp of what seems to be 'going on' in each ad. Reference is made to specific material in a specific text (for example 'Past 8.1/A', 'Present 8.5/A') via use of the relevant spoken (SC) and/or visual (C) contribution number (for example SC.3, V.5). Illustrative citations will therefore be made by reference to <u>both</u> analysed <u>and</u> 'plain' texts (the latter incorporating visual elements), as appropriate.

The detailed results of these complementary approaches are presented in Sections 8.8 to 8.11.

8.8 Presentation of results: Past Text 8.1/A, Persil, 1959

The situation in the analysed Past 8.1A, 'Woman Alone', is wholly that of Direct Address. The primary participants are the advertiser (realised by an anonymous and unidentifiable narrative voice – the voice-over) and the consumer. There is no explicit linguistic manifestation of the presence of the ADDRESSEE via any kind of second-person reference such as pronoun choice (see Section 6.6.1) or interrogative or imperative mood choice realising a question or command (see Section 5.6.2 and also Leech 1966: 110–16). All pronouns are in the third person (*her, she* etc.) and all clauses are either declarative (*this woman is alone*) or moodless (*yet not alone*).

The very first word of the narrative, however, is the demonstrative determiner *this*, which is designed to 'point to' (that is, draw the attention of the viewer to) the woman being portrayed in the ad. (Leech, 1966: 41, notes the prominence of such items in direct address advertising.) *This* is thus being used as an exophoric deictic item (see Section 5.6.1), linking linguistic and visual text and, significantly for current purposes, taking for granted the common situation shared by SPEAKER and ADDRESSEE.

The narrator observes, and invites us to observe, characters performing appropriately in support of the narration. They are not presented as communicating in any way with the viewer, and therefore in Leech's terms no explicit secondary participants intervene. However, their expressions and behaviour illustrate some kind of silent secondary situation which the viewer is invited to take part in. This is examined in some detail below.

There is some small use of written language via the intermittent presentation of the Persil packet (the 'pack shot'; Leech 1966: 42), with its display of the product name incorporated in an expansion of the traditional Persil slogan: [new Persil washes even whiter] (V.6, V.8). This appears to be used to 'punctuate' the narration at significant points – in conjunction with the use of the lexical items *whiteness* and *whiter*, thus underlining the link between the product and this apparently highly desirable quality.

The bulk of the copy, however, consists of spoken text placed under the 'spoken as if not written' dimension (see Section 8.2.1 and Figure 1.1). The speech represented is that of a single speaker (as one continuous contribution) which shows signs of Gregory and Carroll's (1978: 40–3) 'monologuing', that is, speech characteristic of 'educated' speakers, such as the narrator is presented as being. Thus 'there are elements of preparation and repetition in their speaking performances which give them some of the characteristics of written modes' (1978: 41). There is no attempt to give an impression of the narrator producing informal spontaneous speech. The language is quite obviously carefully crafted, creating balanced rhetorical effects in its chosen grammatical and stress patternings (compare Section 6.10) and, in particular, the schematic device of 'antithesis' described by Cockcroft and Cockcroft (1992: 125–6). Thus: *alone – yet not alone; apart from her . . . still a part of her; her strength and their happiness; as a wife . . . as a mother.* Both of the last two juxtapositions also incorporate the brand name *Persil.*

The 'traditional' slogan *Persil washes whiter* rounds off the ad. The use of a closing slogan is very characteristic of Direct Address advertising (see, for example, the Polo Mint ad referred to in Section 8.6.1). It is designed to get over the key parts of the message and in potentially memorable form – it is the 'language of pure salesmanship' (Leech 1966: 45). As Leech notes, such slogans make frequent use of 'unqualified comparatives' (1966: 31), for example *whiter* here. He goes on to observe (1966: 160–1), that such a use is so vague as to be virtually meaningless, citing Quirk's cutting comment:

> whiter than *what* we must ask. Whiter than when washed under precisely similar conditions using every other relevant product on the market? Or merely whiter than when they are washed in cold water without soap? Or perhaps, indeed, just whiter than they were before they were washed?' (Quirk 1962: 223)

As indicated above, the woman and the family whom we are invited to observe do not fit easily into the framework as presented in Section 8.6.3. They cannot be regarded as 'true' secondary participants in Leech's terms since they are actually required to say nothing at all, either to the consumer or to each other. However, they are a necessary resource in providing support for the Direct Address commentary. (As Cook stresses (2001: 54), it is important that the critical viewer should learn 'to argue with pictures' (McLuhan 1964: 246) and not just focus on the 'literal' meaning of copy.)

Past 8.1, therefore, shows the woman looking thoughtful in the midst of her domestic chores (V.2), and we are then given visual access to those thoughts. This shows some analogical connection with Leech's illustration of a Crackerbarrel cheese ad which purports to represent the 'audible thoughts' of a woman in a supermarket (1966: 55). Thus an approximation of a soundless secondary situation is constructed through the consciousness of a pseudo-'secondary participant' – the woman displayed to us – *this woman*. We see her daughter and husband outshining (literally) their fellow pupils/workers (V.3), thus (she hopes) reflecting credit on her for *the care she takes of them*. We also see her husband's thoughtful face and imagine his thoughts about her (and even his colleague's thoughts about her) (V.5), including presumably their (positive) 'judgements' of her (. . . *she is being judged* . . .). Both sets of thoughts are shown to be vindicated at V.7, where husband and wife are seen to be united as a couple and also fully supportive of their (clever) daughter: the visual evidence reinforcing and being reinforced by a progression in the pronouns used at this point from the singular *her* (*strength*) to the plural *their* (*happiness*). (See Section 6.8 for progression of pronoun choice, and also Cook's (2001: 112–18) discussion of a Suburu car magazine ad and the effects of use of *his, hers, theirs.*)

8.9 Presentation of results: Past Text 8.2/A, Kellogg's Corn Flakes, 1956

The situation in Past 8.2A, 'Executive', involves three sequences of Direct Address (consisting of SC.1, 6 and 9) interspersed with two sequences of Indirect Address (SC.2–5 and 7–8). The SPEAKER is an unseen narrator/voice-over (realising the advertiser), who invites the ADDRESSEE (the viewer/consumer) to observe the behaviour and conversations of several secondary participants (via the illustrative Indirect Address sequences) in conveying a particular message. (Contrast the 'soundless' secondary situation discussed in Section 8.8.) The basic aim of the message is to demonstrate the 'before and after' effects of a breakfast which includes Kellogg's Corn Flakes.

8.9.1 Past Text 8.2/A: Direct Address

Several linguistic features typical of Direct Address situations are apparent. Exophoric deictic items open the advertisement (compare Past 8.1/A): *this is how his wife sent him off to work this morning* (SC.1). These set the scene for the whole ad by directing the ADDRESSEE's attention towards the visual elements: the demonstrative pronoun *this* supported by the temporal marker *this morning* which assumes that the viewer and the world being observed share the same time reference (see Section 5.6.1).

In the closing sequence the narrative voice-over produces the product slogan, again typical of the Direct Address situation, *start your day the Kellogg's way* (SC.10). Here there are unambiguous markers of the viewer's ADDRESSEE status since the slogan is realised by an imperative structure which also incorporates the possessive form of the second person pronoun *you*. The slogan reinforces and is reinforced by its word-by-word synchronisation with the same written text in conjunction with the 'pack shot' displaying the product name. All of these features thus conform to expectations for a Direct Address situation.

The central Direct Address sequence, however, (the extended SC.6) introduces some ambiguities. The narrator's initial comment, *his wife's fault really*, represents a reflection on the unfortunate events illustrated in the dramatised dialogue (SC.2–5) – the effects of a 'no Kellogg's' situation – and he goes on to suggest a solution. This is expressed by the use of the base form of the verb *give* in the following: *before his toast and tea give him a good big plate of corn flakes.* It would be possible to regard *give* here as an imperative form being used to realise a suggestion directed at the (neglectful) wife, though the use of a third person pronoun immediately afterwards (*his wife needn't worry*) scarcely supports this interpretation. Alternatively, *give* could be regarded as being directed at the ADDRESSEE, though this would strike a decidedly odd note overall – given that the viewer could hardly in any sense be directly addressed as Mr Jones's wife. (Again, the subsequent use of *his wife* would rule out such an interpretation.)

This use of *give* may, in fact, be deliberately indeterminate and ambiguous, perhaps as an attempt to represent some kind of 'quoted' imperative or a reduced 'base' form indicating 'situational ellipsis' (Quirk et al. 1985: 895–6), to convey something like *(she should) give him.* . . . Such an aim would be consistent with what seems to be an overall attempt by the copywriter to create the impression of 'monologuing' speech – but this time at the spontaneous and colloquial – even 'conversational' – end of the cline suggested by Gregory and Carroll (1978: 40). There are several uses of contractions (Quirk et al. 1985: 1595–7) – *didn't* (SC.1), *hadn't, needn't* (SC.6), situational ellipsis (see above) – *(it's a) good job* . . . (SC.1) *(it's) his wife's fault, really...(he's had) no proper breakfast* . . . (SC.6) as well as the conversational 'hedge' (see Section 4.8) *really* (SC.6). (This therefore contrasts markedly with the carefully constructed, rhetorical, style assigned to the narrator in Past 8.1.)

Of course, this very ambiguity – in terms of whether or not an imperative is being used and, if so, who is the designated Addressee (or ADDRESSEE) – fulfils the valuable function of blurring the distinction between Indirect and Direct Address situations, that is, between the unreal world portrayed in the advertisement and the real world in which the viewer observes/receives it. (See Cook, 2001: 181, on a kind of elliptical bridging of the gap between characters and receivers.) At this point, therefore, the SPEAKER appears to extend the boundaries of the narration about Mr Jones and his world and may (or may not) be bringing the viewer – the ADDRESSEE – into it. It seems that somehow the message does get through to Mr Jones's wife – hence his transformation after a 'proper breakfast' – but how it does so is not shown to the viewer. (Perhaps Mrs Jones watches television ads.) The intriguing use of the simple word *give* in the middle of SC.6 raises questions about how advertisers may try to smuggle in their message, and how subtly the 'identification' Leech refers to (1966: 55) may be encouraged and indeed constructed.

8.9.2   Past Text 8.2/A: Indirect Address

The two interspersed sequences involving Indirect Address are presented in the form of apparently spontaneous Dialogues between Jones and clients and

Jones and his secretary (SC.2–5 and 7–8). They are more straightforward in situational analysis terms, in that the secondary participants are shown to alternate the roles of Speaker, Addressee and Auditor, as appropriate. For example, while Jones is addressing clients the secretary is acting as Auditor as she reacts rather anxiously (V.2) or makes notes (V.7). It will be noted, too, that on two occasions Jones addresses utterances to different Addressees within the same contribution – to Watkins and to his secretary in SC.3, and to Watkins, another client and his secretary in SC.7. (The viewer's situational role throughout both Indirect Address sequences is, of course, as AUDITOR.)

The mini-dramas are enacted in Gregory and Carroll's 'conversing' mode, and in a style consistent with the very traditional social roles expected in an office environment of the 1950s. There is a male boss, with a female secretary in attendance, dealing with a male client, and there is an attempt to represent a type of interaction which is in keeping with the social status, sex and age of the secondary participants (Leech 1966: 49). An appropriately colloquial style is suggested by the frequent use of contractions by all the secondary participants – *can't* (SC.2), *didn't* (SC.4), *I'll* and *that's* (SC.7) – and even a degree of informality – *fix you up, ok* (SC.7).

In spite of such approximations of informality, however, the necessary status differences are observed, for example by the use of formal titles, with the appropriate deference being shown in that particular environment. Thus there is 'non-reciprocity' in the use of address terms between these secondary participants (see Holmes 2001: 269–73, drawing on Laver 1981: 297). Jones addresses the client as *Mr Watkins* (SC.3, 7) but receives *Jones* in return (SC.2, 5). Jones receives *Mr Jones* (SC.4) and *sir* (SC.8) from his secretary, but does not use any form of address to her, merely issuing a bald wh-question *where is that schedule* (SC.3) and a request/command realised by a similarly bald imperative *remind me . . .* (SC.7).

As the Dialogues show, however, 'before Kellogg's' Jones is not fulfilling the working role expected of him: the client is annoyed (SC.2) and the secretary is looking anxious (V.2) and she has to remind Jones that he *didn't complete* an important task (SC.4). 'After Kellogg's' Jones is, of course, transformed and so is his working life. He successfully juggles the various demands made on him (including negotiating two telephone conversations simultaneously) and his secretary performs her appropriate tasks whether or not she is explicitly asked to do so (V.7 and SC.7–8). It should be noted that there is no mention of the product <u>at all</u> by a secondary participant (this is reserved for the final Direct Address sequence) thus avoiding the risk of compromising their authenticity by having them engage in what Leech calls 'the embarrassment of unrealistic sales talk' (1966: 51–2).

The degree of dramatic realism involved in these Indirect Address Dialogue sequences has both social and linguistic interest, and it is considered again in Section 8.13. In the meantime, the exploration of the use of *give* in the Direct Address situation may provide some degree of support for Leech's assertion that the language of Direct (as distinct from Indirect) Address advertising is likely to be 'more rewarding to study' (1966: 38). This point is returned to in Section 8.15.

8.10 Presentation of results: Present Texts 8.3/A to 8.5/A, Persil Tablets, 1998 and 2000

The three Persil Tablets texts, 'Sports Kit Mother', Pregnant Woman' and 'Kidding Woman', have many basic features in common but also a number of interesting and potentially significant differences. They are, therefore, taken as a group, for economy of discussion and also to allow their similarities and differences to be more clearly demonstrated.

It will be seen from both analysed and plain texts that these three advertising situations are constructed in very similar ways indeed:

- Each begins with an Indirect Address sequence representing a Dialogue between two secondary participants – an unseen male interviewer and a woman who addresses all her contributions to camera.

- In each case the Dialogue suggests that this is the continuation of an interview which is ongoing.

- Each ad makes use of colour variation and music for structuring purposes and to underline its message.

- Each includes at some point visual illustration of the tablets themselves (and the net bag in which they are to be used) which presumably is intended to underline the distinction between Persil Tablets and traditional Persil powder.

- Each shows only the right hand of the woman. The left hand, with its possible clue to marital status is kept carefully out of shot. (This receives further consideration in Section 8.14.)

- Each closes with a Direct Address sequence which uses a pack shot and a written slogan, accompanied by a female voice-over speaking (a version of) product name-plus-slogan.

The most notable of these common features, or **themes**, will be described and discussed in turn. Those **variations** which seem to be the most significant will then be identified.

8.10.1 Present Texts 8.3/A to 8.5/A: themes

(a) Indirect Address: Leech discusses Indirect Address situations such as are used here, involving Dialogue in the form of an interview with a so-called 'ordinary consumer' (1966: 53). The most striking feature of the current ads, however, is that the male interviewer is heard but unseen: the viewer sees only the female participant, and through the interviewer's eyes. The viewer, who as primary participant is in fact AUDITOR, is the recipient of the woman's eye contact. The boundaries between the (secondary participant) interviewer and the (primary participant) viewer have thus become blurred. There is little or no contextualising or 'distancing' space around this dialogue in which the viewer can safely or easily act as AUDITOR. The viewer appears to be being

drawn into participation in and identification with the (male) interviewer's gaze, and by extension perhaps with the words he uses: AUDITOR is required almost to 'become' Addressee.

This represents a rather different 'take' on Leech's suggestion that the viewer is being invited to identify with a secondary participant via access to her audible thoughts and to 'see the product through her eyes' (1966: 55). Here we seem to be asked literally to see the 'ordinary consumer' (as embodied in the three different women) through the male interviewer's eyes. In each case the woman tends to take a rise out of the interviewer, though in rather different ways. (The implications of all of these different factors are considered in Section 8.14.)

(b) Direct Address: There is no explicit indication of an assigned ADDRESSEE via the use of a second person pronoun or other marker such as mood choice. Each text in fact chooses moodless structures, or what Leech calls 'disjunctive grammar' (1966: 58), here only noun phrases and adjective phrases, which give (a version of) the product name and a slogan declaring its claimed attributes. However, the presentation of both product and slogan via the use of 'supers' and also a completely 'unanchored' and anonymous voice-over (which belongs to neither of the secondary participants) confirms its 'conventional' Direct Address status (compare discussions in Sections 8.8 to 8.9).

(c) Colour and music: All of the scenes which show the woman interviewee are photographed in muted (sepia-type) colours. Full colour is reserved for the product and/or its (very positive) results: clean clothes blowing on the washing line.

The same 'upbeat' music is used to punctuate each text, marking off Indirect from Direct Address sequences. In each case it accompanies the scene showing the full-colour washing line.

8.10.2   Present Texts 8.3/A to 8.5/A: variations on themes

The three ads show interesting variations on the themes summarised above. Each basic theme is therefore considered separately in order to identify where the main differences between individual texts occur and what these differences might suggest. The three texts will be referred to by their titles, and in abbreviated form as follows: 'Sports Kit Mother' (Present 8.3/A) – SKM; 'Pregnant Woman' (Present 8.4/A) – PW; 'Kidding Woman' (Present 8.5/A) – KW.

(a) Indirect Address: The three 'ordinary consumers' represent different facets of women and their roles and/or what their main demand of a washing powder might be at a particular stage of their lives. This seems to be reflected in the discourse form chosen for the different interviews and also in the particular emphasis adopted in both the Indirect and Direct Address copy.

Each interview is presented as part of a Dialogue which is already in progress (compare Leech 1966: 48). However, each woman is treated differently by the interviewer, and this is shown immediately by his opening utterance in each case.

- SKM is asked a wh-question *how well* . . . , ending in *then*, whose form appears designed to invite her to (continue to) extol the particular virtue of the product which most directly appeals to her, which she duly does.

- PW, on the other hand, is presented by the interviewer with a series of positive statements about the product (Labov's 'requests for confirmation' – 1978: 254), with which she continues to agree. It may be significant, given her pregnant condition, that his opening statement, with its *so* and *they*, indicates that she has already concurred.

- The pattern for KW is different again: the interviewer opens with a wh-question, *why* . . . which suggests she has already said that the product is *great* in some way, but the focus for this woman is on her thought processes: *why do you think*. . . . The woman then goes on to take him at his word and produce her own series of statements about what she thinks are the virtues of the product for her. The interviewer is reduced to merely giving 'minimal responses' (see Section 4.7.2) in support.

(b)   Direct Address: Variations in the way the Indirect Address interviews are represented are paralleled by variations in the type of tablets featured and the way the product is presented and/or spoken about in the Direct Address sequences. Thus, the final, silent, shot of SKM and boys displays a 'super' [Persil tablets] (SKM: V.5) and the voice-over presents the product as *Persil's new tablets* (SKM: SC.5). The pack shot, however, includes the word *Performance*, by displaying [Persil Performance tablets]. The slogan (both written and spoken) is *a great wash – a great deal easier,* offering the promise of at least some escape from the hard work which washing for active children involves.

PW is given the same super [Persil tablets] as SKW for her final, silent, shot (PW: V.4), and a pack shot in which [Persil Tablets] dominates ([the original non-biological] is included but in very small lettering), plus the slogan. In her case, however, the product is described by the voice-over as *Persil's new non-bio tablets* (SC.7), presumably to accord with PW's forthcoming baby's needs (see SC.3, 5). It will be noted that in both SKM and PW the word *new* (the most frequent adjective used in advertising – Leech 1966: 52) is used to characterise the product in the voice-over, both to underline the distinctiveness of the tablets and once again, presumably, to suggest a new solution – whether biological or non-biological – to an old familiar problem. (Unqualified comparatives of the kind used in Past 8.1/A are not used.)

Once again, the treatment of KW differs noticeably from that of the other two women. She is given no final, silent, shot at all (and no added opportunity for display of the product name), her slogan is completely different from the one used for SKM and PW, being *clean soft and fresh* (KW: SC.11), with its possible pun on *fresh*. Most notably too, while the pack shot displays only [Persil] (V.6) the voice-over produces *Persil Performance tablets*. This appears to highlight, and play on, the word *Performance*, whereas the 'performance' angle is kept very low-key for SKM and PW. For KW, of course, the performance implied is likely to be of a sexual nature (see SC.8). Thus the eschewing of *new* and the substitution of such flirtatious innuendo by the interviewee could itself be seen as demonstrating – even embodying – that very 'newness'.

(c)   Colour/visual variation: Each of the women is photographed in muted colour and all three start with serious expressions, with SKM and PW represented as being rather burdened by their domestic responsibilities. (The closing slogan suggests possible rescue.) KW's initial frown, however, shows her concentrating on the interviewer's question – actually doing the 'thinking' being asked of her – and, far from being overburdened, she is shown to have the energy and wit to tease and challenge her interviewer.

There are other, small, variations in the way the three women are treated in terms of colour shifts, but these seem to be less significant for current purposes.

8.11   Presentation of results: Present Text 8.6/A, Kellogg's Corn Flakes, 2000

Present 8.6A, 'Early Man', presents this ad as alternating sequences of three Indirect and three Direct Address situations. The Indirect Address sequences feature a single secondary participant as Speaker – the 'early man' of the title – whom the viewer observes evolving from a primitive state (before Corn Flakes) to a civilised one (after Corn Flakes). (The ad shows some parallels, therefore, with Past 8.2/A of 1956.)

The man is alone throughout, and his spoken contributions (one in each of the three sequences) consist only of appropriately primitive grunts (transcribed as *uggghh*). They are thus addressed to no one in particular – and in any case seem to be occurring before human communication has begun. In terms of the framework, however, the *uggghh*s have been considered to be operating within a secondary situation of (potential) 'Dialogue' rather than acting as a Monologue addressed to the viewer. The viewer, therefore, has been assigned the role of AUDITOR in these sequences.

This analysis would seem to be supported when the intervening sequences are considered. Here a female voice-over (which appears to be acting as SPEAKER) implicitly addresses the viewer (as ADDRESSEE) by commenting on the man's appearance and behaviour and using exophoric caption-type devices (compare Past 8.1/A and 8.2/A) which draw attention to the various scenes displayed, for example: *early man . . . and it's not a pretty sight* (SC.2, 4). This culminates in *amazing – Neolithic to modern man . . .* (SC.6), which accompanies the series of images reminiscent of an anthropological chart demonstrating the evolutionary stages from ape through *Homo erectus* to *Homo sapiens* (V.14). The same voice-over then segues into stereotypical Direct Address format, producing the slogan *have you woken up to Kellogg's Corn Flakes* (at the end of SC.6), which accompanies the corresponding written version and a pack shot. (The slogan, of course, chooses the explicit second person pronoun as well as a yes–no interrogative structure. It also puns on the connection between *early man* and *woken up*.) It seems clear, therefore, that each of these three sequences is indeed a Direct Address sequence.

The role assigned to the woman's voice, however, is not clear in every respect. There seems to be some blurring of the boundaries between Direct and Indirect Address in that the woman's narration does not show quite the anonymity and impersonality expected of the disembodied voice-over (Leech 1966: 37), even as modified in Past 8.2/A (see Section 8.9). Instead there are signs of the individual personality and credibility usually devised for secondary participants (1966: 49), even of a slight regional accent. The voice is describing ironically, even affectionately, the behaviour of a particular 'early man' while observing him in his natural habitat. An alternative analysis of Present 8.6 could in fact regard it as almost entirely an Indirect Address situation, having the form of a Monologue by an (unseen), presumably fictional, female secondary participant (as Speaker) commenting, with heavy though indulgent irony, on the early morning behaviour of a particular male creature (perhaps her partner), with further-embedded (illustrative) Indirect Address 'Dialogue' sequences of the kind already outlined. On this reading, and for the 'first-embedded' Indirect Address sequences, the viewer would, of course, be assigned the role of ADDRESSEE.

A problem with this analysis is that the abrupt movement by the 'same' woman into very clear and traditional Direct Address sales talk mode in the final stages would create a certain dissonance, even discomfort, in analytical terms (compare the 'embarrassment' referred to in Section 8.9). A simpler analysis, therefore, would maintain the Indirect/Direct alternations as originally proposed and regard the 'blurring' of participant roles as a deliberate creative act on the part of the copywriter. Thus an informal and humorous style has been created for the (female) persona representing the advertiser (acting as SPEAKER) in consequence of which any very clear distinction between the roles of Addressee and ADDRESSEE virtually disappears. (See the Kellogg's Corn Flakes (Past 8.2/A) discussion of *give* in Section 8.9 and possibly comparable blurring.)

Like the three Present Persil Texts 8.3/A to 8.5/A (see Section 8.10), this ad makes interesting use of combinations of visual, musical and spoken elements to punctuate, enhance and underline its message. Here, however, they seem to be even more complex and subtle. At different points visual composition is juxtaposed with sound, music and/or spoken text to create witty, often anachronistic, effects. Thus, in the opening stages, the dark primeval forest (V.1) is accompanied by the stirring and familiar music used for a decidedly futuristic film (V.2). The [645BC] is first transformed to [Before Corn Flakes] and then to a digital clock whose electronic alarm proceeds to beep (V.3–5), thus bringing 'early man' literally into the picture. This primitive creature can only deal with the beeping alarm by thumping it in cliché cave-man fashion (V.7).

Meanwhile, the man has produced his first sounds and has been formally introduced to the viewer (SC.1–4). His *uggghhs* might be regarded as being primitive indications of a future capacity for dialogic communication, though at this stage he is clearly shown to be incapable of practical tasks let alone discerning the purpose of the expression of articulated thought. (Berry's, 1989: 152, label 'externalised mental process' for speech (see Section 3.7.4) seems particularly apt here.) The woman's ironic and often punning commentary, with its anachronistic images, continues: *early man* becomes *the hunter–gatherer*, who is seen exploring a fully equipped modern (and spotless) kitchen. He appears to find the vital food by accident (*instinct?*), when a cupboard door opens, apparently all by itself, and reveals the Kellogg's Corn Flakes packet (V.10). The sight (with its visual pun on light dawning – V.11) produces his final *uggghh* (SC.5). This is the transitional moment, of course: the animal-like devouring of his first bowl of corn flakes (V.13) brings about his awakening (*helps him to wake up*) and starts the transformation (V.14), which is presumably reinforced by another helping of corn flakes at a subsequent, more civilised-looking, breakfast (V.15). Unsurprisingly, once the crouching and ape–like *early man* has woken up and become *modern man* he does not attempt a form of communication (speech) which would be regarded as inappropriate to his currently solitary state (V.15).

The most traditional, even stereotypical, form of Direct Address seems to be confined to the end of the final sequence – the close–up of the product packet in V.15 and, especially, the pack shot and the written and spoken versions of the slogan (V.16–17 and SC.6). Again, however, the choice of Mode is given an added role in taking up and building on earlier parts of the overall message. The SPEAKER continues to communicate with the viewer (the ADDRESSEE) via speech, but the written language that is now added is displayed to the viewer (V.16) in two distinctive ways: darkness gives way to light (compare V.10–11), and the source of that light – the Corn Flakes packet – is shown as elevated above the viewer. (Kress and van Leeuwen, 1996: 397, discuss the way an image may be viewed: 'a low angle makes [the subject] imposing and awesome'.) The viewer is thus placed in the lower position of *early man*, but may perhaps aspire to *wake up*, stand up and become *modern man* (compare V.14). The viewer is in fact made to experience – to participate in – the perception that the written language is truly an even more 'enlightened' and 'higher' form of communication than speech. The spoken reiteration of the slogan shows the viewer <u>both</u> the means to that end <u>and</u> the enjoyment of the reward: consumption of the product.

This may of course be an over–interpretation of the data, but it does seem that variations across and within the overall Mode dimension are being exploited in this ad to emphasise and enrich the message being conveyed. When combined with the other visual and aural strategies described they create a remarkably complex, subtle and hugely enjoyable television advertisement. The ad also shows both fascinating parallels and marked contrasts with the corresponding 1956 Kellogg's ad (Past 8.2/A) discussed in Section 8.9. These are considered again in Sections 8.12 and 8.13.

8.12 Summary of findings: types of Address – Past v. Present

Given the very small amount of data and the particular analytical approach adopted, quantitative results can serve only a limited purpose. Table 8.1 does, however, enable direct comparisons to be made between the six ads in terms of relative choice of Direct and Indirect Address in proportion to total words (spoken and written) in each case. Table 8.2 then groups Past and Present texts to give an overall comparison.

As Table 8.1 shows, both of the two Past texts use notably more words to present their message than any of the Present texts; they are also, of course, longer in terms of time (see 'plain' texts for respective running times). The Present texts make greater use of music and visual effects, including colour (not available to the Past texts) to get their messages over.

The proportions of words allocated to Direct v. Indirect Address across individual texts and Past v. Present show no very striking patterns. (All of the Indirect Address in the data was in the form of Dialogue: there were no instances of Monologue.) Table 8.2 does, however, show a tendency towards lesser Present use of Direct Address in comparison to Past (54.7 per cent compared with 68.4 per cent). This consequent preference for forms of Indirect Address may represent a movement away from the more obvious hard-sell approach. This tendency holds even when the almost 100 per cent proportion of Direct Address in Present 8.6A (see Table 8.1) is taken into account. The blurring of roles in this ad – see Section 8.11 – would therefore seem to be consistent with the general 'indirect' trend. The three Persil Tablets texts (Present 8.3A to 8.5A) give the clearest support for the trend – especially, and unsurprisingly perhaps, 'Kidding Woman' (Present 8.5A) which has over three-quarters Indirect Address (most of it allocated to the woman herself).

Table 8.1 Summary of findings: Direct v. Indirect Address in proportion to total words used in each text

	Total words	Direct Address		Indirect Address			
				Monologue		Dialogue	
		Number	%	Number	%	Number	%
8.1A	88	88	100				
8.2A	162	83	51.2			79	48.8
8.3A	60	22	36.7			38	63.3
8.4A	54	25	46.3			29	53.7
8.5A	53	12	22.6			41	77.4
8.6A	78*	75	96.2			3	3.8
	495	305	61.6			190	38.4

* The (very faint) copyright super in Present 8.6 (V.12) was excluded from both analysis and word count.

Table 8.2 Summary of findings: Direct v. Indirect Address – Past v. Present texts

| | Total words | Direct Address | | Indirect Address | | | |
| | | | | Monologue | | Dialogue | |
		Number	%	Number	%	Number	%
Past	250	171	68.4			79	31.6
Present	245	134	54.7			111	45.3
	495	305	61.6			190	38.4

The connections between types of Address and gender of participants are considered in Section 8.13.

8.13 Summary of findings: participants and gender – Past v. Present

Table 8.3 summarises the assignment of gender to each of the primary and secondary participants in each ad. Even though the amount of data is inevitably very limited, some interesting patterns emerge, the most notable being the shift from male to female for the voice of the primary participant as SPEAKER (that is, for the advertiser). Both of the Past ads (that is, both products) use male voices, whereas all four of the Present ads (both products) use female voices. The cajoling voice mentioned by Leech is now female, though in most cases it retains its total anonymity and impersonality.

The exception is the voice-over in 'Early Man' (Present 8.6/A). As the discussion in Section 8.11 suggests, the impression of an individual personality, with some kind of connection to the secondary participant, threatens to blur the distinction between primary and secondary situations. This represents, of course, a progression of the relatively informal style assigned to the voice-over in Past 8.2/A (see Section 8.9), but the injection of a sense of an individual personality is a notable change. (How far this is emphasised by the very fact

Table 8.3 Summary of participants and gender assignment in each ad

| | Total participants | Direct Address (primary participants) | Indirect Address (secondary participants) | | | |
| | | | Monologue | Dialogue | | |
			Participant 1	Participant 1	Participant 2	Participant 3
8.1A	1	M				
8.2A	4	M		M	M	F
8.3A	3	F		M	F	
8.4A	3	F		M	F	
8.5A	3	F		M	F	
8.6A	2	F		M		
Total	16	2M/4F		5M	1M/3F	1F

that the voice is female is hard to say.) The sense of a possible 'real woman', therefore, has some parallels with the creation of convincing 'ordinary consumers' as secondary participants (see below).

Of the total of ten secondary participants who make spoken contributions to the ads, six are male and only four are female, the allocation in the Past texts being two males to one female and in the Present texts four males to three females. On the face of it, therefore, there has been little change in the tendency to give males a greater share of attention. The Past texts are, however, notable in that the most significant woman (the wife) in each case is given no voice at all: she is seen but not heard, 'addressed' but not consulted. The one female voice actually heard is that of the obedient secretary in Past 8.2/A, and it may be significant that the <u>order</u> of roles in which she is represented is first as Auditor, then as Addressee and only then as Speaker. The analysis of the Present texts, however, has shown that there has been a marked change in the treatment of both male and female secondary participants. On this evidence men are no longer being treated as authority figures who require deference and/or care and cosseting by others (principally women). Men in the Present texts may eventually manage to feed themselves (8.6/A), though they tend to be regarded by women with irony, indulgence and a degree of humorous resignation – bordering on contempt – if they just don't seem to 'get it' (8.3/A to 8.6/A).

Women with families are still likely to carry the burden of responsibility for getting the washing done (see Section 8.4) and the ads show them accepting this: they want it to be done well and appropriately, which is where the product comes in (8.3/A to 8.4/A). However, a little flattery of the women is built in too: they are portrayed as spirited and independent-minded and ready to state what they need (in addition to the product of course), whether or not they are likely to get it (8.3/A to 8.4/A again). There is a limit to how far they are prepared to accept direction about this – especially perhaps from a man (contrast Past 8.1/A). The discourse pattern given to 'Pregnant Woman' (Present 8.4/A), however, suggests she has already conceded defeat in this particular aspect of the sex war (see Section 8.10.2): Persil Tablets may be her only salvation.

Women may, of course, be free of family responsibilities for whatever reason. They may, indeed, be truly independent and sexy with it (Present 8.5/A), and with a job of their own which means they leave their partner to get himself successfully off to work in the mornings (Present 8.6/A) (contrast Past 8.2/A). It seems, therefore, that all of the roles portrayed or implied by the secondary participants in the Present ads are intended to reinforce (and be reinforced by) the knowledgeable authority accorded to women by the allocation of a female voice to the primary participant – the SPEAKER.

8.14 Overall discussion of findings: identifying the ADDRESSEE?

As Leech notes, television is 'perhaps the least selective of (advertising) media' (1966: 63), and, as has been shown, none of the ads examined gives any clear indication of its intended audience. How far then is it possible to identify its actual ADDRESSEEs? The consumer is ultimately unknown and the variously designed messages can only be assumed to be constructed 'as if' the consumer is 'known'. Is it possible, therefore, to use the analyses in Sections 8.8 to 8.11 and the discussion in Sections 8.12 to 8.13 to suggest how the ADDRESSEE might be identified?

In both Past 8.1/A (Woman Alone) and Past 8.2/A (Executive) the advertiser (the voice of the product) is male. There is no explicit indication of the gender of the Addressee. Each ad merely asks the viewer to observe the 'successful' wife and/or mother and to learn how this can be achieved (learning the hard way in the case of Executive) – via consumption of the product. Both ads seem to be designed to instil aspiration and/or guilt in a woman viewer (who is encouraged to identify with the wife illustrated – Leech 1966: 55), and envy and/or discontent in a husband/male partner (who similarly identifies). Woman's subservience is in effect justified to all family members (including the woman herself), since by consumption of the product she is ensuring – and achieving satisfaction through – others' success (see Section 8.4).

The Present texts (8.3/A to 8.6/A) however present a notable change: women are given the authoritative voice on domestic matters. The ADDRESSEE is still, of course, unknown, but it is apparent that the viewer's role as AUDITOR (a kind of INDIRECT ADDRESSEE?) assumes great significance in the Present ads (see Section 8.12 and the move towards Indirect Address). The viewer sees (some) men starting to do domestic tasks for themselves, at least with women's help (Early Man). Responsibility, however, usually stays with women and this is especially so for the 'good mother' (Sports Kit Mother and Pregnant Woman). This is so, too, for the indulgent partner (Early Man) (who can be presumed to have cleaned the spotless kitchen and provided the Corn Flakes in the first place?), and of course for the independent woman herself (Kidding Woman) (no 'role-sharing' for her apparently). (Kidding Woman could almost be Early Man's partner, indulging in a little mild flirtation at the interviewer's expense.) The consumer in the Present texts (in marked contrast to the Past texts) is in fact given no explicit or implicit indication of the marital status of participants – or indeed of any kind of partner at all.

Present 8.3/A to 8.5/A thus move away from instilling guilt into a woman ADDRESSEE, while continuing to show her the way (via the product) towards making her life easier and happier – even to 'having it all'. They appear to be being directed at a wide range of (youngish) women viewers who are presumably expected to self-select, identifying with the particular women portrayed or implied (Leech 1966: 55) and projecting on to them a part of themselves (Cook 2001: 181).

Male viewers can similarly self-select and identify/project according to their current state, whether in a partnership or solo. The blurring of roles in the Past Executive ad (see discussion in Section 8.9) comes up to date in the corresponding Kellogg's Early Man ad (see Section 8.11), where the fictional and 'real' worlds of Addressee and ADDRESSEE appear to merge. A comparable, even more notable, blurring seems to be built in to the three Persil Tablets ads

(Present 8.3/A to 8.5/A) (see Section 8.10). The self-selection process allows (indeed encourages) a male viewer to identify with the interviewer (to 'become' both Addressee and ADDRESSEE) and 'get the message' – whichever aspect might fit his circumstances, including its debunking conclusion.

This discussion moves some way towards suggesting how the advertiser constructs the likely ADDRESSEE of both Past and Present texts. What is most noticeable, however, in the Present ads when compared with the Past ones is their humour. The solemnity which seems to lie behind the two Past texts is replaced by a light touch in all the Present ones. Given that the latter group of texts has, inevitably, a rather narrow scope, a surprisingly wide range of social roles and characteristics has been reflected – and in an entertaining and non-judgemental way – at least so far as the women are concerned! Manufacturers, salesmen and all the other personae presumed to be manifested in 'the advertiser' still want to promote and sell the product but, on the evidence of the Present texts, they appear (on the surface at least) to take themselves a little less seriously and the consumer a little _more_ seriously. They approach their ADDRESSEEs from a position closer to respect, crediting them with intelligence, discrimination and, above all, good humour.

8.15 Conclusion

This chapter has carried out very detailed analyses of a small amount of data in its comparison of Past and Present television advertisements and its conclusions can therefore only be modest. It has, however, produced some interesting findings.

The majority of the analytical concepts put forward by Leech in 1966 appear to be still valuable and highly relevant. The ads examined show notable changes of approach and emphasis, but it is remarkable how many of the conventions are still being followed, even if in a modified fashion. The notable shift in the direction of Indirect Address, and the ways in which it is manifested in these texts, does place a question mark over Leech's claim (1966: 38) that the language of Direct Address advertising 'is more rewarding to study'. This study indeed suggests some of the ways in which the language of Indirect Address might be systematically – and very fruitfully – explored.

In the closing stages of his book Cook assesses how far advertising can be placed alongside other art forms such as music and literature, especially poetry. He acknowledges the extent to which it may be compromised by its ideological content and 'its central mercenary core', but he concludes: 'Advertising can focus and redefine ideas about language, discourse, art and society, and in this respect its study is well worthwhile' (Cook 2001: 237). The overall findings of this chapter would support this view.

8.16 Suggestions for further work

(a) Other features which could be systematically investigated for these and/or comparable texts include:

- personal pronouns used by all participants (compare Section 6.8) in relation to both (type of) Address and gender;

- accent features assigned to different participants/roles, Past v. Present (for example RP v. 'non-RP' and/or 'southern' v. 'northern' features – compare Section 7.9). Such an investigation could be related more precisely to the apparent 'social status, sex and so on' (Leech 1966: 49) of participants.

Informants (see Section 1.2.6) could be asked to give their intuitive responses to the ads (including perceptions of ADDRESSEE/s in each case) as a complement or alternative to the speculative Section 8.14.

(b) The same basic framework (adapted as necessary) could be applied to other kinds of advertisements, including print advertisements, and for other kinds of products. Product type (Field) could be built in:

- as a deliberately varying variable – tangible goods such as cosmetics or electrical goods compared with intangibles such as films or holidays;

- as a controlled variable – say, cars or alcoholic drinks – with deliberate variation in perceived targeted consumer, in terms of income/social status/gender (Tenor). (The latter might be gauged via approaches to informants.)

CHAPTER 9

New Language Forms

9.1 Introduction

This chapter adopts a rather different approach from that of the rest of the book. It attempts to take account of some relatively new forms of language as a consequence of rapidly developing technology and to consider how far these may be related to the more 'traditional' frameworks and approaches already expounded. While what follows will thus be very much more speculative in nature, it should at the same time be seen to be consistent with – and evolving from – the principles which underpin both the individual studies and the book as a whole.

9.2 The aims of the chapter

A number of writers have identified – and have begun to explore and describe – some of the changes in function and form of written language as a consequence of technological developments and the rise of the internet (see, for example, Baron 2000; Carter et al. 2001; Crystal 2001). This area is still, however, relatively unmapped territory. In this final chapter, therefore, the 'real texts' will be taken as a starting point and an attempt made to use them to build towards a larger theory.

The examples to be cited are few in number, very short, and restricted to emails, text messages and internet chat: there will be no examination of, for example, interactive message boards and the like. Senders and receivers of the messages represented by the data vary in age and relationship to each other, and the texts have been approached with no 'general expectations' or formally stated 'specific areas of enquiry'. All of the examples are, however, 'real texts' occurring in identifiable situations and having intrinsic interest. More importantly, they may serve as a basis for identifying some possible patterns of occurrence, including perhaps permutations of significant situational variables and chosen forms of expression. With this in mind, I want to explore:

(a) how far such texts can be related to the governing framework of the book as represented in Figure 1.1, or to an extension or development of that framework;

(b) what specific linguistic features of the individual texts may suggest about their likely place within the proposed extended framework (with connections being made to earlier chapters where possible);

(c) what the findings might suggest for further work in this area.

9.3 Description of the data

Examples of each type of text are reproduced in turn and in approximately similar form. Brief contextual details are given as appropriate, including some limited specification of variables. There has been a very small amount of editing of the data, with names in particular being disguised as necessary.

The broad initial presumption will be that Mode is 'written' in each case: communication is via 'the graphic channel' and there is '–visual contact' between participants (see the situational scales presented in Section 1.1.6.3 as Figure 1.2). Transmission of each message is swift – probably a matter of seconds at most. The message itself appears on a 'screen' of some kind and is essentially ephemeral (it is far from the permanence suggested by Hasan's 'graven image'), though both emails and text messages can be saved at least for a time, and the former can be readily printed off and transformed into hard copy. Emails and text messages are usually preceded by an announcement of the name of the sender and (possibly) some indication of the subject of the message.

9.3.1 Emails

Texts **9.1** and **9.2** are two short emails, each composed on a conventional keyboard and sent (and received) via home computer in a domestic setting. Each was addressed to me by a member of my family (Tenor – participants long known to each other – literally 'familiar') and each is very broadly concerned with aspects of the sender's work (Field).

Text 9.1 (received March 2002) is from my sister, who lives in the USA. She has sent me (also via email) reproductions of some of her paintings and I have confirmed receipt, including in the following terms: *They're a bit skewiff and I think that at least one is upside down but they look pretty good to me (tricky standing on my head to view them but . . .).*

Text 9.1

Yes, the whole page may be upside down. I'm sorry. And since the pictures were loose on the scanner bed they 'moved' a little when I put the lid down.

One of these days I'll figure out how to work with one picture at a time and correct the color specifically. I'll have to sort out and let you have the actual sizes of the finished pieces so you would have some idea.

Lots of love. GJ

Text 9.2 (received September 2002) is from my son, who lives in Nottingham.

Text 9.2

well, i've got more good news . . . i passed my wxyz today, i have beeen revising like mad though . . . and to top it all they're gonna send me on a proper pqrs trainers course, blimey . . . take it easy . . . we'll pop and see u nex weekend if u not around this . . .

e x

9.3.2   Text messages

Texts 9.3 and **9.4** were composed and received via mobile telephone. (I was allowed privileged access to messages received by others, from which these two were selected.) Both the sending and receiving of text messages can take place in virtually any type of setting and in the midst of almost any kind of surrounding discourse. The activity is relatively brief (see below) and it can be confidential and unobtrusive (the arrival of a message can be indicated by an audible signal or merely by vibration). Keying and text presentation conventions vary according to type and age of telephone, but the full range of letters and symbols, including those for punctuation, are usually available. All, however, impose constraints on quantity of text entered and transmitted and consequent length of any individual message, typical text limits being 160 characters, including spaces.

The texts were received in September and October 2002 respectively and each represents a message between young people (age group 20s–30s) who know each other very well, the first being female to female and the second female to male (Tenor).

Text 9.3 was sent by W, in Ireland, to her close friend J, in Nottingham. W is responding to a message from J which suggested a visit to her in the near future, and she is confirming all is well (Field).

Text 9.3

NO PROBS . . . WILL U B BRINGING Z? WE'LL HAVE A GOOD NITE OUT ORGANISED 4 YA! XX LUV U

Text 9.4 requires a rather more extensive specification of context, but it does demonstrate a particular practical virtue of the text messaging Mode. Z was in a taxi on his way out for what was likely to be a very late evening. He telephoned his partner J to tell her he had discovered he had forgotten his house key. J did not want to have to wait up for him, but was uneasy about using the telephone (within earshot of the taxi driver) to arrange to leave a key for him to find. She therefore said she would send him a text message for this purpose (Field):

Text 9.4

THE KEY IS UNDER THE SILVER SLOP BUCKET. STICK YR HAND UNDER THE FENCE ON THE LEFT NEAR THE PLANT. LUV U. X

(It may be prudent to comment here that this strategy and location is no longer used!)

9.3.3 Internet chat

Texts 9.5–9.9 appeared in a particular (and particularly crowded) computer-accessed 'chat room' site during the same evening in October 2002. They are noticeably more fragmented than the previous texts cited. Many different participants were contributing to the chat, and the cited examples were in fact selected by me on the purely practical basis that they could be accurately noted and extracted from the ongoing (and very fast-flowing) stream of utterances, few of which could be reliably related to each other. Most appear to involve 'orientating' utterances as participants enter the chat room (Texts 9.5–9.8), though one (Text 9.9) does constitute at least one 'exchange' (see

Section 4.7.1). (Carter et al. 2001: 276–7 cite a 'chat-log' consisting of a more extended sequence of utterances.) The examples do, nevertheless, serve to illustrate some notable features of internet chat.

The Field is approximately constant across all examples – each seeming to be concerned with the early social stages of 'meeting' someone new (though see discussion of Text 9.9 in Section 9.5.3) and having the initial aim of 'just chatting'. From the Tenor perspective, participants (who have been allocated the identifying letters K to P) are apparently males and females of approximately similar ages, the specific chat room being intended for a 20s–30s age group. It should be remembered, however, that both age range and gender of participants are ultimately unknown since individuals can present themselves in any way they wish. This is so even if a gender-indicative first name is used - a choice made in fact by participants L (female) and P (male). (I myself entered this chat room as a 'guest', using a (female) pseudonym; I am not a participant in any of the cited texts.)

Given the immediacy possible in internet chat, participants occupy the same temporal Setting (note the exophoric deictic references (Section 5.6.1) to *tonight* and *2nite*) but they remain in their separate spatial Settings, for example their respective domestic environments (compare the telephone situation in Chapter 4). In linguistic and psychological terms, however, participants behave <u>as if</u> they are inhabiting the <u>same</u> spatial Setting – that is, the notional chat room where they 'meet' (see exophoric deictic references to *here* and *ere*). This may, therefore, be regarded as corresponding informally to Hymes's 'scene' (Section 1.1.6.4). The texts are:

Text 9.5

K: so how is everyone in here tonight?

Text 9.6

L: any I wanna chat

Text 9.7

M: hi n e one from Norwich in ere?

Text 9.8

N: hi any girls up 4 a good time 2nite#?

Text 9.9

O: p ru ok
P: I'm good o
[...]
O: were ru p

9.4 Extension of the overall framework of Figure 1.1

Given that the data samples presented in Section 9.3 involve 'written' Mode and communication via the graphic channel, the most significant nodes of Figure 1.1 are likely to be those appearing under WRITING . . . intended to be READ. It will be apparent, however, from just a preliminary inspection of the individual texts that they differ in the extent to which they can be processed entirely by the eye: some require, to a greater or lesser extent, the 'sounding' of particular written forms, that is, to be processed via the ear (compare the texts in Chapter 7). The more specific nodes, therefore, would seem to be 'writing intended to be read' and 'writing intended to be read but as if heard'. These two nodes have therefore been extracted and reformulated as part of a diagram presented as Figure 9.1. Thus, 'to be read as if heard' and 'to be read' are placed at either end ('western' and 'eastern') of a line representing the horizontal axis of the diagram. This horizontal axis should thus be regarded as a scale or continuum on which each individual text might be placed – compare the scales presented in Figure 1.2.

The vertical axis of the diagram can also be regarded as a scale, this time represented by the 'two-way . . . one-way'/'degree of shared process' scale suggested in Figure 1.2, with 'one-way' placed at the most northerly point and 'two-way' at the most southerly. The significant factors here in suggesting a placing on the vertical scale would seem to be whether an individual text (or, perhaps, elements within that text) may signal:

- the 'presence' of an addressee

- how far that addressee is (or is presented as being) 'known' – that is, as a specific or as a more general addressee

- how far the addressee is (or appears to be) presented as having shared in the creation of the meaning of that particular text (or element/s within that text)

The two axes of Figure 9.1 will be seen to form Quadrants A, B, C and D.

9.5 The cited texts and the extended framework

This section will consider some of the principal features of each of the texts cited in Section 9.3, which, in view of their potential for cross-fertilisation of the characteristics of written and spoken language, I propose to term 'crossover' texts. The discussion will make brief reference, as appropriate, to frameworks and/or findings presented in earlier chapters, and the kinds of features identified will be used as evidence for the suggested 'placing' of a particular text within a particular quadrant of Figure 9.1.

Thus, a text which 'crosses over' to a notable extent, that is, which contains a number of 'spoken' features, will fall towards the western end of the horizontal axis. If that text also contains a number of indicators of 'two-way' communication it will fall to the southern end of the vertical axis. Notional lines

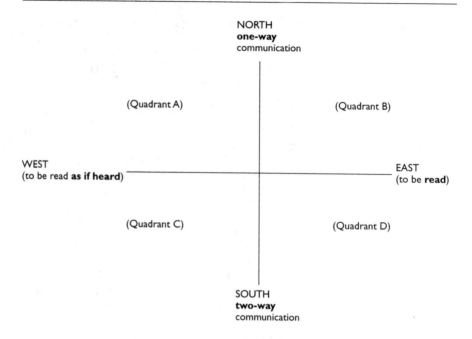

Figure 9.1 Suggested extension of overall framework as presented in Figure 1.1 to accommodate 'crossover' texts

drawn from the points on the two separate axes will meet at a particular point – that is, in Quadrant C. If a text contains a similar number of indicators of 'two-way' communication but predominantly 'written' features (so falling towards the eastern end of the horizontal axis) it will be placed in Quadrant D.

Suggested 'placings' in each case are inevitably approximations and there has been no attempt at mathematical precision. Nevertheless, such an approach may offer a potentially illuminating 'way in' to this type of data.

9.5.1 The emails

Texts 9.1 and 9.2 show some notable differences in the extent to which they adopt the formal conventions of the graphic channel, including spelling, punctuation and paragraphing. Text 9.1 could almost be a traditional ('to be read') letter in this respect. Text 9.2, on the other hand, eschews several of the conventions while retaining others: it adopts its own (transcript-like) spelling and punctuation in places, for example by its use of *gonna* and 'anti-capitals', but it makes careful use of apostrophes. (Anti-capitals could, of course, be influenced by the conventions attaching to email address itself, though see Section 2.13 and the kinds of choices made by the poet e e cummings.)

Particular forms in Text 9.2 are used to represent particular words, for example the letter *u* is, in effect, 'sounded' in order to represent the word (pronoun) 'you'. The word 'next' is represented as *nex* before *weekend*. This could, of course, be a simple error (see Section 9.6 below), but it would, in fact, be consonant with the frequent elision of the /t/ phoneme in such a linguistic environment in informal <u>speech</u> (see Section 7.17).

So far as the vertical axis is concerned, both Texts 9.1 and 9.2 signal the 'presence' of the addressee, specifically by using variants of the pronoun *you* (Section 6.6.1) and in each case the *you* makes deictic exophoric reference to a specific, known, addressee (Section 5.6.2, criterion 3 for identifying 'Addressee'). Text 9.2 also chooses an 'interactive' grammatical mood, specifically an imperative (Section 5.6.2), *take it easy*.

The texts differ, however, in the extent to which the addressee is presented as having shared in the creation of meaning. Text 9.1 shows clear evidence of such sharing, with GJ's elliptical *Yes* . . . requiring recourse to the message I had sent earlier the same day for its full interpretation (Section 5.6.2, criteria 2(i)(ii)). The speed of transition of email, with its potential for equally speedy response, would seem to increase the scope for elliptical sharing of this kind. Text 9.2 on the other hand shows no real evidence of comparable sharing: the reference to *if u not around this (weekend)* relates to something communicated several days earlier (to the effect that I was likely to be out at the weekend), but it has the appearance of a relatively independent 'initiating utterance' (Section 5.6.2, criterion 4).

On the evidence presented, therefore, the two email texts could be placed approximately as shown in Figure 9.2. Both are in southern quadrants, but Text 9.1 is in Quadrant D (extreme East and South) and Text 9.2 in Quadrant C (roughly Central West and less South than Text 9.1).

9.5.2 The text messages

Texts 9.3 and 9.4 show some similarities in the degree to which they adopt the conventions of the graphic channel. Both happen to choose upper case consistently throughout, rather than the alternatives of all lower case (as Text 9.2) or combined upper and lower case (Text 9.1) Both use traditional punctuation features such as question and exclamation marks and full stops, arguably optional in conveying meaning (especially perhaps the last). Both use some abbreviated forms and/or spellings (*PROBS, NITE, YA, LUV* in Text 9.3, and *YR, LUV* in Text 9.4), these being consistent with brevity and economy of space (see Section 9.3.2). Both use the 'sounded letter/number' strategy identified in Text 9.2: *U* (you), *B* (be), *4* (for). Both use the conventional symbols for kisses – *X* (compare Text 9.2).

Text 9.4 is intriguing in its frequent use of the definite article (for example *THE KEY, THE FENCE, THE LEFT* and so on). Absolute clarity of meaning – essential in the circumstances, of course – would have been equally served in far fewer words, and with no full stops. The whole message represents a delightful mix of the conventions of the latest technology and old-fashioned syntactic pedantry.

So far as the vertical axis is concerned, both Texts 9.3 and 9.4 signal the presence of the specific addressee (J and Z respectively) via several uses of variants of the pronoun *you*. In addition, each one chooses an 'interactive' grammatical mood (compare Text 9.2), thus reinforcing that presence: Text 9.3 uses an interrogative (*WILL U B BRINGING Z?*) and Text 9.4 an imperative (*STICK YR HAND UNDER THE FENCE . . .*).

As with email, the speed of transition of text messages increases the scope for process sharing. The texts differ, however, in this respect. Text 9.3 shows clear evidence of such sharing, with W's *NO PROBS* requiring recourse to the earlier message from J about her proposed visit for its full interpretation (compare the discussion of Text 9.1 above). Text 9.4 on the other hand provides no comparably clear evidence (compare Text 9.2). The use of the initial definite reference <u>*THE KEY*</u> . . . does suggest a link with previous discourse ('the key already spoken/known about') (Section 5.6.1), though it is arguable – and certainly in this context – that *KEY UNDER SILVER SLOP BUCKET* would convey precisely the same message.

On the basis of this evidence Texts 9.3 and 9.4 would both seem to fall into Quadrant C. Text 9.3, however, would be placed both further West (more '. . . to be heard') and further South (more explicitly two-way) than Text 9.4 (see Figure 9.2).

9.5.3   The internet chat

Texts 9.5–9.9 differ in the extent to which they observe graphic conventions. K and P (in Texts 9.5 and 9.9 respectively) use entirely 'written' forms, including (in K's case) the question mark. The remainder choose a mixture of

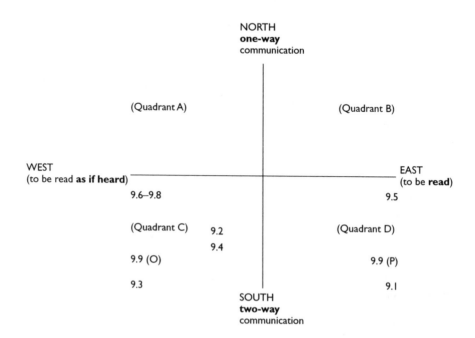

Figure 9.2   Suggested placings of crossover texts in Figure 9.1

conventional and 'sounded' forms, the latter comparable to those found in email Text 9.2 and, especially, the text messages. For example, names of letters and/or numbers are used to represent words or parts of words, thus *n e* (any), *r u* (are you), *1* (one), *4* (for), *2* (to-). Lower case is chosen virtually throughout (even for the vocatives *p* and *o* in Text 9.9), the exceptions being *Norwich* (Text 9.7) and *I'm* (Text 9.9).

Likely positions on the vertical axis are more difficult to estimate. Only O uses the pronoun *u* which, together with the vocative *p* (Section 5.6.2, criterion 1), gives a clear signal of the 'presence' of a specific addressee, reinforced by use of interrogative mood (to realise two questions, a yes–no and, later, a wh-question – Section 5.6.2). P's response to the first question, including the use of the vocative *o*, provides evidence of shared process, and confirms a strong two-way interpretation for all three utterances of Text 9.9. It suggests, indeed, that these two participants had already 'met' – either earlier in the ongoing discourse or, possibly, in the same chat room on an earlier occasion.

The remainder of the examples pose (interactive) questions, most being realised by situationally elliptied forms, probably involving the omission of the operator *does/is/are* (Quirk et al. 1985: 898–9) (Texts 9.6–9.8 respectively) and with or without an explicit question mark. The exception is Text 9.5 which appears in its 'full' interrogative form. Two (Texts 9.7 and 9.8) preface their questions with the greeting *hi*. All, however, use some kind of marker of indefiniteness to refer to a potential (and therefore non-specific) addressee, whether pronoun (for example variants of *anyone*) or determiner (*any (girls)*) (Crystal 1996: 150 and 128–9). This seems to be consistent with the speculative, introductory (and hopeful) nature of such communication.

On the evidence presented, these particular examples can be placed approximately as shown in Figure 9.2, all being in southern quadrants and just Text 9.5 and P's contribution to Text 9.9 in the 'to be read' Quadrant D. There are signs in fact that K's status (Text 9.5) is rather different from that of all the other participants. The combination of full 'written' forms together with the all-embracing indefinite pronoun *everyone* and the conjunct *so* (Section 4.8) suggests that her/his role could be one of general 'moderator' of the chat room.

9.6   Other features of the crossover texts

The crossover texts display notable features in addition to those discussed in Section 9.5. The most striking of these, perhaps, are those which seem to involve keying or spelling mistakes – what might be termed 'performance errors'. Examples of such 'errors' are *beeen, nex* (Text 9.2) (though see Section 9.5.1 for a comment on the latter), *ere* (Text 9.7) (which <u>could</u>, of course, be a representation of 'zero /h/' as discussed in Section 7.14.2), *2nite#* (Text 9.8), *were* (Text 9.9).

Errors may arise as a direct consequence of speed of mechanical input: expression via the graphic channel is being attempted in the same way, and at the 'same' speed, as expression via the phonic channel. While it must be acknowledged that the general keyboard and other skills of individual participants can be factors here, speed of thought (and speech) is always going to exceed that of the hand – whether a pen or a keyboard is used. The likelihood of 'performance errors' is thereby increased. Further, such errors may well be felt <u>not</u> to warrant the kinds of editing procedure described and illustrated by Halliday (1994b: 63–6), especially in the environments in which these crossover texts have been produced. There would appear to be a direct relationship, therefore, between the occurrence (and persistence because unedited) of performance errors, spontaneity of production, and informality of relations between participants well known to each other.

Consideration of the effects of spontaneity and informality in any situation returns us once more to the scales set out in Figure 1.2. The significant ones this time are the spontaneous . . . prepared and the informal . . . formal scales. Choices along these scales are, of course, likely to be influenced as much by Tenor relations (and, to a lesser extent, Field) as by Mode considerations. It may be useful, therefore, to identify features in the crossover texts which appear to be indicative of 'informality'. Some have already been referred to in Section 9.5, for example those involving 'sounding'. Others are:

- forms of the first person singular pronoun *I* (Section 6.6.1) (Texts 9.1, 9.2, 9.9);

- conventional contractions (Section 8.9) such as *I'm, I'll* (Texts 9.1, 9.9), *i've, they're* (Text 9.2). (Note though, *I have beeen revising* . . . in Text 9.2, where use of the full form <u>could</u> serve the purpose of giving intentional prominence or stress to *have* (note the *though*) in the context of his having passed the exam.)

- situational ellipsis, involving the omission of 'understood' elements (Section 8.9.1), for example the auxiliary *'re* in *if u ('re) not around this* . . . (Text 9.2) (compare the omission of operator in forms realising questions, mentioned in Section 9.5.3);

- lexical/idiomatic choices such as slang or exclamations, for example *blimey, take it easy, pop* (Text 9.2), *STICK* (Text 9.4), *up 4 (a good time)* (Text 9.8);

- use of endearments such as (variants of) *love* (Texts 9.1, 9.3, 9.4).

It is not clear quite how the spontaneity/informality scales may be related directly to each other, although a fruitful start might be to juxtapose them crosswise in a similar way to that adopted for Figure 9.1. A possible placing on both horizontal and vertical scales could then be carried out for each crossover text, using the evidence of clusters of particular indicators from each category and thus arriving at an approximate correlation between degrees of 'spontaneity' and 'informality'. It should be emphasised, however, that an <u>appearance</u> of, for example, 'informality' can be more or less consciously adopted or specifically created, and therefore in effect 'prepared'. This might in fact be a manifestation of a deliberately constructed persona, for example for the purposes of internet chat or, indeed, for the representation of the speech of a fictional character – compare the account of Gregory and Carroll's original distinctions within Mode in Section 1.1.3 – or of the narrator in Chapter 7.

Further investigation of these two scales, and their possible relationship to those in Figure 9.1, is beyond the scope of this exploratory chapter. They may, however, make useful contributions towards the building of an overall theoretical framework for analysing these – and analogous – crossover texts.

9.7 Suggestions for more systematic studies involving crossover texts

This chapter has explored how far a very limited sample of particular texts might be related to the overall framework of the book, and it has sketched out the beginnings of a theoretical approach to the systematic study of crossover texts.

The ephemeral nature of some of the data has practical implications for its collection for full research purposes, and this may be particularly so for the control of variables – especially in the case of internet data. Nevertheless, it is clear that suitable material <u>can</u> be found and interesting questions are waiting to be asked and – perhaps – answered. Initial strategies to this end might, therefore, involve the following:

- collection of an eclectic range of data taken from different (crossover) Mode variations – email, text messages, samples of internet chat and other phenomena – and from a range of situations;

- approximate placing of each individual text on a version of the framework suggested by Figure 9.1;

- identification of some possible patterns of occurrence, for example approximate position on the 'to be read' axis (and in particular quadrants) according to age and/or gender of participants and relationships between them (Tenor), in conjunction with purpose of communication (Field);

- consideration of other features found in the texts, as explored in Section 9.6.

The principles and procedures expounded in Chapter 1 might then be drawn upon to devise a structured approach to the material initially collected, to inform the collection of additional (more controlled) data, and to arrive at a framework for its analysis. Possible approaches might involve:

(a) control of (crossover) Mode (for example email <u>or</u> text messaging) and (perhaps) Field with deliberate variation in Tenor (for example age <u>or</u> gender and/or familiarity of sender);

(b) control of Tenor (age/gender of participants) and variation in (crossover) Mode (for example email v. text messaging);

(c) control of Tenor and (crossover) Mode with variation in Field (for example emails between the same participants for 'work' v. 'social' purposes);

(d) control of Tenor and (perhaps) Field with variation in (overall) Mode (for example email and/or text messaging v. answer phone/voice mail);

(e) (attempted) control of Tenor (age/gender of participants) and variation in (overall) Mode (for example internet chat v. a 'real' telephone conversation).

An analytical framework (based on the kinds of features suggested in Sections 9.5 and 9.6) could be applied to each text, identifying the areas in which they might (or might not) differ. The precise method of analysis and calculation of results would have to be decided according to the type of feature involved. A carefully thought-out adaptation of the 'actuals v. potentials' method presented in Section 7.10 might be suitable for some features, for example standard written v. 'sounded' forms. The basis for calculation would also have to be decided, whether numbers of words, contributions and so on (see Section 1.2.10), including what would count as a 'word'.

To take approach (a) as an example, it would seem that on the (very) small evidence presented in Sections 9.3 and 9.5, there may be some correlation between age group of sender and degree of preference for 'spoken' forms. The suggested difference is most clearly shown in Texts 9.1 and 9.2 (these texts were <u>not</u>, of course, controlled for gender). A more systematic approach to data collection and a carefully devised and rigorously applied analytical framework (following the principles and practices recommended in Chapter 1) would enable this kind of general impression to be explicitly examined.

Finally, it might be possible to use the approach sketched out in this chapter to reconnect Fig.9.1 with the original Fig.1.1 and thus with more 'traditional' written texts. The specific texts examined in Chapters 2 and 3, for example, would seem to be clearly placed in Quadrant B, the narrative of Chapter 7 in Quadrant A and its quoted dialogue in Quadrant C. Detailed analysis could presumably suggest more delicate placing/s <u>within</u> a quadrant in each case. This kind of approach might thus provide a useful 'way in' to a range of written texts, whether 'literary' or journalistic – including perhaps the informal, 'oral', news reporting referred to in Section 3.16.

9.8 Conclusion

This final chapter has, I hope, proved to be a natural development from all that has gone before. Both chapter and book have sought:

• to use real texts grounded in very specific situations to explore interesting areas, both linguistic and social;

• to suggest ways in which detailed textual analysis might be carried out in order to identify patterns of occurrence of particular linguistic features;

- to discover how texts and patterns of occurrence might be related to some overall theories of language use;

- to suggest how those theories might be developed and applied to analogous texts and situations, signalling new paths which might be followed.

Finally, to move explicitly into 'two-way' mode, all of these aims will, I hope, combine to a single end – to light the spark of adventure and encourage <u>you</u> to take that leap of the imagination and set off on your own journey of linguistic discovery.

Appendix 1
Analysed Texts

1.1 Literary narrative: sentences, clauses, noun phrases

Key to Texts 2.1A and 2.2A: identification of sentences, clauses and noun phrases

Sentences numbered in sequence.

Clauses shown between double vertical lines; clause elements between single vertical lines; square brackets show embedded clauses and/or clause elements; $S^{1, 2}$ match grammatical and notional S elements; round brackets show S elements occurring within V elements; notes via [1,2] (bold).

Noun phrases (including embedded) shown in curly brackets; 'first stratum' noun phrases underlined; notes via [a,b].

Text 2.1A: Dickens

```
             S         V    C    Cj        S      V    C     Cj
1. ||{The raw afternoon} | is | rawest, || and | {the dense fog} | is | densest, || and | {the

           S        V         C
muddy streets} | are |  muddiest, || near[a] {that leaden-headed old obstruction},

─────────────────────────────── A ───────────────────────────────
{appropriate ornament for {the threshold of {a leaden-headed old corporation}}} :

{Temple Bar}||. [1]


      Cj        A                A                                    A
2. || And | hard by {Temple Bar}, | in {Lincoln's Inn Hall}, | at {the very heart of {the

       V        S                         A
fog}} | sits | {the Lord High Chancellor} | in {his High Court of Chancery}||.
```

A V (S¹) S¹ C A V (S²) S²
3. ||Never | can (there) come | {fog} | too thick,|| never | can (there) come | {mud} and

C ——A—— V A O
{mire} | too deep, [[to assort | with {the groping and floundering condition [[which|

S V
{this High Court of Chancery}, {most pestilent of {hoary sinners}[b]},| holds, | {this

A A
day}, | in {the sight of {heaven} and {earth}}}]]]]. [2, 3, 4]

Summary of sentence/clause analysis: Dickens

Sentence 1: [SVC] + [SVC] + [SVC] A
Sentence 2: + AAAVSA
Sentence 3: [AV(S^1) S^1C] [AV(S^2)S^2C] A
[VA[. . . OSVAA]] [5]

Notes to Text 2.1A: Dickens

Sentences and clauses

1 Analysed as what Q et al. call 'interpolated coordination': there are three coordinated SVC clauses in sentence 1, with the A element standing outside the coordination structure and applying simultaneously to all of them (Q et al.: 950, 976–7)

2 Sentence 3 has another example of interpolated coordination, this time of comparative constructions where *too* expresses 'excess' (Q et al.: 1140–2), with the *to*-infinitive clause *to assort with* . . . providing the comparative A element for both preceding clauses and expressing a blend of time and result (Q et al.: 1144–6, 1079, 1109); . . . *to assort with* . . . has been interpreted as meaning *to match, to agree (with)* . . . (Cassell 1997: 82)).

3 Each of the coordinated clauses features existential *there*, which has been analysed as empty or 'dummy' grammatical subject (Crystal 1996: 218–9) with the 'notional' subject postponed until after the verb *(can) come* (Q et al.: 1403, 1408–9). The notation has followed Berry (1996) in assigning matching superscripts to each pair of grammatical and notional S elements to indicate their interdependence.

4 Round brackets are used to show that the grammatical subject occurs within the V element, the subject–verb inversion being brought about by the marked placing of the A element *Never* in first position (Q et al.: 1379–81).

5 The summarising notation for sentence 3 is intended to show that the A element (see note 2 above) begins at *to assort with* . . . and extends to the end of the sentence. It consists of a non-finite VA clause, with its own A element being a 'process adjunct of manner' (Q et al.: 556), answering the question 'how'/'in what way'.

The A element is realised by a prepositional phrase (Crystal 1996: 180–7), consisting of the preposition *with* followed by its complement *the groping and floundering condition which*. . . . The prepositional complement is a noun phrase which embeds an OSVAA relative clause (see also Section 2.9).

Noun phrases

a   The extensive A element at the end of sentence 1 (see note 1 above) is realised by a prepositional phrase consisting of the preposition *near* followed by a series of <u>three</u> noun phrases acting in apposition (Crystal 1996: 144–5), with *that leaden-headed . . .* and *appropriate ornament . . .* being 'attributes' of the proper name *Temple Bar*. The 'first stratum' noun phrase *appropriate ornament . . .* has, of course, two embedded noun phrases within its postmodification, one inside the other, as indicated.

b   *most pestilent of hoary sinners* in sentence 3 has been interpreted as a noun phrase in apposition to, and expressing an attribute of, the immediately preceding *this High Court of Chancery*.

Text 2.2A: Tarner

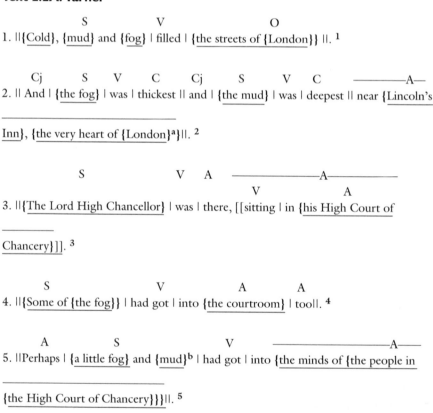

          S   V   O
1. ||{Cold}, {mud} and {fog} | filled | {the streets of {London}} ||. ¹

      Cj   S   V   C   Cj   S   V   C   ————A—
2. || And | {the fog} | was | thickest || and | {the mud} | was | deepest || near {Lincoln's

Inn}, {the very heart of {London}ᵃ}||. ²

                  S   V   A   ——————————————A——————————
                                                      V   A
3. ||{The Lord High Chancellor} | was | there, [[sitting | in {his High Court of

Chancery}]]. ³

          S   V   A   A
4. ||{Some of {the fog}} | had got | into {the courtroom} | too||. ⁴

      A   S   V   —————————————————A——
5. ||Perhaps | {a little fog} and {mud}ᵇ | had got | into {the minds of {the people in

{the High Court of Chancery}}}||. ⁵

Summary of sentence/clause analysis: Tarner

Sentence 1:   SVO

Sentence 2:   + [SVC] + [SVC] A
Sentence 3:   SVAA[VA]
Sentence 4:   SVAA
Sentence 5:   ASVA

Notes to Text 2.2A: Tarner

Sentences and clauses

1   Three coordinated noun phrases are together acting as subject (S) (Crystal 1996: 144, 196) of the verb *filled*.
2   An instance of 'interpolated coordination' (see note 1 to Text 2.1A), this time of just <u>two</u> SVC clauses.
3   The non-finite VA clause *sitting* . . . has been analysed as an embedded 'subjectless supplementive clause' (Q et al.: 1123–7) realising an A element occurring in final position in the main clause and 'supplementing' the space adjunct *there*. Q et al. note that 'there may be considerable indeterminacy as to the semantic relationship to be inferred' (p. 1123), though they note that *–ing* clauses 'tend to suggest a temporal link' (p. 1124).
4   *too* has been analysed as an 'additive subjunct', something additional to, and immediately following, the A element *into the courtroom* (Crystal 1996: 174–5; Q et al.: 604–9)
5   *Perhaps* has been analysed as a 'content disjunct' (Crystal 1996: 176–7) making an observation about the truth of the remainder of the clause or a value judgement about its content.

Noun phrases

a   *the very heart of London* in sentence 2 has been regarded as being in apposition to, and expressing an attribute of, the preceding proper name *Lincoln's Inn* (see note **a** to Text 2.1A).
b   *fog* and *mud* in sentence 5 have been regarded as coordinated noun phrases having article and postdeterminer in common (*a little*), together acting as grammatical subject of *had got* (Crystal 1996: 144, 196–9) (compare note 1 above).

Key to Tables 2.1 and 2.2: Noun phrase structures

Embedded noun phrases shown in square brackets.

Simple noun phrases (S) determiner+head or head alone; all other structures regarded as **Complex (C)**.

Notes to Table 2.1: Dickens

1   Proper names and titles such as those appearing in this text (and also Text 2.2) can arguably be analysed in different ways, for example as det+premod+head+postmod. It was decided to follow Crystal (1996: 111), at least to some extent, by regarding such constructions as consisting of a <u>single</u> headword, though with a separately analysed determiner. The latter decision was partly on the grounds of Dickens's

own variation of determiner choice, as in *his/this High Court of Chancery*. It does not, of course, affect the simple/complex designation since <u>either</u> analysis would regard them as simple noun phrases.

2 *very* in sentence 2 is being used as a restrictive adjective rather than an intensifying adverb (Q et al.: 431).

Table 2.1 Dickens

Sentence	Determiner	Premodification	Head	Postmodification	S/C
I	the	raw	afternoon		C
I	the	dense	fog		C
I	the	muddy	streets		C
I	that	leaden-headed old	obstruction		C
I		appropriate	ornament	for the threshold of a leaden-headed old corporation	C
I	[the		threshold	of a leaden-headed old corporation]	C
I	[[a	leaden-headed old	corporation]]		C
I			Temple Bar[1]		S
2			Temple Bar		S
2			Lincoln's Inn Hall		S
2	the	very[2]	heart	of the fog	C
2	[the		fog]		S
2	the[1]		Lord High Chancellor		S
2	his		High Court of Chancery[1]		S
3			fog		S
3			mud		S
3			mire		S
3	the	groping and floundering[3]	condition	which this High Court of Chancery, most pestilent of hoary sinners, holds, this day, in the sight of heaven and earth	C
3	[this[1]		High Court of Chancery]		S
3		[most pestilent	[4]	of hoary sinners]	C
3		[[hoary	sinners]]		C
3	[this		day]		S
3	[the		sight	of heaven and earth]	C
3			[[heaven]]		S
3			[[earth]]		S

3   *groping* and *floundering* in sentence 3 are participles (Crystal 1996: 136) which act in 'linked' (or 'syndetic') coordination to premodify the headword *condition* (pp. 196–8).

4   This analysis has regarded *most pestilent of hoary sinners* in sentence 3 as involving ellipsis, that is the omission of elements which are recoverable from context (Q et al.: 883–900). Interpretation of the elided head of the noun phrase is postponed, requiring recourse to the postmodifying element (that is *sinner/s* or, possibly, *hoary sinner/s*), and thus involving 'cataphoric ellipsis'. Q et al. note (p. 895) the 'stylistically marked effect that often results from cataphoric ellipsis'.

Table 2.2   Tarner

Sentence	Determiner	Premodification	Head	Postmodification	S/C
I			Cold		S
I			mud		S
I			fog		S
I	the		streets	of London	C
I			[London]		S
2	the		fog		S
2	the		mud		S
2			Lincoln's Inn		S
2	the	very[1]	heart	of London	C
2			[London]		S
3	the[2]		Lord High Chancellor		S
3	his		High Court of Chancery[2]		S
4			Some[3]	of the fog	C
4	[the		fog]		S
4	the		courtroom		S
5	a little[4]		fog		S
5	(a little)		mud		S
5	the		minds	of the people in the High Court of Chancery	C
5	[the		people	in the High Court of Chancery]	C
5	[[the		High Court of Chancery]]		S

Notes to Table 2.2: Tarner

1   compare note 2 to Table 2.1.

2   see note 1 to Table 2.1.

3   *Some* in sentence 4 has been regarded as a pronoun which is acting as head, rather than as a predeterminer followed by *of* (Q et al.: 383–4).

4   *(a) little* in sentence 5 has been analysed as a postdeterminer (quantifier) rather than a premodifier, the equivalent of 'small' (Crystal 1996: 134–5).

1.2 Newspaper reports: clauses, Transitivity and Voice

Key to Text 3.1A

Clauses shown between double vertical lines; clause elements between single vertical lines; square brackets show embedded clauses and/or clause elements

Extract A (*The Times*)

               S   V   A

||Mr Ian MacGregor, the National Coal Board chairman,| was knocked | to the ground

————————————————— A —————————————————

cj   S   V   A   A

[[as | angry miners | surged | round him | at the Ellington Colliery, Northumberland,|

—————

  A

yesterday]]. [1]

Extract B (*Sun*)

           S   V   A   A

||Coal chief Ian MacGregor, 71, | was flattened | yesterday | by a mob of rampaging

miners||. [2]

Extract C (*Daily Mail*)

           S   V   A   A

||Coal Board chief Ian MacGregor | was knocked | to the ground | unconscious |

  A   ————————————A————————————

             cj   S   V   A

yesterday   [[when | mob fury | erupted | during a pit visit]].

Extract D (*Guardian*)

               S   V   A   –

                                                            cj

||The chairman of the National Coal Board, Mr Ian MacGregor, | said | last night [[that

———————————————————— O ————————————————————

S   V   C   —————————————— A ——————————————

                    cj   V   A   A

| he | was | fit and well [[after |being knocked | to the ground | earlier in the day | by

—————

—————

  A

protesting pitmen]]]]. [3, 4]

Extract E (*Daily Star*)

S	V	A	A	A

‖ Coal Board chief Ian MacGregor | was battered | to the ground | yesterday | by a mob

of angry miners‖.

Extract F (*Daily Telegraph*)

S	V	A

‖ Mr Ian MacGregor, National Coal Board chairman, | was knocked | stunned | to the

A	A	S	V	O

ground | by a surging mob of 400 miners [[who | had thrown | eggs and slices of

A	A

bread,]] at Ellington Colliery, Northumberland, | yesterday ‖. [5, 1]

Notes to Text 3.1A: clauses

1   In some extracts single clause elements are realised by two noun phrases acting in either apposition or coordination (Crystal 1996: 144–5), for example the S element in Clause 1 of Extract A (*Mr Ian MacGregor, the National Coal Board Chairman* – apposition) and the O element in Clause 2 of Extract F (*eggs and slices of bread* – coordination). (See also notes to Text 2.1A.)

2   It would be possible to regard the added *,71,* after *Coal chief Ian MacGregor* in Extract B as a very-much-reduced non-restrictive relative clause (see note **5** for fuller explication), the equivalent of *who is 71*. It provides additional information about, but is not essential to identifying, the unique individual Ian MacGregor. Quirk et al. 1985: 289–90 comment on the possibility of a comparable non-restrictive modification of a personal name, though their cited examples involve premodification: *the inimitable Henry Higgins [Henry Higgins, who is inimitable]*. They do refer elsewhere to 'non-restrictive modification . . . .in post-head position' (1985: 1242) but subsequently cited examples feature 'full' relative clauses (for example 1985: 1257–8) or prepositional phrases such as *This course, on English grammar, starts . . .* which they call 'rare and rather awkward' (1985: 1285–6). For simplicity of analysis *,71,* has been regarded as coming within the noun phrase acting as the S element of the clause, and has therefore been analysed as a postmodifier (see Section 2.6.3 for a description of noun phrase structures). Such an analysis is not, however, unproblematic. (A possible alternative approach to approximately comparable structures appears in Berry 1989: 98–9. I am grateful to Margaret Berry for her personal communication, November 2001, which explored some of the questions raised by this data.)

3   In Extract D the finite clause beginning at *that he was fit and well . . .* and continuing to the end of the extract has been analysed as direct Object of *said*, and therefore an embedded O element within the main clause (Crystal 1996: 54–5 and 200–2). It should be noted that a Hallidayan analysis would treat this as a separate 'hypotactic (dependent) projection clause' (see B&B: 202–5) rather than as an element of the main ('projecting') clause.

4   The non-finite clause *after being knocked* . . . in Extract D has been analysed as a further-embedded clause acting as an A element within the already-embedded O element (see note **3**).

5   In Extract F, the status of the final two A elements *at Ellington Colliery, Northumberland* and *yesterday* is potentially ambiguous, since they could be regarded as acting within <u>either</u> the main clause <u>or</u> the relative clause beginning at *who had thrown eggs and slices of bread*. Whatever its final boundary, the meaning of the clause itself is ambiguous. It could be regarded either as restricting the reference to the specifically mentioned group of miners (*a surging mob of 400 miners* rather than any other miners who might have been there) or as merely providing optional extra information. A decision has to be made between analysing it as a restrictive or a non-restrictive relative clause (Crystal 1996: 140–3). In the first case the clause would be regarded as postmodifying *miners* and therefore coming within the very complex noun phase beginning at *a surging mob*. In the second it would be regarded as a separate, optional, clause. In written texts punctuation frequently gives a clue (Crystal 1996: 142), and the fact that there is a comma after *bread* but no comma after *miners* would encourage the 'restrictive' interpretation. On balance, however, this seemed counter-intuitive. The decision was therefore taken to regard the clause as a <u>non</u>-restrictive relative clause – *who had thrown eggs and slices of bread* – that is, as adding optional but not essential information. The analysis reflects this and, as a further consequence, regards *at Ellington Colliery, Northumberland* and *yesterday* as A elements in the <u>main</u> clause. An alternative interpretation is, however, acknowledged. (It should be noted that B&B's account of 'defining and non-defining relative clauses' and the decisions which may have to be made (pp. 186–90) corresponds closely with Crystal's. They also make the useful comment that a '(non-defining relative clause) is grammatically dependent on the dominant clause, but (is) not an integral part of it'.)

Key to Text 3.1B

Transitivity, Voice as shown (see frameworks in Sections 3.7 and 3.8).

Extract A (*The Times*)

Clause 1 (Passive)

Mr Ian MacGregor the National Coal Board chairman	Participant 1 (Goal)
was knocked	Process (Material)
to the ground	Circumstance (location – where)
as angry miners . . .	Circumstance (time – when)

Clause 2 (Active)

as	subordinating conjunction (time)
angry miners	Participant 2 (Actor)
surged	Process (Material)
round him	Circumstance (location – where)
at the Ellington Colliery, Northumberland	Circumstance (location – where)
yesterday	Circumstance (time – when)

Extract B (*Sun*)

Clause 1 (Passive)

Coal chief Ian MacGregor, 71,	Participant 1 (Goal)
was flattened	Process (Material)
yesterday	Circumstance (time – when)
by a mob of rampaging miners	Participant 2 (Actor)

Extract C (*Daily Mail*)

Clause 1 (Passive)

Coal Board chief Ian MacGregor	Participant 1 (Goal)
was knocked	Process (Material)
to the ground	Circumstance (location – where)
unconscious	Circumstance (manner – how)
yesterday	Circumstance (time – when)
when mob fury erupted . . .	Circumstance (time – when)

Clause 2 (Active)

when	subordinating conjunction (time)
mob fury	Participant (3) (Actor?/Behaver?)
erupted	Process (Material?/Behavioural?) [1]
during a pit visit	Circumstance (time – when)

Extract D (*Guardian*)

Clause 1 (Active)

The chairman of the National Coal Board Mr Ian MacGregor	Participant 1 (Sayer)
said	Process (Verbal)
last night	Circumstance (time – when)
that he was . . .	Participant (4) (Reported)

Clause 2 (Active)

that	content-less complementiser (B&B: 164)
he (Ian MacGregor)	Participant 1 (Carrier)
was	Process (Relational+Attributive)
fit and well	Attribute
after being . . .	Circumstance (time – when)

Clause 3 (Passive)

after	subordinating conjunction (time – when)
(ellipted) (he (Ian MacGregor))	(Participant 1 (Goal))
being knocked	Process (Material)
to the ground	Circumstance (location – where)
earlier in the day	Circumstance (time – when)
by protesting pitmen	Participant 2 (Actor)

Extract E (*Daily Star*)

Clause 1 (Passive)

Coal Board chief Ian MacGregor	Participant 1 (Goal)
was battered	Process (Material)
to the ground	Circumstance (location – where)
yesterday	Circumstance (time – when)
by a mob of angry miners	Participant 2 (Actor)

Extract F (*Daily Telegraph*)

Clause 1 (Passive)

Mr Ian MacGregor National Coal Board chairman	Participant 1 (Goal)
was knocked	Process (Material)
stunned	Circumstance (manner – how)
to the ground	Circumstance (location – where)
by a surging mob of 400 miners	Participant 2 (Actor)
at Ellington Colliery, Northumberland	Circumstance (location – where)
yesterday	Circumstance (time – when)

Clause 2 (Active)

who	Participant 2 (Actor)
had thrown	Process (Material)
eggs and slices of bread	Participant (5) (Goal)

Notes to Text 3.1B: Transitivity and Voice

1 B&B (pp. 125–6) acknowledge the 'bottom of the barrel' nature of Behavioural Processes and their potential overlap with some Material Processes (see Section 3.7.5). The particular instance in Clause 2 of Extract C *(mob fury) erupted* has a notionally abstract entity *(fury)* (though with animate associations via *mob*) being 'agent' of a process more usually occurring in a non-volitional, inanimate context (volcanoes 'erupt'). This relates interestingly to the account of Transitivity systems given by Berry (1989: 149–53). Berry identifies 'event processes' as a sub-type of 'material process' and quite distinct from 'action processes' (1989: 151), citing such examples as: 'A stream flows through that part of the valley', and 'The car backfired noisily'. She comments: 'In the case of event processes, there is no question of their having been brought about <u>intentionally</u> since inanimate participants do not possess free wills' (emphasis added). She also comments on the effects of 'untypical' combinations of processes and participants (1989: 155). In Extract C an 'event' type of process is combined with an animate-associated participant. Davidse (1999: 31–4) also focuses on 'intentionality', characterising it as a <u>relation</u> between Agent and process in intransitive clauses (original emphasis), and she identifies 'absence of intentionality' as being inherently associated with an inanimate Actor. However we actually label the components of *mob fury erupted* in Extract C, it is clear that specific choices can create many layers of meaning.

1.3   Women's talk: Minimal Responses, Hedges and Hesitations

Key to analysis

Minimal Responses underlined – <u>mm</u>; notes via [1], [2]
Hedges bold – **I mean** | **presumably**; notes via [a], [b]
Hesitations bold, underlined – **<u>um</u>**; notes via [i], [ii]

Text 4.1A: Phone

1	H:	[<u>h</u>- how's it going
2	R:	[oh[1]
3	H:	[I gather you're having **a bit of** a tiring time
4	R:	**well** – yeah – it's **<u>um</u>** – it's **almost**[a] like a full – teaching load **in a way**	**I mean**
5		**I sort of** preparation-wise I'm spending a long time - preparing – lectures and
6		seminars and things
7	H:	<u>yeah</u>
8	R:	**<u>um</u>** – the travelling's not very nice
9	H:	no I gathered you've got a lot of travelling
10	R:	<u>oh yes</u>[2]
11	H:	[<u>urr</u>
12	R:	[( ) **well** nearly two hours a day – **well** two hours there and **sort of** two
13		hours back
14	H:	<u>oh</u>
15	R:	**in actual fact** it does take me two hours when I walk up to the
16		station
17	H:	<u>oh dear</u>[3]
18	R:	( ) very good – oh to be in Nottingham – (this is) what I keep saying to
19		myself
20	H:	oh **really** – do you miss it **a bit**
21	R:	**well** – yes I do – **<u>um</u>** London's not **really**[b] – to me not all it's cracked up to be
22		or I haven't found it yet but **maybe** it **just** takes a few months to settle into it
23	H:	<u>mm</u>
24	R:	**<u>um</u>** I'm **actually** applying H for a Tefl course postgrad at Birmingham
25	H:	*are* you
26	R:	yeah — **well** — this job would be o.k. if it was full time **really**
27	H:	<u>yeah</u>
28	R:	**you know** I — at first I <u>I</u> was getting **a bit** bored **sort of** staying at home and
29		– **I mean** I'd **quite** like to go into Tefl **I think** ( ) **well** I was talking to C about
30		it and she thinks it's good to get some kind of Tefl qualification **anyway**[c]
31	H:	<u>mm</u>
32	R:	so
33		I'm **<u>um</u>** applying to do **<u>um</u>** the RSA preparatory course in Tefl at English
34		International House – that's **<u>um</u>** – a part-time course in the evenings two evenings
35		a week – **hopefully** if I get on that that'll[i] be **sort of** next term Tuesdays and

36 Thursdays so then I'll be able to teach Tefl in the summer holidays   [( )
37 H: oh [that **that**'s
38 in London you mean or
39 R: **well** I'll do the course in London yeah
40 H: yeah
41 R: you've got to pay for it but – I
42 thought it was worth it (well) **you know**
43 H: mm
44 R: and then if I liked it I could either stay on at D and – do the RSA – Diploma
45 course which is the higher course
46 H: mm
47 R: **um** and **just I sort of** carry on like that or
48 else – if I get on Birmingham postgrad do **do** that and then do it permanently
49 H: mm — [mm
50 R: [yeah – yeah
51 H: [oh
52 R: [it's difficult because I don't **really**[d] want to give up a **a a** job I've got **you**
53 **know** that's **sort of** permanent and it's not badly paid
54 H: [no
55 R: [so it'd be silly to **sort of** give it up without something – else
56 H: yeah of course – and it'll be good experience won't it – for you **I mean** – [for
57 **for** a year or so
58 R: [yeah
59 – yeah – [yeah[4]
60 H: [**I mean I presumably** that would mean you'd be there for a year wouldn't
61 it
62 R: **well** yes (and I'd) yeah I'd **I'd** be there till – July
63 H: [yeah yeah
64 R: [yeah yeah[5] – and the teaching's **quite** nice
65 H: [is it
66 R: [apart from the bloody phonetics
67 H: yeah I gathered you were doing phonetics – B said
68 R: [yeah
69 H: [so that's **a bit of** a pain
70 R: **well** I'll **I'll** have to do a course in it for next year – **I mean** – when I do the
71 Tefl course **hopefully** – **I mean** that will cover the phonetics anyway[e]
72 H: yes
73 R: **um** so I'll **probably** feel **a bit** better about it
74 H: yeah[6] – [**well** it's
75 R: [but this year's not been very good at all
76 H: oh

Notes to Text 4.1A: Phone

Minimal Responses

1   *oh* (**line 2**) has not been analysed as an MR since some kind of response is required
    by the preceding question (it is +predicted). *Oh* is not really an adequate reply as it

stands: it appears to be functioning to allow R time to formulate a full response, which in fact begins at **line 4.**

2 *oh yes* (**10**) has been analysed as a single response (there is no break between them).

3 *oh dear* (**17**) – compare Coates' *oh my god* (1989: 100).

4 The first of R's three yeahs in **58–9** appears to be a response to H's tag question *it'll be good experience won't it – for you . . .* , but it is spoken simultaneously with H's immediately following *for for a year or so.* R's second *yeah* therefore replaces the first one and functions in the same way. Her third *yeah* (which in fact overlaps with H's utterance at **60**) has been regarded as responding to *for a year or so.* (It is, of course, arguable that the various stages of H's tag question actually <u>require</u> a response – that is, that R's responses should be regarded as +predicted. This analysis has regarded them as –predicted, and thus as minimal responses.)

5 R's *yeah*'s (**64**) occur simultaneously with H's two MRs and appear to be reinforcing her own statement at **62**.

6 yeah (**74**) has not been analysed as an MR, given H's following *well it's* (which is overlapped by R's utterance at **75**).

Hedges

a *almost* (**4**) has been analysed as a hedge modifying *like*, the latter acting as a (non-hedging) preposition of comparison (Q et al.: 661–2) having as complement *a full teaching load.* (The context is, of course, what might be considered the workload expected in a part-time job.)

b *really* (**21**) has been regarded here as being potentially mobile (. . . *really London's not – to me not all it's cracked up to be* . . .) that is, the negative element is not an essential part of the hedge (contrast **52**). This analysis seems to be supported by the occurrence of the second *not* before *all it's cracked up to be*. . . .

c *anyway* (**30**) has been analysed here as a non-optional element <u>within</u> the clause beginning at *it's good to get* . . . reporting what C thinks, rather than acting as R's own comment on the statement. It thus acts as an informal concessive and 'non-hedging' conjunct (Q et al.: 636), making the link between getting a Tefl qualification and what C thinks is good (compare note e below, and contrast Face **37** where *anyway* <u>has</u> been analysed as a hedge).

d the negative particle (**52**) is an essential element in arriving at a 'hedge' analysis, since *really want* would classify *really* as a booster (compare Face **5**).

e *anyway* (**71**) has been analysed as a non-optional element <u>within</u> the clause beginning *that will cover* . . . (compare note c above).

Hesitations

i There is no repetition here, of course, although the two that's in **35** both refer to the same part-time course: the first *that* is complement of the preposition *on* while the second is subject of *'ll be.*

Text 4.2A: Face

1 R: **I think** part of the problem's been that I've been so tired **basically** – and I
2 hadn't **really** taken on board what the job involved
3 H: what *does* it involve

4   R: oh right[1]
5   H: **I mean** cos I'm **not really**[a] sure
6   R: yeah yeah **well** it's taken *me* quite[b] a while to **sort of** find out but a lot of it is
7   to do is working with newly arrived refugees that have been in that have come
8   into the country within the last two years – and it's **really** to help them with the
9   resettlement process in schools to make sure that they adjust the adjustment
10 process is as smooth as possible – and it's to try and **um** – help with the **the**
11 schools with their induction and admission procedures so it's making sure that the
12 schools – create that very – comfortable and warm secure environment cos a lot
13 of these children are **quite**[c] I **you know** traumatised and they might not have been
14 in school for several years or they've had a (disruptive) education and **er** so it's
15 **really** to make them feel welcomed into the school environment
16 H: but it's they're all – actually[d] in your school all the time
17 R: yeah yeah **well** the **the** (other) difficulty with refugee children is that a lot of
18 them are placed in temporary accommodation because of their – asylum status and
19 **er** there's a very high – is it transition rate **you know** a high **mobil-** is it mobility
20 movement problem **you know** the refugee population is always shifting so it's
21 often very hard for schools to keep tabs on where the children go cos they might
22 start at the school and a couple of months later **just** disappear and nobody knows
23 where they've gone to – cos there's no [tabs being kept on them
24 H: [oh   oh   mm
25 R: very often – so
26 another part of the job is to make sure that the **the** right questions are actually[d]
27 asked at the interview because obviously we need to find out more information
28 than if you're working if it's **just** I **like**[e] a monolingual child – so **like**[e] have they
29 had – formal education before – **um** — have they had schooling **perhaps** in another
30 country – **I mean** cos some of the children **like**[e] – ones that come from Somalia
31 some of them have now **c-** just[f] come to this country from Holland – for example
32 we've got two families who've lived in Holland for the last six years
33 H: oh
34 R: and –
35 goodness knows how they've done it but they've come here – I don't know if
36 they're going to be sent back I don't know but they could be because it's that third
37 country rule **you see** I – **anyway**[g] so it's questions like that and **er** what sort of[h]
38 accommodation they're living in – do they have a social worker are they on
39 income support – all these other questions need to be asked **you know** – are they
40 registered with doctors are they having emotional behaviour problems that we
41 need to know about the child and you might not get it all at interview it might
42 come in dribs and drabs [and things
43 H: [(oh oh)   but – (   ) you have to do that
44 R: well no no[2]
45 H: (oh)
46 R: but my **my** role is to **sort of** I– **kind of** — not ad*vise* the schools
47 but **er** to make sure that the right questions (   ) or to put those sort of[h] questions
48 down for the schools to consider – **um** – cos a lot of teachers don't feel
49 comfortable in asking a refugee child what their refugee status is – **you see** they
50 think it's **a bit of** a thorny – issue and one that can make ( ) problems but I **I**
51 personally don't see a problem (with it myself)

Notes to Text 4.2A: Face

Minimal Responses

1 R's *oh right* (**4**) is a required response (+predicted) to H's preceding wh-question and has not, therefore, been analysed as a minimal response.

2 R's *well no no* (**44**) would not have been regarded as a minimal response even without the *well* since it reverses the polarity of the preceding utterance, H's *you have to do that*.

Hedges

a the negative particle (**5**) is an essential element in arriving at a 'hedge' analysis, since *really sure* would involve *really* as a booster (see also Phone **52**).

b *quite (a while)* (**6**) has been regarded here as being closer to a maximiser than a compromiser or diminisher, and therefore has not been analysed as a hedge. (Q et al.: 385 suggest 'quite a few' would indicate 'a considerable number'.)

c *quite* (**13**) has been analysed as a hedge on the basis that 'fairly' would seem to be a more likely substitute here (than, for example, 'completely').

d *actually* (**16, 27**) would seem to be non-mobile, the scope of each being restricted to emphasising particular elements within their respective clauses: *in your school all the time* and *asked* respectively.

e the three instances of *like* (**28, 30**) – each analysed as a hedge – are not easy to categorise. They appear to be informal examples of what Q et al.: 635 term 'appositive conjuncts', having a meaning equivalent to 'for example'.

f *just* (**31**) has been regarded as a subjunct acting as a Time adverbial (Crystal 1996: 175) and therefore has not been analysed as a hedge. The children and their families have *just* ('recently') come to this country after having been in Holland for the last six years.

g *anyway* (**37**) has been analysed as a hedge, being an informal and slightly deprecating conjunct linking different, and syntactically independent, stages of her account at this point.

h neither of the instances of *sort of* in **37** and **47** has been analysed as a hedge. Each has been regarded as an informal post-determiner (Crystal 1996: 134), with R referring to the kinds of questions asked, *what sort of accommodation . . . , . . . those sort of questions . . .* (There are no signs of even the smallest hesitation at either point which would suggest a hedging interpretation.)

I.4 Children's talk: Deixis and Addressee

Key to analysis

Deixis   endophoric items underlined – <u>it</u>; presumed meaning – [<u>the water</u>]
exophoric items bold – **there**; presumed meaning – [[<u>direction indicated</u>]]
notes via [1, 2]

Addressee as shown; criteria 1–4 as in Section 5.6.2; notes via [a, b]

Text 5.1A: Talk

		Deixis	Addressee
1	A	I like Ilkeston baths	R+H 4
2	R	yeah I	A 2ii
3	H	Ilkeston – where's Ilkeston baths	A 2ii A+R 4[a]
4	R	er – I don't know – next to Victoria Park	H 2i
5	A	yeah	R+H 2ii[b]
6	R	right next to Victoria Park	H 2i
7	H	oh yes ( )	R 2ii
8	R	it [Ilkeston]'s got a big sl- it [Ilkeston]'s got a slide what goes about – twenty metres – down —- it [the slide] goes like this [[the action demonstrated]] – oooh ((gesture demonstrates action))	H 4
9	A	no about fifty metres – it [the slide]'s big	R 2ii
10	R	yeah big	A 2ii
11	A	R you know that [the mutually known about] shower at the end of it [the slide]	R 1,3,4
12	R	((laugh)) there's[1] a shower just as you come in	A 2ii, H 4[c]
13	A	well when we went with Scouts last Wednesday [[the Wednesday before the day on which currently speaking – that is, 24 June 1992]]	R 4[d]
14	R	yeah	A 2ii
15	A	we blocked the end of it [the slide] near that [previously mentioned] shower and everyone kept barging into us – then you know the man up at top who watches you go down – the one (on net) – he [the man] come down blowing whistle – down slide — with his [the man's] shorts and T-shirt on ((laugh))	R 3,4
16	R	yeah there's[1] like a sprinkler what comes down right in your face at end but then you go into a big – erm	A 2ii, H 4[e]
17	A	(right) it [the water]'s only about that [[the extent demonstrated]] deep ((gesture demonstrates depth))	(R 2ii), H 4
18	R	yeah and then you go into water and it [the water] splashes right up all in your face	A 2ii, H 4
19	A	yeah	R 2ii
20	H	and that [the shower/the splashing]'s before you go in is it [tag]	R+A 2ii, 4[f]
21	A	no that [the shower/the splashing]'s after you that [ditto]'s when you're coming out	H 2i, 4
22	R	it [the shower/the splashing]'s just like – you go right into a (pool/puddle) of water about this [[the extent demonstrated]] ( ) ((gesture demonstates depth?))	H 4[g]
23	A	there's[1] a dead dark park and you – dead dark part	H 4
24	R	yeah and then	A 2ii, H 4[h]
25	A	and you get stuck there [in the dead dark part] if you don't push hard enough cos there's[1] like a bar at the beginning and you have to swing on that [the bar] to get down	H 4

26	R	yeah and if you don't go down	A 2ii, H 4
27	A	on your back	H 4
28	R	flat on your back	H 4
29	A	then you stop	H 4
30	R	you stop half way through – – and then you have to keep pushing yourself off	H 4
31	A	and there's[1] disco lights	H 4
32	H	(so) if you sit up – you slow up	R+A 4
33	R	yeah	H 2ii
34	A	yeah	H 2ii
35	R	but if you lie on your back you come to this [previously mentioned] dark part and then next thing you're still in dark part and all water's sprinkling in your face	H 4
36	A	I know – you go down on your back and you go down dead fast	R 2ii, H 4
37	R	I know	A 2ii
38	A	you do it [the going down the slide] in about ten seconds	H 4[i]

Notes to Text 5.1A: Talk

Deixis

1   (contributions 12, 16, 23, 25, 31) Instances of existential *there* (Crystal 1996: 218–9; see also note **3** to Text 2.1A) rather than adverb of place *there* (25).

Addressee

a   (3) H's *Ilkeston* is a response to A, but the subsequent question has been regarded as being addressed to both boys, since R's contribution at 2 suggests that he has knowledge of Ilkeston baths (subsequently confirmed) (thus two Addressing utterances).

b   (5) A confirms R's response to H's question at 3, hence R+H 2ii.

c   (12) R's laugh is a response to A's 11 but the information about the shower is clearly for H's benefit.

d   (13) A's use of *well* signals the link with 11 and the continuation of his narrative for R's benefit.

e   (16) compare 12. The pronoun *you* has been regarded as the general or 'generic' *you* (Q et al.: 353–4) – see also 18, 20, 22 and so on.

f   (20) H responds to preceding contributions from both R and A about the shower/splashing, hence 'R+A'.

g   (22) The use of anaphoric pronoun reference has not been regarded as constituting a response to A's 21, though R's contribution develops from and is related to the several preceding ones centring on the shower and/or the splashing. It is clearly intended to tell H something she does not know (but A does).

h   (24) R's *yeah* is a response to A's 23, and he begins to continue the account for H's benefit with his *and then*. He is interrupted, however, by A's own continuation at 25.

i   (38) compare **g**.

Text 5.2A: Task

		Deixis	Addressee
1	R	camping is **here** [[in the area currently in]]	A+H D[a]
		((reading from screen))	
2	A	west ((commentary?))	R+H D[b]
3	R	come on (A)	A 4 (1)[c]
4	H	west	A 2ii
5	R	I'm staying over a couple of minutes – I am	A+H 4
6	A	what to complete **this** [[the game currently being played]]	R 2ii, 4
7	R	yeah	A 2i
8	H	have you only got to get one more	R+A 3,4
9	R	yeah	H 2i
10	H	oh well ( )	R 2ii
11	A	when we've found this [the previously mentioned] clue	
		it [the clue]'s the last[1] clue	H 4[d]
12	H	oh	A 2ii
13	R	we're nearly . . .	A+H D . . .
14	A	hang on where we got to go to – lifeboat ( )	R 4[e]
15	R	yeah we're **there** [[at the place indicated]] **at the moment**	
		[[at the time of speaking/at this point in the game]]	
		– so (if I was)	A 2ii,4
16	H	yes	R 2ii
17	A	we're **here** [[at the place indicated]]	R 4[f]
18	R	yes – so ( ) go right up **there** [[in the direction	A 2ii,4
		indicated]] – to the castle	
19	H	can you get round to the lifeboat station that	
		[previously mentioned] way	R+A 4
20	A	yeah — it [the previously mentioned way]'s the only way	
		you can get	H 2i,4
21	H	(you haven't got any . . .)	
22	A	that [the previously mentioned way]'s the only way you	H 4
		can get	
23	H	(there aren't any devils) (devils there)	
24	R	I've found a I've found a route by em [the devils]	H 2ii,4
25	H	oh	R 2ii
26	A	west – that [west]'s **that** [[the direction indicated]] way	
		now [[at this point in the game]] we need to look ( )	R+H D
27	H	( ) ((reading from screen?))	
28	A	I wish **this** [[currently being used]] computer	
		was faster ((banging keyboard))	R+H 4
		–(6)–	
29	R	(Lord) what you doing ( )	A 3,4
30	H	(north) ((reading from screen?))	
		(north)	
31	A	I can't see – R	R 1,4
		– yeah	H? 2ii?

		– **now** [[<u>at this point in the game</u>]] we need to go west	R+H 4
32	H	where are you **now** [[<u>at this point in the game</u>]]	A 3,4
33	A	just **there** [[<u>in the place indicated</u>]]	H 2i
34	H	oh — oh I see – oh I see you've got to go round **that** [[<u>currently being indicated</u>]] um– (no no no) – west	A 2ii
35	A	**he** [[<u>R</u>]] keeps marking where we are and I keep thinking <u>they</u> [the markings made]'re traps ((i.e. on written map))	H 3,4g
36	H	yes – <u>it</u> [what you're doing]'s very confusing R ((laugh))	A 2ii R 1,4

Notes to Text 5.2A: Task

Deixis

1 (11) *last* here is a 'general ordinal' postdeterminer (Q et al.: 262; Crystal 1996: 134; and see Section 2.6.3), not a temporal indicator of the kind used in Talk 13.

Addressee

a (1) R appears to be reading aloud from the computer screen.

b (2) This has not been regarded as a genuine suggestion as to the next move they should make, since the responsibility for operating the computer keyboard is A's and he does not appear to be actually consulting R and H (hence the D coding) (see also 26).

c (3) The Addressee is presumed to be A in his role as keyboard operator (code 4); tentative support for this decision is provided by the slightly uncertain hearing of A's name – hence the placing of code 1 in round brackets.

d (11) R is presumed to know this (see 9), hence H as Addressee.

e (14) A's *hang on* interrupts R's 13 while he (A) considers what he/they should do next.

f (17) A is checking with R where they are on the written map which R is in charge of (see 35).

g (35) A's use of the pronoun *he* (to refer to R) confirms the Addressee is H (hence the code 3 in addition to 4).

1.5 Political speeches: pronouns and lexical and grammatical repetition

Key to analysis

Pronouns bracketed, bold, with person specified via [1, 2, 3] – [**them**[3]]

Lexical repetition bold, with overall alphabetical order specified via superscript – **Conservatives**[4], **Labour**[8]

Grammatical repetition underlined – <u>because [**we**[1]]</u>

Text 6.1A: Blair

1 and [**I**[1]] say to [**you**[2]] [**my**[1]] **party**[11] – be strong and of good **courage**[6] –the

2 **Labour**[8] **party**[11] that first won support from the **British**[1] **people**[13] – that was

3 new[10] Labour[8] then – 1945 was new[10] Labour[8] – 1964 was new[10] Labour[8] –
4 both new[10] Labour[8] because both had the courage[6] to take the values of the
5 Labour[8] party[11] and *use* [them[3]] not for the world[23] as [it[3]] was but for the
6 world[23] as [they[3]] wanted[21] [it[3]] to be – and new[10] Labour[8] now ready in 1995
7 to build new[10] Britain[1] — during those VJ day celebrations [I[1]] was on the
8 platform with Tory[19] ministers and as [we[1]] walked down the Mall there were
9 thousands of people[13] there holding [their[3]] Union Jacks[20] – and [it[3]] became
10 clear – to the horror of the Tories[19] – that most of [them[3]] were Labour[8]
11 ((laughter)) and [they[3]] were waving[22] and shouting and urging [me[1]] to get[7] the
12 Tories[19] out ((laughter)) ((applause))

13 these are [our[1]] people[13] – [they[3]] love this country[5] just as [we[1]] do and [it[3]] is
14 because [they[3]] love this country[5] that [they[3]] look for [us[1]] to change [it[3]] – so
15 let [us[1]] say with pride – [we[1]] are patriots[12] – this is the patriotic[12] party[11]
16 because [it[3]] is the party[11] of the people[13] – and as the Tories[19] wave[22] [their[3]]
17 Union Jacks[20] next week [I[1]] know what so many people[13] will be thinking – [I[1]]
18 know what the people[13] want[21] to say to those Tories[19] – [it[3]] is no good
19 waving[22] the fabric of [our[1]] flag when [you[2]]'ve spent sixteen years tearing
20 apart[18] the fabric of the nation[9] ((applause))

21 tearing apart[18] the bonds that tie communities together and make [us[1]] the
22 United Kingdom – tearing apart[18] the security[15] of those people[13] – clutching
23 [their[3]] Union Jacks[20] swelling with pride at [their[3]] victory over tyranny yelling
24 at [me[1]] to get[7] the Tories[19] out because [they[3]] want[21] security[15] because [they[3]]
25 want[21] to leave a better world[23] for [their[3]] children[2] and [their[3]]
26 grandchildren[2] than [they[3]] created for [themselves[3]] and [they[3]] know the
27 Tories[19] can't do [it[3]] – decent people[13] — good people[13] — patriotic[12] people[13]
28 — and when [I[1]] hear people[13] urging [us[1]] to fight for [our[1]] people[13] [I[1]] tell
29 [you[2]] *these are [our[1]] people[13]* ((applause))

30 [they[3]] *are* the majority – and [we[1]] will serve[16] [them[3]] and build that new[10]
31 Britain[1] – that young country[5] for [their[3]] children[2] and [their[3]] families and
32 [I[1]] make [them[3]] this promise now – that [I[1]] will do all that [I[1]] can to get[7] these
33 Tories[19] out and [I[1]] will devote every breath that [I[1]] breathe every sinew of
34 [my[1]] body to ensuring that [your[2]] grandchildren[2] do get to live in that new[10]
35 Britain[1] in a new[10] and better world[23] – discipline – courage[6] – determination –
36 honesty – this victory can be won – the prize is immense – [it[3]] is new[10] Britain[1]
37 – one Britain[1] – the people[13] united by shared values shared aims – a government
38 governing for *all* the people[13] – and the party[11] – this party[11] – the Labour[8]
39 party[11] – new[10] Labour[8] – founded by the people[13] backed truly as the people's[13]
40 party[11] – new[10] Labour[8] – new[10] Britain[1] – the party[11] renewed[10] – the country[5]
41 reborn – new[10] Labour[8] – new[10] Britain[1] ((applause))

Text 6.2A: Major

1 Mr Chairman — after four terms why a fifth – why should [we[1]] be elected for a
2 fifth time to serve[16] [our[1]] nation[9] – because in a shifting world[23] only [we[1]] will

3   build a safe future for [**our**[1]] people[13] and heal the **scars**[14] of the past – <u>because</u>
4   [**we**[1]]'re building a more **secure**[15] economy as the enterprise centre of Europe –
5   <u>because</u> [**we**[1]]'re reforming public **service**[16] to make [**it**[3]] more accountable to the
6   public who pay for [**it**[3]] – <u>because</u> [**we**[1]] **stand**[17] for **choice**[3] and excellence in
7   education and [**we**[1]] are in the midst of the biggest revolution in education since
8   Rab Butler — <u>because</u> [**we**[1]] will retain the old rock-solid guarantee of the health
9   **service**[16] free at the point of delivery – and where improvement in the health
10 **service**[16] is necessary [**it**[3]] won't be treated as a sacred cow [**we**[1]] will seek to
11 improve [**it**[3]] – <u>because</u> defence and **security**[15] of the realm in [**our**[1]] streets and
12 beyond [**our**[1]] streets are of *paramount* concern <u>to [**us**[1]]</u> and to [**our**[1]] **party**[11] and
13 to [**your**[2]] government – [**we**[1]] **Conservatives**[4] are <u>for the individual not the state</u>
14 <u>for **choice**[3] not direction</u> <u>for ownership not dependence</u> <u>for liberty not for control</u>
15 – these are the enduring things – the cornerstones of [**our**[1]] beliefs – the reasons
16 that [**you**[2]] and [**I**[1]] joined the **Conservative**[4] **party**[11] and are meeting here today
17 – [**we**[1]] have worked <u>for [**them**[3]]</u> – cared <u>for [**them**[3]]</u> fought <u>for [**them**[3]]</u> over the
18 years – [**we**[1]] are building in this **country**[5] the greatest success for this **nation**[9]
19 that [**we**[1]] have known in [**our**[1]] lifetime – [**we**[1]] will not surrender [**them**[3]] to a
20 lightweight alternative – [**we**[1]] carry the **scars**[14] of battle – that is true – but [**they**[3]]
21 are honourable **scars**[14] – [**we**[1]] know that no other **party**[11] can win the battles for
22 Britain[1] that lie ahead – so when [**you**[2]] go home – refreshed and uplifted [**I**[1]] hope
23 by this conference – remember these things and ask the people[13] on the doorstep
24 – <u>would taxes be higher or lower under **Labour**[8]</u> – <u>would inflation be higher or</u>
25 <u>lower under **Labour**[8]</u> – <u>would there be more or less **choice**[3] under **Labour**[8]</u> –
26 <u>would [**our**[1]] defence be more **secure**[15] under **Labour**[8]</u> – <u>would [**our**[1]]</u>
27 <u>constitution be safe under **Labour**[8]</u> – [**you**[2]] and [**I**[1]] have only to ask the question
28 and the echo from [**our**[1]] **country**[5] will provide the answer – [**we**[1]] **stand**[17] –
29 [**we**[1]] **Conservatives**[4] – [**we**[1]] **stand**[17] for a wise and kindly way of life that is
30 rooted deep in [**our**[1]] history – [**our**[1]] hopes for [**our**[1]] **country**[5] aren't tired –
31 [**our**[1]] ambitions aren't dim – [**our**[1]] message to [**our**[1]] fellow **country**[5]men is
32 clear – millions of [**them**[3]] have yet to make up [**their**[3]] minds the **choice**[3] is
33 [**theirs**[3]] – [**our**[1]] **nation's**[9] future is at stake and [**we**[1]] **Conservatives**[4] – who
34 have **served**[16] [**our**[1]] **country**[5] in office for longer and better than any other
35 democratic political **party**[11] in the world[23] – [**we**[1]] **Conservatives**[4] are here and
36 in the future [**we**[1]] **Conservatives**[4] **stand**[17] ready to **serve**[16] on behalf of the
37 **nation**[9] [**we**[1]] love ((applause))

1.6   Dialect narrative: dialect and accent features

Key to Text 7.1A: Dialect features

Potential/actual features in upper case, with type of feature specified via superscripts:

a   past tense of irregular verbs
b   relative pronouns
c   possessive pronouns (first person)
d   adverbs without *–ly*
e   unmarked plurality after numeral

f   preposition *on* for *of*

g   definite article

Text 7.1A: Dialect features

1   *Now I'll tell yer about OUR[c] Ada.*

2   OUR[c] Ada loved ter go ter school, specially wenT[g] Teacher took [g] class inter [g]
3   fields unT[g] woods. She soon lont alT[g] names aT[g] flowers, leaves onT[g] trees, un
4   grasses. I thort grass WER[a] just grass un orlT[g] same. OnT[g] dark nights when we
5   couldn't go ert to play she'd be doin drawins ON[f] um, REAL[d] clever WER[a] OUR[c]
6   Ada.

7   Ada WER[a] four YEAR[e] older than me, un five YEAR[e] older than Dollie, THE[g]
8   youngest, Bill WER[a] somewhere in between. InT[g] summer when we WER[a] little,
9   unT[g] sun WER[a] shining, she'd tek us a walk on Sunday afternoons. OUR[c] Mam
10   ud say to her 'Tek OUR[c] Bill with yer', but we dint want him we us cos we
11   WER[a] orlus up to summat. Anyroad, he said he dint want to go with lasses, he'd
12   sooner go ter [g] farm. We'de go ter Newstead Abbey, yer could go round by
13   Newstead pit, but [g] favourite walk WER[a] ovva [g] Misk-Hills ter Beauvale. It
14   WER[a] a long way un we'de getta bit tired, un Ada would let us rest for a bit. She'd
15   be tellin us abert wild flowers un things, un if we WER[a] good she'd show us some
16   Bee-orchids, but we WER'nt[a] to touch um, not to tell anybody, it WER[a] a secret.

17   One Sunday, we had little Audrey with us from next door, her Mum ud asked Ada
18   if she'd tek her with us. Her husband liked her out uT[g] road on Sunday afternoon.
19   I don't know why cos she WER[a] such a quiet kid, un well mannered anorl. We
20   WER[a] cummin back through Annesley park, we WER[a] orl tired, OUR[c] Ada said
21   ter hurry up or we'd be late for US[c] tea, un she'd got ter get ready for Chapel.
22   We'd just got by [g] 'Badger' goin towards Mutton hill when OUR[c] Dollie said
23   'What's that in that front garden?' It WER[a] a hearse. Ada TOLD[a] us it WER[a] a
24   funeral car, WHAT[b] yer go in when yer dead. We all went nearer ter have a
25   proper look, little Audrey let ert a yell, then we could see a man layin in it, we
26   soon RUN[a] off. We'd gone up [g] road a bit when we SAW[a] Bobby Brown on his
27   bike cummin towards us. OUR[c] Ada shouted to him, 'Please sir, there's a man
28   layin in a hearse inna front garden'. 'Yer what ME[c] lass?' he said, un she TOLD[a]
29   him again, 'Un he's not in a coffin, is he dead?' [g] Bobby laughed un said, 'He's
30   only asleep', un not to be frightened, 'Its only old man Jones, he often as a sleep
31   innit on Sunday afternoons'. We could still hear him laughing as he peddled
32   away, I said to OUR[c] Ada what a nerve she'd got talkin to a bobby, but then that
33   WER[a] her, nowt bothered OUR[c] Ada.

Glossary of lexical items

orlus (line **11**)   always (compare H&T: 92)
summat (**11**)   something
lasses (**11**)   girls (note possible implication of female persona of narrator?)

pit (**13**)   colliery or coal mine

Badger (**22**)   familiar reference to The Badger Box, a local public house (see also Text 7.3)

Bobby, bobby (**26, 29, 32**)   policeman

layin (**25, 28**)   lying (H&T: 74 comment on the regionally widespread use of *lay* for *lie*)

nowt (**33**)   nothing

Key to Text 7.3A: Accent features

Potential occurrences/environments in upper case, with type of feature specified via superscripts:

a   /ʊ/ for RP /ʌ/
b   /æ/ for RP /ɑː/
c   /n/ for RP /ŋ/ in suffix *–ing*
d   zero (0) for RP /h/
e   [ʔ] for definite article
f   [æː] for RP /aʊ/
g   [ɛː] or [ɒ] for RP /ɜː/

Actual pronunciations shown in square brackets [n], [0]

Text 7.3A: Accent features

1   NOW[f][æː] *I'll tell yer* aBOUT[f][æː] OUR[f][æː] *Ada.*

2   OUR[f][æː] Ada LOVEd[a][ʊ] goIN[c][n] ter school, specially wenT[e][ʔ] Teacher took
3   [e][ʔ] CLASS[b][æ] inter [e][ʔ] fields unT[e][ʔ] woods. She soon LONT[g][ɒ] alT[e][ʔ]
4   names aT[e][ʔ] FLOWERS[f][æu], leaves onT[e][ʔ] trees, GRASSes[b][æ]. I thort
5   GRASSes[b][æ] wer JUST[a][ʊ] GRASS[b][æ] un orlT[e][ʔ] same. OnT[e][ʔ] dark nights
6   when we couldn't go ERT[f][æː] to play she'd be doIN[c][n] drawINS[c][n] on um, real
7   clever wer OUR[f][æː] Ada.

8   Ada wer four year older than me, un five year older than Dollie, THE[e][ðə]
9   YOUNGest[a][ʊ], Bill were SOMEwhere[a][ʊ] in between. InT[e][ʔ] SUMMer[a][ʊ]
10   when we wer little, unT[e][ʔ] SUN[a][ʊ] wer shinING[c][n], she'd tek US[a][ə] on a
11   walk on SUNday[a][ʊ] AFTernoons[b][æ]. OUR[f][æː] Mam ud say 'Tek OUR[f][æː]
12   Bill with yer', but we dint want Him[d][0] cos He[d][0] wer orlus gettIN[c][n] UP[a][ʊ] to
13   SUMMat[a][ʊ]. Anyroad, He[d][0] said He[d][0] dint want to go with [ʔ] 1 lasses,
14   He'd[d][0] sooner go ter [e][ʔ] farm. We'de go ter Newstead Abbey, yer could get
15   ROUND[f][æː] by [ʔ] 1 Newstead pit then, BUT[a][ʊ] [e][ʔ] favourite walk wer ovva [e][ʔ]
16   Misk-Hills[d][0] ter Beauvale. It wer a long way un we'de getta bit tired, un
17   Ada would let US[a][ə] rest for a bit. She'd be tellIN[c][n] US[a][ə] aBERT[f][æː] wild
18   FLOWERS[f][æu] un things, un if we wer good she'd show US[a][ə] SOME[a][ʊ]
19   Bee-orchids, BUT[a][ʊ] we not to TOUCH[a][ʊ] um, un not tell anybody else, it wer
20   OUR[f][æː] secret.

21 One SUNday^{a[ʊ]}, we Had^{d[0]} little Audrey with US^{a[ʊ]} from next door, HER^{d/g[0]/}
22 [ɛː] MUM^{a[ʊ]} ud ASKed^{b[æ]} Ada if she'd tek US^{a[ʊ]} with US^{a[ə]}. HER^{d/g[0]/[ɛ]}
23 HUSband^{dd/a[0]/[ʊ]} liked HER^{d/g[0]/[ə]} OUT^{f[æː]} uT^{e[ʔ]} road on SUNday^{a[ʊ]}
24 AFTernoon^{b[æ]}. I can't think why cos she wer a right quiet kid, un well
25 mannered anorl. We wer CUMMIN^{a/c[ʊ]/[n]} back through Annesley park, un we
26 wer orl tired, OUR^{f[æː]} Ada says HURRy^{d/a[0]/[ʊ]} UP^{a[ʊ]} or we'll be late for
27 US^{a[ʊ]} tea, I've got to get ready for ^{[ʔ]} 1 Chapel anorl. We'd JUST^{a[ʊ]} got by ^{e[ʔ]}
28 'Badger Box' goIN^{c[n]} towards Mutton^{a[ʊ]} Hill^{d[0]} when OUR^{f[æː]} Dollie said
29 'What's that in that FRONT^{a[ʊ]} garden?' It wer a HEARSE^{d/g[0]/[ɛː]}. Ada says
30 it wer a funeral car, what yer go in when yer dead. We all went nearer ter Have^{d[0]}
31 a proper look, little Audrey let OUT^{f [æː]} a yell, then we could see a man layIN^{c[n]}
32 in it, we soon RUN^{a[ʊ]} off. We'd gone UP^{a[ʊ]} ^{e[ʔ]} road a bit when we saw
33 Bobby BROWN^{f[æː]} on His^{d[0]} bike CUMMIN^{a/c[ʊ]/[n]} towards US^{a[ʊ]}. OUR^{f[æː]}
34 Ada SHOUTed^{f[æː]} to Him^{d[0]}, 'Please SIR^{g[ɛə]}, there's a man layIN^{c[n]} in a
35 Horse^{d[0]} inT^{e[ʔ]} FRONT ^{a[ʊ]} garden of that HOUSE^{d/f[0]/[æː]}. 'Yer what me
36 lass?' He^{d[0]} said, un she told Him^{d[0]} again, 'Un He's^{d[0]} not in a coffin, is He^{d[0]}
37 dead?' ^{e[ʔ]} Bobby LAUGHed^{b[æ]} un said, 'He's^{d[0]} only asleep', un not to be
38 frightened, 'Its only old man Jones, He^{d[0]} often AS^{d[0]} a sleep innit on SUNday^{a[ʊ]}
39 AFTernoons^{b[æ]}'. We could still Hear^{d[0]} Him^{d[0]} LAUGHING^{b/c[æ]/[n]} as
40 He^{d[0]} peddled away, I said to OUR^{f[æː]} Ada what a NERVE^{g[ɛː]} you've got
41 talkIN^{c[n]} to a bobby, BUT ^{a[ə]} then that wer OUR^{f[æʊ]} Ada, nowt bothered
42 HER^{d/g[0]/[ɛə]}.

Notes to Text 7.3A: Accent features

1 Three 'unpredicted' realisations of the definite article occur in **13**, **15** and **27** (see discussion in Section 7.12.2).

I.7 Television advertisements: address situation and participant roles

Key to analysis

Situation bold – **Direct/Indirect Address**
Indirect Address indented
Situation type within Indirect Address regular – Monologue/Dialogue
Primary participants upper case – SPEAKER, ADDRESSEE, AUDITOR
Secondary participants upper and lower case – Speaker, Addressee, Auditor

Past Text 8.1A: Persil, 1959, 'Woman Alone'

Direct Address
primary participant (advertiser) as SPEAKER
primary participant (consumer) as ADDRESSEE
1. Voice over (male): this woman is alone – yet *not* alone — even though her family may be apart *from* her they are still a part *of* her – being judged by the care she takes of them – being judged by how clean and white she keeps their clothes – just

as she is being judged by that same whiteness
((close-up of packet)): [New Persil washes even whiter]
so Persil is part of *her* strength and *their* happiness — as a wife she uses Persil – as
a mother she uses Persil
((close-up of packet)): [New Persil washes even whiter]
Persil washes whiter

Past Text 8.2A: Kellogg's Corn Flakes, 1956, 'Executive'

Direct Address
primary participant (advertiser) as SPEAKER
primary participant (consumer) as ADDRESSEE
1. Voice-over (male): this is how his wife sent him off to work this morning – good
job she didn't see him two hours later

> **Indirect Address**
> Dialogue involving secondary participants (all fictional)
> secondary participant (man – Jones) alternating as Addressee and Speaker
> secondary participant (telephone voice – Watkins) alternating as Speaker
> and Addressee
> secondary participant (secretary – unnamed) alternating as Auditor,
> Addressee and Speaker
> primary participant (consumer) as AUDITOR
> 2. Telephone voice (male): really Jones I can't wait any longer – you
> promised me that quote today
> 3. Jones: just a moment Mr Watkins
> ((to secretary)) where is that schedule
> 4. Secretary (female): you didn't complete Mr Jones
> 5. Telephone voice (Watkins): I told you Jones I can't wait

Direct Address (primary participants as above)
6. Voice over: his wife's fault really – he's had almost nothing since supper twelve
hours ago – no proper breakfast – he said he hadn't time – what nonsense – before
his toast and tea give him a good big plate of corn flakes – delicious — after a
breakfast like that his wife needn't worry

> **Indirect Address** (secondary participants as above, with addition of a
> fourth, unseen, secondary participant as Addressee via 'second telephone')
> 7. Jones ((into first telephone)): I'll fix you up Mr Watkins – yes just hold on
> ((into second)): I'll take that five hundred – yes today – goodbye ((replaces
> receiver))
> ((returning to first)): that's ok Mr Watkins – not at all – goodbye ((replaces
> receiver))
> ((to secretary)): well that's quite a good day's work – remind me to take
> some flowers home to my wife
> 8. Secretary: yes sir ((makes note))

Direct Address (primary participants as above)
9. ((close–up of packet)): [Kellogg's Corn Flakes]
((written text)): [Start *your* day the Kellogg's way]
Voice-over: start *your* day the Kellogg's way ((word-by-word in sync with written
text))

Present Text 8.3A: **Persil Tablets, 1998, 'Sports Kit Mother'**

Indirect Address

Dialogue involving secondary participants (both fictional)
secondary participant (male voice) alternating as Speaker and Addressee
secondary participant (woman) alternating as Addressee and Speaker
primary participant (consumer) as AUDITOR

1. ((male voice)): how well do these new Persil tablets clean then
2. Woman ((to camera)): they get the boys' sports things lovely and clean
3. ((male voice)): but all washing powders do that don't they
4. Woman: oh yeah – and how many dirty sports kits have you washed recently

Direct Address

primary participant (advertiser) as SPEAKER
primary participant (consumer) as ADDRESSEE

5. ((written text)): [Persil tablets]

((close-up of packet)): [Persil Performance tablets]

((written text)): [a great wash, a great deal easier]

Voice-over (female): Persil's new tablets – a great wash – a great deal easier

Present Text 8.4A: **Persil Tablets, 1998, 'Pregnant Woman'**

Indirect Address

Dialogue involving secondary participants (both fictional)
secondary participant (male voice) alternating as Speaker and Addressee
secondary participant (woman) alternating as Addressee and Speaker
primary participant (consumer) as AUDITOR

1. ((male voice)): so they clean brilliantly
2. Woman ((to camera)): yeah
3. ((male voice)): they're dermatologically tested
4. Woman: mhmm
5. ((male voice)): and the tablets give your clothes a (sort of) Persil
softness – what more could you ask for
6. Woman: some help with the ironing?

Direct Address

primary participant (advertiser) as SPEAKER
primary participant (consumer) as ADDRESSEE

7. ((written text)): [Persil tablets]

((close-up of packet)): [Persil the original non-biological tablets]

((written text)): [a great wash, a great deal easier]

Voice-over (female): Persil's new non-bio tablets – a great wash – a great deal easier

Present Text 8.5A: **Persil Tablets, 2000, 'Kidding Woman'**

Indirect Address

Dialogue involving secondary participants (both fictional)
secondary participant (male voice) alternating as Speaker and Addressee
secondary participant (woman) alternating as Addressee and Speaker
primary participant (consumer) as AUDITOR

1.   ((male voice)): why do you think Persil's Performance Tablets are such a great way to wash
2.   Woman ((to camera)): well – they don't just clean brilliantly
3.   ((male voice)): right
4.   Woman: they leave clothes soft
5.   ((male voice)): uhuh
6.   Woman: they freshen
7.   ((male voice)): yeah
8.   Woman: and they do wonders for your love life
9.   ((male voice)): really
10. Woman: no-o-o – only kidding

Direct Address

primary participant (advertiser) as SPEAKER

primary participant (consumer) as ADDRESSEE

11. ((close-up of packet)): [Persil]

((written text)): [clean, soft and fresh]

Voice-over (female): Persil Performance tablets – clean soft and fresh

Present Text 8.6A: **Kellogg's Corn Flakes, 2000, 'Early Man'**

Indirect Address

'Dialogue' involving one secondary participant (fictional)

secondary participant ('early man') as Speaker

primary participant (consumer) as AUDITOR

1.   Man: uggghh

Direct Address

primary participant (advertiser) as SPEAKER

primary participant (consumer) as ADDRESSEE

2.   Voice-over (female): early man

   Indirect Address (participants as above)

3.   Man: uggghh

Direct Address (participants as above)

4.   Voice-over: and it's not a pretty sight — even the simplest of tasks seem beyond his primitive brain — the hunter-gatherer's first instinct is to find food

((close-up of packet)): [Kellogg's Corn Flakes]

   Indirect Address (participants as above)

5.   Man: uggghh

Direct Address (participants as above)

6.   Voice-over: particularly if it helps him to *wake up* – [1]

amazing — Neolithic to modern man in the time it takes to eat a bowl of Kellogg's Corn Flakes

((close-up of packet)): [Kellogg's Corn Flakes]

((close-up of packet)): [Kellogg's Corn Flakes] preceded by [Have you woken up to]

Voice-over: Have you woken up to Kellogg's Corn Flakes

Note

[1] The (very faint) super appearing in V.12 has been excluded from the analysis

Appendix 2
Selective Glossary

The Glossary defines technical terms as used in this book, other than those which are fully explained in the body of the text. (The latter can be found via the Index.)

abstract noun intangible or unobservable phenomenon or concept, e.g. *thought, happiness* (contrast **concrete** noun, an observable object or entity, e.g. *house, pencil*).

adjuncts adverbials (A elements) which relate directly to the meaning of the V element of the clause or to the whole sentence. Their status is approximately equal to that of the other clause elements (contrast conjuncts, disjuncts and subjuncts – *see* Section 4.8).

animate noun living being or creature, human or non-human, e.g. *child, cat* (contrast <u>in</u>**animate** noun: object or entity without life, e.g. *car, book*).

apposition the acting together, within the same clause element, of two (or more) noun phrases having the same basic meaning. The relationship may be one of equivalence (for example where one NP gives the name and another the professional status of the same individual) or of attribution (where one NP expresses a quality or characteristic of the other).

asyndetic coordination *see* **coordination**

base form of verb *see* **non-finite**, under **finite verb phrase**

collocation the tendency for regular co-occurrence of particular lexical items (**collocates:** the other lexical items with which a given item occurs).

common noun *see* **proper noun**

concrete noun *see* **abstract noun**

congruent approximately equivalent to **unmarked** (in its figurative sense – *see* **marked/unmarked**).

coordination the joining of units that have the <u>same</u> grammatical status within the sentence, for example two (or more) clauses, noun phrases, adjectives. The coordination may be made explicit via use of a linking conjunction such as *and* ('syndetic coordination') or may be left implicit, e.g. commas may be used ('<u>a</u>syndetic coordination').

declarative (clause)   *see* **mood**

dummy grammatical subject   an 'empty' (dummy) item in initial subject (S) slot in a clause; used as a way of focusing attention on a later, usually extensive, part of the clause. The 'dummy' item is frequently the so-called 'existential *there*'.

ellipsis   the non-specification, or 'leaving out', of a part of a sentence (or utterance), usually because it is assumed to be readily recoverable from elsewhere in the text (textual ellipsis) or to be understood from the immediate situation (situational ellipsis).

existential *there*   *see* **dummy grammatical subject**

finite verb phrase   the verb (V) displays contrasts according to linguistic environment, such contrasts being in tense (present or past time), number and person (in relation to subject (S)), mood (mainly declarative (SV) or interrogative (VS)). Thus: *Jack is happy; they walked home; are they happy*. A **non-finite** verb phrase displays <u>none</u> of these contrasts, its restricted range of forms remaining the same whatever its environment. These forms are the **participle** forms *–ing* and *–ed* (*she is <u>walking</u>; they are <u>walking</u>; she has <u>walked</u>; they have <u>walked</u>*) and the **base/infinitive** form (*she'll <u>walk</u>; they'd like to <u>walk</u>*).

glottal stop   the vocal tract is closed by the vocal folds, causing a compression of air, which is then released in the form of a small explosion.

imperative (clause)   *see* **mood**

inanimate noun   *see* **animate noun**

infinitive form of verb phrase   *see* **non-finite**, under **finite verb phrase**

interrogative (clause)   *see* **mood**

marked/unmarked   that which is **unmarked** (in a figurative sense) is regarded as the most expected, most usual, most common form or usage in a particular context; that which is **marked** is <u>less</u> expected, less usual, less common. (It should be noted that **marked** can also be used in a more restricted and literal sense to mean the inclusion of specific linguistic material, for example to signal a topic jump (*see* Section 4.13.2) or the use of *–s* to 'mark' plural meaning after a numeral (*see* Section 7.8). Chapter 7, in fact, makes use of <u>both</u> the literal <u>and</u> figurative meanings of these terms.)

modal auxiliaries   particular kinds of auxiliary verbs. They cannot be used as main verbs and they have very limited formal variation. The principal modals are *can, could, may, might, must, shall, should, will, would*. Other, 'marginal', modals include *need, ought to, used to*.

mood   term used to characterise the structure of, and ordering of elements within, a clause: declarative (SV); interrogative (VS), imperative (V). These mood choices typically realise statements, questions, commands respectively, though there is no necessarily direct relationship between the grammatical <u>form</u> of an utterance and its function in context. 'Moodless' structures have no V element (compare Leech's 'disjunctive grammar'; Section 8.10.1).

morpheme   the smallest grammatical unit. It realises the whole or a part of the structure of a word, for example the word *sing* consists of a single morpheme (it can stand alone); *singing* consists of <u>two</u> morphemes – *sing* plus the suffix *ing* (*ing* cannot stand alone).

non-finite verb phrase   *see* **finite verb phrase**

operator   the <u>first</u> auxiliary verb in a verb phrase. The operator can go before the main verb to form an interrogative, e.g. *is Molly happy?, shall we go?*

participles   *see* **non-finite**, under **finite verb phrase**

phoneme   a meaningful sound unit which distinguishes between different <u>words</u>, e.g., in the 'same' environment, /f/ as in *fan* compared with /v/ as in *van*.

polarity   a choice between positive and negative meaning, e.g. *is* v. *isn't*.

prepositional phrase   the combination of a preposition (e.g. *of, in, to, with, by, for*) and a 'prepositional complement' (usually a noun phrase).

prop *it*   *it* used with very general and fairly empty meaning, e.g. *it's raining*.

proper noun   the name of a specific person, place, publication and so on, e.g. *Joan, Sean O'Casey, Dublin, The Guardian*. (All other nouns are **common nouns**.)

syndetic coordination   *see* **coordination**

tag question   typically an interrogative (VS) structure added to a statement expressed in declarative (SV) form (for example *Rowan is happy, isn't he?*). In most tags the operator is the same as that in the declarative; the subject is a pronoun which repeats, or has the same referent as, the subject of the declarative; the polarity of the declarative is reversed in the interrogative.

unmarked   *see* **marked/unmarked**

wh-question   begins with a question word such as *where, when, how, why, who*, usually followed by an interrogative (VS) structure (*where are you going?*). Such questions allow for a range of possibilities in response (*see* also Stubbs's 'X-question'; Section 5.6.2).

yes–no question   begins with an interrogative (VS) structure (*are you going to town?*) which is designed to limit the scope for a reply, apparently to *yes* or *no*.

Bibliography

Anderson, P. M. (1987) *A Structural Atlas of the English Dialects* (Beckenham: Croom Helm).

Atkinson, J. M. (1984) *Our Masters' Voices: The Language and Body Language of Politics* (London: Methuen).

Baron, Naomi S. (2000) *Alphabet to Email: How Written English Evolved and Where It's Heading* (London: Routledge).

Bell, A. (1984) Language style as audience design. *Language and Society*, 13: 2, 145–204.

Bell, A. (1991) *The Language of News Media* (Oxford: Blackwell).

Bell, A. (1997) Language style as audience design. In N. Coupland and A. Jaworski (eds) (1997) pp. 240–50.

Berry, M. (1987) Projects in Modern English Language. Department of English Studies, University of Nottingham.

Berry, M. (1989) *Introduction to Systemic Linguistics – I: Structures and Systems – Reprints in Systemic Linguistics, No. 1.* Department of English Studies, University of Nottingham. (First published by Batsford, 1975.)

Berry, H. M. (1996) Grammar 1–8: Descriptive frameworks and exemplified passages for Modern English Language, Language and Context I, Department of English Studies, University of Nottingham.

Bloor, T. and Bloor, M. (1995) *The Functional Analysis of English: A Hallidayan Approach* (London: Arnold).

Brazil, D. C. (1969) Kinds of English: spoken, written, literary. *Educational Review*, 22:1, 78–92.

Brazil, D. (1983) Kinds of English: spoken, written, literary. In M. Stubbs and H. Hillier (eds) (1983) pp. 149–66.

Brazil, D. (1995) *A Grammar of Speech* (Oxford: Oxford University Press).

Brown, G. and Yule, G. (1983) *Discourse Analysis* (Cambridge: Cambridge University Press).

Burton, D. (1981) Analysing spoken discourse. In M. Coulthard and M. Montgomery (eds) (1981) pp. 61–81.

Butler, C. (1998) Statistics. In A. Wray et al. (1998) pp. 255–64.

Cameron, D. (ed.) (1990) *The Feminist Critique of Language: A Reader* (London: Routledge).

Cameron, D., McAlinden, F. and O'Leary, K. (1989) Lakoff in context: the social and linguistic functions of tag questions. In J. Coates and D. Cameron (eds) (1989) pp. 74–93.

Carter, R. (1982a) Introduction to R. Carter (ed.) (1982) pp. 1–17.

Carter, R. (1982b) Style and interpretation in Hemingway's 'Cat in the Rain'. In R. Carter (ed.) (1982) pp. 65–80.

Carter, R. (ed.) (1982) *Language and Literature: An Introductory Reader in Stylistics* (London: George Allen & Unwin).

Carter, R. (1998) *Vocabulary: Applied Linguistic Perspectives*, 2nd edn (London: Routledge).

Carter, R., Goddard, A., Reah, D., Sanger, K. and Bowring, M. (2001) *Working with Texts: A Core Book for Language Analysis*, 2nd edn (London: Routledge).

Carter, R. and Nash, W. (1990) *Seeing through Language* (Oxford: Blackwell).

Carter, R. and Simpson, P. (eds) (1989) *Language, Discourse and Literature: An Introductory Reader in Discourse Stylistics* (London: Unwin Hyman).

Cassell (1998) *The Cassell Concise Dictionary* (London: Cassell).

Channell, J. (1994) *Vague Language* (Oxford: Oxford University Press).

Coates, J. (1989) Gossip revisited: language in all-female groups. In J. Coates and D. Cameron (eds) (1989) pp. 94–122.

Coates, J. (1993) *Women, Men and Language*, 2nd edn (London: Longman).

Coates, J. (1994) No gap, lots of overlap: turn-taking patterns in the talk of women friends. In D. Graddol, J. Maybin and B. Stierer (eds) (1994) pp. 177–92.

Coates, J. (1996) *Women Talk* (Oxford: Blackwell).

Coates, J. and Cameron, D. (eds) (1989) *Women in Their Speech Communities: New Perspectives on Language and Sex* (London: Longman).

Cockcroft, R. and Cockcroft, S. (1992) *Persuading People: An Introduction to Rhetoric* (Basingstoke: Palgrave Macmillan).

Cook, G. (2001) *The Discourse of Advertising*, 2nd edn (London: Routledge).

Coulthard, M. and Ashby, M. C. (1975) Talking with the doctor. *Journal of Communication*, 25:3, 240–7.

Coulthard, M. and Montgomery, M. (eds) (1981) *Studies in Discourse Analysis* (London: Routledge).

Coupland, N. and Jaworski, A. (eds) (1997) *Sociolinguistics: A Reader and Coursebook* (Basingstoke: Palgrave Macmillan).

Crawford, M. (1995) *Talking Difference: On Gender and Language* (London: Sage).

Crystal, D. (1996) *Rediscover Grammar*, rev. edn (Harlow: Longman).

Crystal, D. (2001) *Language and the Internet* (Cambridge: Cambridge University Press).

Crystal, D. and Davy, D. (1969) *Investigating English Style* (London: Longman).

cummings, e. e. (1963) *selected poems, 1923–1958* (Harmondsworth: Penguin).

Davidse, K. (1999) *Categories of Experiential Grammar – Monographs in*

Systemic Linguistics No. 11, Department of English and Media Studies, Nottingham Trent University.

Delin, J. (2000) *The Language of Everyday Life* (London: Sage).

Dickens, C. (1992) *Bleak House*, retold by Margaret Tarner (Oxford: Heinemann).

Dickens, C. (1998) *Bleak House*, Oxford World's Classics (Oxford: Oxford University Press).

Drury, I. (1998) Fred's gorra big 'it for issen. *Nottingham Evening Post*, 31 July 1998, p. 3.

Edwards, V., Trudgill, P. and Weltens, B. (1984) *The Grammar of English Dialect: A Survey of Research* (London: ESRC).

Eggins, S. (1994) *An Introduction to Systemic-Functional Linguistics* (London: Pinter).

Fairclough, N. (1995) *Media Discourse* (London: Arnold).

Fairclough, N. (2000) *New Labour, New Language?* (London: Routledge).

Fairclough N. (2001) *Language and Power*, 2nd edn (London: Longman).

Fisher, E. (1993) Characteristics of children's talk at the computer and its relationship to the computer software. *Language and Education* 7:2, 97–114.

Fishman, P. (1990) Conversational insecurity. Reprinted in D. Cameron (ed.) (1990) pp. 234–41.

Fowler, R. (1989) Polyphony in *Hard Times*. In R. Carter and P. Simpson (eds) (1989) pp. 77–93.

Fowler, R. (1991) *Language in the News: Discourse and Ideology in the Press* (London: Routledge).

Fowler, R., Hodge, B., Kress, G. and Trew, T. (1979) *Language and Control* (London: Routledge & Kegan Paul).

Freeborn, D. with French, P. and Langford, D. (1993) *Varieties of English: An Introduction to the Study of Language*, 2nd edn (Basingstoke: Palgrave Macmillan).

Garvey, C. (1975) Requests and responses in children's speech. *Journal of Child Language*, 2, 41–63.

Garvey, C. (1984) *Children's Talk* (London: Fontana).

Geis, M. L. (1982) *The Language of Television Advertising* (London: Academic Press).

Ghadessy, M. (ed.) (1988) *Registers of Written English: Situational Factors and Linguistic Features* (London: Pinter).

Giles, H. and Coupland, N. (1991) *Language: Contexts and Consequences* (Milton Keynes: Open University Press).

Gimson, A. C. (1989) *An Introduction to the Pronunciation of English*, 4th edn, revised by S. Ramsaran (London: Edward Arnold).

Goffman, E. (1976) *Gender Advertisements* (London: Palgrave Macmillan).

Goffman, E. (1981) *Forms of Talk* (Philadelphia: University of Pennsylvania Press).

Goodman, S. and Maybin, J. (1999) *Study Guide: E300 English Language and Literacy*. School of Education, The Open University.

Graddol, D. and Boyd-Barrett, O. (eds) (1994) *Media Texts: Authors and Readers* (Clevedon: Multilingual Matters in association with the Open University).

Graddol, D., Cheshire, J. and Swann, J. (1994) *Describing Language*, 2nd edn (Buckingham: Open University Press).

Graddol, D., Maybin, J. and Stierer, B. (eds) (1994) *Researching Language and Literacy in Social Context* (Clevedon: Multilingual Matters in association with the Open University).

Gregory, M. J. (1967) Aspects of varieties differentiation. *Journal of Linguistics*, 3, 177–98.

Gregory, M. and Carroll, S. (1978) *Language and Situation: Language Varieties and their Social Contexts* (London: Routledge).

Halliday, M. A. K. (1970) Language structure and language function. In J. Lyons (ed.) (1970) pp. 140–65.

Halliday, M. A. K. (1973) *Explorations in the Functions of Language* (London: Arnold).

Halliday, M. A. K. (1978) *Language as Social Semiotic: The Social Interpretation of Language and Meaning* (London: Arnold).

Halliday, M. A. K. (1989a) see M. A. K. Halliday and R. Hasan (1989) pp. 3–49.

Halliday, M. A. K. (1989b) *Spoken and Written Language*, 2nd edn (Oxford: Oxford University Press).

Halliday, M. A. K. (1994a) *An Introduction to Functional Grammar*, 2nd edn (London: Edward Arnold).

Halliday, M. A. K. (1994b) Spoken and written modes of meaning. In D. Graddol and O. Boyd-Barrett (eds) (1994) pp. 51–73.

Halliday, M. A. K. (1999) *Learning How to Mean: Explorations in the Development of Language – Reprints in Systemic Linguistics No. 5.* Department of English and Media Studies, Nottingham Trent University. (First published by Edward Arnold, 1975.)

Halliday, M. A. K. and Hasan, R. (1976) *Cohesion in English* (London: Longman).

Halliday, M. A. K. and Hasan, R. (1989) *Language, Context, and Text: Aspects of Language in a Social-Semiotic Perspective*, 2nd edn (Oxford: Oxford University Press).

Harris, S. (1987) Court discourse as genre: some problems and issues. *Occasional Papers in Systemic Linguistics*, 2, 35–73.

Hasan, R. (1989) see M. A. K. Halliday and R. Hasan (1989) pp. 51–118.

Hasan, R. (1994) The texture of a text. In D. Graddol and O. Boyd-Barrett (eds) (1994) pp. 74–89.

Heritage, J. and Greatbatch, D. (1986) Generating applause: a study of rhetoric and response at party political conferences. *American Journal of Sociology*, 92:1. (Cited in R. Wooffitt (1996).)

Hillier, H. (1992) *The Language of Spontaneous Interaction between Children aged 7–12: Instigating Action – Monographs in Systemic Linguistics No. 4.* Department of English Studies, University of Nottingham.

Hillier, H. (1993a) Lawrence and the Eastwood dialect – representation and reality. Paper presented to 'Literature and Language', a Conference to mark the retirement of Professor Norman Page, University of Nottingham, May 1993.

Hillier, H. (1993b) D. H. Lawrence and the dialect of Eastwood. Paper presented to a Conference for the Society of Teachers of Speech and Drama, Nottingham, August 1993.

Hillier, H. (1993c) Introduction to *The Daughter-in-Law*. Paper presented to a Lawrence and Language Colloquium, University of Nottingham, September 1993.

Hillier, H. (1994) The Eastwood dialect – then and now. Paper presented to the D. H. Lawrence Society, Eastwood, Nottingham, September 1994.

Hillier, H. (1995) Choice within the verbal group of a non-standard grammar: the case of the disappearing auxiliary. Paper presented to the 7th International Systemic Functional Workshop, 'Language as Choice', University of Valencia, Spain, July 1995.

Hillier, H. (1996) Social class, gender and linguistic choice in *The Merry-Go-Round*. Paper presented to the 6th International D. H. Lawrence Conference, University of Nottingham, July 1996.

Hillier, H. (1998) Interpersonal meaning potential within a non-standard grammar – towards a systemic description. Paper presented to the 10th Euro-International Systemic Functional Workshop, University of Liverpool, July 1998.

Hodge, B. (1979) Newspapers and communities. In R. Fowler et al. (1979) pp. 157–74.

Hodge, R. and Kress, G. (1993) *Language as Ideology*, 2nd edn (London: Routledge).

Hoey, M. (1991) *On the Surface of Discourse – Reprints in Systemic Linguistics No. 3*. Department of English Studies, University of Nottingham. (First published by Allen & Unwin, 1983.)

Holmes, J. (1995) *Women, Men and Politeness* (London: Longman).

Holmes, J. (2001) *An Introduction to Sociolinguistics*, 2nd edn (Harlow: Longman).

Hughes, A. and Trudgill, P. (1996) *English Accents and Dialects: An Introduction to Social and Regional Varieties of English in the British Isles*, 3rd edn (London: Arnold).

Hutchinson Softback Encyclopedia (1992) (Oxford: Helicon).

Hymes, D. (1977) *Foundations in Sociolinguistics* (London: Tavistock). (Cited in J. Maybin (ed.) (1994).)

Hymes, D. (1994) Toward ethnographies of communication. Edited from Chapters 1 and 2 of D. Hymes (1977) and reproduced in J. Maybin (ed.) (1994) pp. 11–22.

Kress, G. R. and van Leeuwen, T. (1996) *Reading Images: the Grammar of Visual Design* (London: Routledge).

Labov, W. (1978) *Sociolinguistic Patterns* (Oxford: Blackwell).

Lakoff, R. (1975) *Language and Woman's Place* (New York: Harper & Row).

Laver, J. (1981) Linguistic routines and politeness in greeting and parting. In F. Coulmas (ed.) *Conversational Routine* (The Hague: Mouton) pp. 289–304. (Cited in J. Holmes (2001).)

Leech, G. N. (1966) *English in Advertising: A Linguistic Study of Advertising in Great Britain* (London: Longman).

Leech, G. N. and Short, M. H. (1983) *Style in Fiction: A Linguistic Introduction to English Fictional Prose*, corrected edn (London: Longman).

Levinson, S. C. (1983) *Pragmatics* (Cambridge: Cambridge University Press).

Lyons, J. (ed.) (1970) *New Horizons in Linguistics* (Harmondsworth: Penguin).

McLuhan, M. (1964) Keeping upset with the Joneses. In M. McLuhan, *Understanding Media: the Extensions of Man* (London: Routledge & Kegan Paul). (Cited in G. Cook (2001).)

McTear, M. (1985) *Children's Conversation* (Oxford: Blackwell).

Mason, M. (1982) Deixis: a point of entry to *Little Dorrit*. In R. Carter (ed.) (1982) pp. 29–38.

Maybin, J. (1994) Children's voices: talk, knowledge and identity. In D. Graddol, J. Maybin and B. Stierer (eds) (1994) pp. 131–50.

Maybin, J. (ed.) (1994) *Language and Literacy in Social Practice* (Clevedon: Multilingual Matters in association with the Open University).

Maybin, J. and Mercer, N. (eds) (1996) *Using English: from Conversation to Canon* (London: Routledge and Open University Press).

Milroy, L. (1987) *Observing and Analysing Natural Language: a Critical Account of Sociolinguistic Method* (Oxford: Blackwell).

Ochs, E. (1979) Methodology in child language: transcription as theory. In E. Ochs and B. B. Schieffelin (eds) (1979) pp. 43–72.

Ochs, E. and Schieffelin, B. B. (eds) (1979) *Developmental Pragmatics* (New York: Academic Press).

Packard, V. (1960) *The Hidden Persuaders* (Harmondsworth: Penguin).

Page, N. (1988) *Speech in the English Novel*, 2nd edn (Basingstoke: Palgrave Macmillan).

Preisler, B. (1986) *Linguistic Sex Roles in Conversation: Social Variation in the Expression of Tentativeness in English* (Berlin: Mouton de Gruyter).

Psathas, G. and Anderson, T. (1990) The 'practices' of transcription in conversation analysis, *Semiotica*, 78:1–2, 75–99.

Quirk, R. (1962) *The Use of English* (London: Longman). (Cited in G. N. Leech (1966).)

Quirk, R., Greenbaum, S., Leech, G. and Svartvik, J. (1985) *A Comprehensive Grammar of the English Language* (London: Longman).

Sacks, H., Schegloff, E. and Jefferson, G. (1974) A simplest systematics for the organisation of turn-taking for conversation. *Language*, 50, 696–735.

Scollins, R. and Titford, J. (1976a) *Ey Up Mi Duck, Part One* (Ilkeston: Scollins & Titford).

Scollins, R. and Titford, J. (1976b) *Ey Up Mi Duck, Part Two* (Ilkeston: Scollins & Titford).

Sebba, M. (1993) *Focussing on Language: a Student's Guide to Research*

Planning, Data Collection, Analysis and Writing Up (Lancaster: Definite Article Publications).

Shepherd, V. (1990) *Language Variety and the Art of the Everyday* (London: Pinter).

Short, M. (1996) *Exploring the Language of Poems, Plays and Prose* (London: Longman).

Simpson, P. (1993) *Language, Ideology and Point of View* (London: Routledge).

Sinclair, J. McH. and Coulthard, R. M. (1975) *Towards an Analysis of Discourse: the English Used by Teachers and Pupils* (Oxford: Oxford University Press).

Stubbs, M. (1980) *Language and Literacy: the Sociolinguistics of Reading and Writing* (Henley-on-Thames: Routledge).

Stubbs, M. (1983a) *Discourse Analysis: the Sociolinguistic Analysis of Natural Language* (Oxford: Blackwell).

Stubbs, M. (1983b) *Language Schools and Classrooms*, 2nd edn (London: Methuen).

Stubbs, M. (1983c) The sociolinguistics of the English writing system: or why children aren't adults. In M. Stubbs and H. Hillier (eds) (1983) pp. 279–89.

Stubbs, M. (1999) Whorf's children: critical comments on Critical Discourse Analysis. Paper presented at BAAL Annual Meeting, Swansea, September 1996. (Reprinted in S. Goodman and J. Maybin (1999) pp. 109–17.)

Stubbs, M. and Hillier, H. (eds) (1983) *Readings on Language, Schools and Classrooms* (London: Methuen).

Stubbs, M., Robinson, B. and Twite, S. (1979) *Observing Classroom Language*. Block 5, Part 1, P232, Language Development (Milton Keynes: Open University Press).

Swann, J. (1989) Talk control: an illustration from the classroom of problems in analysing male dominance of conversation. In J. Coates and D. Cameron (eds) (1989) pp. 124–40.

Tarner, M. (1992) *(Retelling of) Bleak House by Charles Dickens* (Oxford: Heinemann).

Traugott, E. C. and Pratt, M. L. (1980) *Linguistics for Students of Literature* (New York: Harcourt Brace Jovanovich).

Trew, T. (1979a) Theory and ideology at work. In R. Fowler et al. (1979) pp. 94–116.

Trew, T. (1979b) 'What the papers say': linguistic variation and ideological difference. In R. Fowler et al. (1979) pp. 117–56.

Trudgill, P. (1997) Acts of conflicting identity: the sociolinguistics of British pop-song pronunciation. In N. Coupland and A. Jaworski (eds) (1997) pp. 251–65.

Trudgill, P. (1999) *The Dialects of England*, 2nd edn (Oxford: Blackwell).

Upton, C. and Widdowson, J. D. A. (1996) *An Atlas of English Dialects* (Oxford: Oxford University Press).

Vestergaard, T. and Schrøder, K. (1985) *The Language of Advertising* (Oxford: Blackwell).

Weber, J. J. (1989) Dickens's social semiotic: the modal analysis of ideological structure. In R. Carter and P. Simpson (eds) (1989) pp. 95–111.

Wetherill, F. (1998) *Our Mam un t'Others: Memories of a mining family from 1930s onwards* (Teversal: Teversal Living Memory Group (c/o P. Sapey, Elbur House, Fackley Road, Teversal, Sutton-in-Ashfield, Nottingham, England)).

Williamson, J. (1978) *Decoding Advertisements: Ideology and Meaning in Advertising* (London: Marion Boyars).

Wilson, J. (1990) *Politically Speaking* (Oxford: Blackwell).

Wooffitt, R. (1996) Rhetoric in English. In J. Maybin and N. Mercer (eds) (1996) pp. 122–44.

Worthen, J. (1991) *D. H. Lawrence: The Early Years 1885–1912* (Cambridge: Cambridge University Press).

Wray, A., Trott, K. and Bloomer, A. (1998) *Projects in Linguistics: A Practical Guide to Researching Language* (London: Arnold).

Subject Index

References to definitions or explanations of technical terms as used in this book are printed in bold. Where entries have many references, within and/or across chapters, those which are significant within a particular chapter are also printed in bold. Some abbreviations are used in cross references, for example, 'TV ads' for 'television advertisements'.

abstract v. concrete nouns, 28, 48, 141, 232, **250**
accent, 17, 200
   of Erewash Valley/Kirkby, 154–5, 156, 159–60, 160–1, 163–5, 165–71, 172, 245–6
   of RP, 158–9, 160, 171, 173, 174, 207
   see also consonants; dialect; vowels
accidental recording, 11, 63, 64
   see also data collection
action processes, 232
   see also processes (transitivity)
active v. passive voice, xix, 42, **45–6**, 47, 47–8, 53–5, 230, 231, 232
actor, **43**, 45, 46, 47, 48, 230, 231, 232
   see also participant roles (transitivity)
acts (in discourse), 72, 74
   see also discourse analysis
actually, 76, 77, 78, 237
   see also hedges
addressee, 5, 7, 100, 101–2, **104–5**, **105–6**, **110–15**, **116**, 117, 131, 132, **187–9**, 190, 191, 193–6, 199, **204–6**, 213, 215, **237–41**, 246–9
   see also audience design; participant roles (ethnography)
addressee relationship, 23, 148
address in advertising situation *see* direct v. indirect address
addressing utterances, **104**, 105–6, 110–15, 239

addressor, 5, 7, **104**, **105–6**, 110–15, 116, 117, 187, 190
   see also participant roles (ethnography)
address terms, 195
adjacency pairs, 72
   see also conversation analysis
adjectives, 27, 28, 127, 157, 197, 226
adjuncts, 27, 32–3, 45, 223, 225, **250**
Adventures of Huckleberry Finn, The, 173
adverbials, 17, **27**, 30, 32–4, 42, 76, 103, 139, 223, 225, 230
   complexity of, 30, 31–2
   meanings of, 27, 223, 237
   mobility of, 77–8
   numbers of, 27, 30
   positioning of, 27, 30, 31, 32, 34, 77, 78, 223, 225
   realisations of, 32–4
adverbs, 33, 103, 127, 157, 160, 161, 162, 226, 239, 243–4
   without -*ly*, 157, 160, 161, 162, 243–4
advertisements, 118, 144, 174, 207
   see also television advertisements
advertiser (as primary participant), 176, 177, 186, **187**, **189–90**, 191, 193, 200, 203, 206
advertising situation, 16, 185–90
   see also direct v. indirect address; primary v. secondary situation
agency, 41, 42, 46, 47–8, 52–4, 55–7, 232

Name Index

It will be seen that, in the interests of brevity within the main text, references having more than two authors are cited as ' . . . et al.', e.g. 'Quirk et al.' In this index, however, each individual author's name is included, and in the following form: surname followed by initial/s, e.g. 'Greenbaum, S.'. Other names are given in full, e.g. 'Blair, Tony'.